APPROACHES TO QUALITATIVE RESEARCH

MW01098123

APPROACHES TO QUALITATIVE RESEARCH

AN OXFORD HANDBOOK OF QUALITATIVE RESEARCH IN AMERICAN MUSIC EDUCATION

Volume 1

Edited by
COLLEEN M. CONWAY

LIBRARY OF
CONGRESS
SURPLUS
DUPLICATE

OXFORD
UNIVERSITY PRESS

OXFORD
UNIVERSITY PRESS

Oxford University Press is a department of the University of Oxford. It furthers
the University's objective of excellence in research, scholarship, and education
by publishing worldwide. Oxford is a registered trade mark of Oxford University
Press in the UK and certain other countries.

Published in the United States of America by Oxford University Press
198 Madison Avenue, New York, NY 10016, United States of America.

© Oxford University Press 2020

All rights reserved. No part of this publication may be reproduced, stored in
a retrieval system, or transmitted, in any form or by any means, without the
prior permission in writing of Oxford University Press, or as expressly permitted
by law, by license, or under terms agreed with the appropriate reproduction
rights organization. Inquiries concerning reproduction outside the scope of the
above should be sent to the Rights Department, Oxford University Press, at the
address above.

You must not circulate this work in any other form
and you must impose this same condition on any acquirer.

CIP data is on file at the Library of Congress
ISBN 978-0-19-092089-0

1 3 5 7 9 8 6 4 2

Printed by Marquis, Canada

CONTENTS

PREFACE

APPROACHES TO QUALITATIVE RESEARCH IN AMERICAN MUSIC EDUCATION

> Music takes us out of the actual and whispers to us dim secrets that startle
> our wonder as to who we are, and for what, whence and whereto.
> —Ralph Waldo Emerson (1969, 37)

Music education researchers who are looking to understand the "dim secrets that startle our wonder" look to qualitative research. *Approaches to Qualitative Research: An Oxford Handbook of Qualitative Research in American Music Education* is a resource for music education researchers, music education graduate students, and P–12 music teachers. I begin this Preface by locating qualitative research in music education within the larger field of qualitative research in social sciences and humanities research, within qualitative research in education, and within music education research in general.

LOCATING MUSIC EDUCATION QUALITATIVE RESEARCH

At the macro level, music education research is situated within the larger body of qualitative research in social science and humanities research. Denzin and Lincoln (2011) suggested that:

> Sometime during the last two decades, critical qualitative inquiry came of age, or more accurately, moved through another historical phase. Out of the qualitative-quantitative paradigm wars of the 1980's there appeared, seemingly overnight, journals, handbooks, textbooks, dissertation awards, annual distinguished lectures, and scholarly associations. All of these formations were dedicated to some form of qualitative inquiry. (ix)

In the summer of 2011 my colleague Ann Marie Stanley from Louisiana State University and I attended the Ethnographic and Qualitative Research Conference held annually in Cedarville, Ohio. This gathering attracts qualitative researchers from all over the world and from diverse backgrounds within social science and humanities research. The keynote speaker, Douglas Bilken from Syracuse University, talked about how it is now "routine" for qualitative researchers to "locate themselves through a sharing of their history in relation to the settings/contexts, issues, vocabularies, identities, and other factors associated with their topic of inquiry" (Ethnographic and Qualitative Research Conference Program, 3). This *Handbook of Qualitative Research in American Music Education* will help music education researchers locate ourselves as a music education community within this larger communities of researchers.

Denzin and Lincoln (2011) also refer to the term "locating" and devote the first five chapters in their most recent *Handbook* to what they label "Locating the Field." In addition to the Denzin and Lincoln *Handbooks of Qualitative Research* (1994, 2000, 2005, 2011), Sage also has *Handbooks* of Grounded Theory, Ethnography, Interviewing, Narrative Inquiry, Performance Studies, Critical and Indigenous Methodologies, and many other texts on qualitative research aimed at assisting readers in locating the field. The Sage qualitative texts by Creswell (2018), Maxwell (2013), and Patton (2015) are commonly cited within music education research and are located within this larger field of social science and humanities research. Key journals that may be of interest to music education researchers within this larger body of social science and humanities research include: *Journal of Contemporary Ethnography*; *Journal of Ethnographic and Qualitative Research*; *The International Review of Qualitative Research*; and *Qualitative Inquiry*.

QUALITATIVE RESEARCH WITHIN EDUCATION

One of the strongest opportunities for music education researchers to locate ourselves within the field of educational research has been through the American Educational Research Association (AERA). Since the mid-1990s, the music education special interest (SIG) group has been a welcome place for researchers to, as Biklin suggested, "locate" ourselves through a sharing of our history in relation to the settings/contexts, issues, vocabularies, identities, and other factors associated with our topic of inquiry. Although Music SIG meetings have been largely attended by those within music education and the arts, music education researchers have been involved in many other AERA SIGs and Divisions, several of which are devoted specifically to qualitative research. Qualitative SIGs and mostly qualitative SIGs within AERA include: action research, arts-based educational research, lives of teachers, narrative inquiry, qualitative research, self-study of teacher education, and teacher as researcher. Many of the authors in this text have held leadership roles within these various organizations of AERA.

As will be discussed in chapter 2, early music education qualitative researchers were introduced to qualitative research through their work in colleges of education. Music education qualitative research begins appearing in our journals later than the early work of qualitative researchers in general education.

Research texts and resources for qualitative research in education are numerous. Some of these sources seem to be regularly cited in music education research including: Denzin and Lincoln (2011); Merriam (1998 and 2009); Merriam and Tisdell (2016); Seidman (1990, 1997, 2006); and Stake (1995, 2010). Music education researchers should also be aware of the following qualitative journals in general education: *Qualitative Studies in Education* and the *International Journal of Qualitative Studies in Education*.

QUALITATIVE RESEARCH WITHIN MUSIC EDUCATION

Koji Matsunobu and Liora Bresler's first chapter in this book examines qualitative research within music education and suggests: "The past 20 years have been a coming of age for qualitative research in music education. From a marginal, pariah methodology, qualitative research has become a legitimate, central methodology, with its own conferences, research journals, and venues" (1). With regard to music education conferences, it seems as if we are now at the point where qualitative research can be found at all types of music education conferences. Whether within the National Association for Music Education (NAfME), AERA, or smaller conferences such as the University of South Florida's Suncoast Symposium or Michigan State University's New Directions in Music Education, conference presentations in music education now regularly include reports of qualitative research.

In chapter 2 of this volume Chad West and I examine and report on the number of qualitative research studies published within the *Journal of Research in Music Education*, the *Bulletin of the Council for Research in Music Education* and the *Journal of Music Teacher Education*. Although the number of qualitative publications is not nearly equal to the number of quantitative publications in music education, qualitative researchers clearly have a strong and growing presence in these journals.

Chapter 2 includes a report on the University of Illinois qualitative research conferences held in the early 1990s. In more recent years, the Narrative Inquiry in Music Education (NIME) venue has been well attended by qualitative researchers and has led to important music education qualitative research publications (Barrett and Stauffer 2009, 2012). Additional qualitative sources within music education are examined in chapter 2 and include: Bresler (1995); Bresler and Stake (1992); and Flinders and Richardson (2002).

BOOK ORGANIZATION

The book includes 11 chapters that together describe the history, epistemological views, theoretical frameworks, and types of qualitative research common in music education.

One of the biggest challenges for authors was to capture the "moving target" that represents qualitative research. Understandings about research and terminology for qualitative research have changed much in the past two decades such that it was challenging for authors to settle on specific recommendations.

Key Criteria for All Qualitative Researchers in Music Education

Although qualitative studies differ with regard to topics and designs, there are consistent headings that appear in most qualitative studies including: research questions; past research and/or frameworks; approaches to design; sampling; data collection and analysis; and goodness criteria. This section of the Preface examines some of these common aspects of qualitative studies.[1]

Research Questions

All aspects of a study, including design, data collection, analysis, and presentation of findings, are guided by the research questions. Qualitative researchers have a responsibility to share their research questions and carefully describe how they guided data collection, analysis and presentation of findings. Chapter 1 of this text examines some of the specific issues that tend to lead researchers to what one might call "qualitative questions"; while chapter 3 reminds readers that epistemological assumptions are a part of the research process right from the development of initial questions. Chapter 4 considers how various theoretical frameworks may interact with the development of study questions. It is important to remember that research questions often emerge and change throughout the process of research, which I believe is one of the most exciting aspects of doing research in a qualitative way.

Past Research, Conceptual Framework, Personal Framework, Theoretical Framework

Most researchers review past research literature and develop research questions based on that literature. However, in some qualitative studies, researchers outline research questions before a search of past literature. In these types of studies, literature is consulted after data have been collected so that knowledge of what past researchers have found in relation to a phenomenon does not hinder the researchers' ability to see what is most meaningful in the data. This order of process is particularly common in teacher research, action research, and practitioner inquiry (see chapter 9).

Chapters 3 and 4 provide extended discussions of epistemology (chapter 3) and theoretical frameworks (chapter 4) and their interaction with the work of qualitative researchers. Although not all studies state specific frameworks, all research includes assumptions on the part of the researcher, and researchers have a responsibility to address these assumptions in their work and share with readers how these assumptions influenced the design, implementation, and analysis in the study.

APPROACHES TO DESIGN

In the "History of Qualitative Research in American Music Education" (chapter 2), Chad West and I document that early qualitative researchers rarely discussed the type of qualitative research, but often referred to their work as simply qualitative. In recent years within music education it has been more typical to state a design. Specific designs for qualitative research are addressed throughout this volume.

Matsunobu and Bresler (chapter 1) discuss the nonlinear nature of design decisions:

> Qualitative researchers normally do not bring a fixed research design to fieldwork because they need to respond to the constraints and possibilities of each field. Research strategies are often emergent and subject to change in the research process (Hammersley and Atkinson 2007; Patton 2002). For example, initial research questions—often generated from etic points of view in the abstract context of scholarship rather than the realities of the settings—are refined over the course of research to make sense in the reality of each setting. Research is often guided by emergent questions. Some predetermined, a priori categories for data analysis and codes may be kept, while others will be generated in the process of data analysis. Similarly, literature review needs to respond to emerging issues (Eisenhart 1998). The researcher goes back and forth between theoretical and empirical data to refine understandings and interpretations. Because of this emergent process of qualitative research, methodological explanation is often provided in retrospect. (Barone 2001; Vidich and Lyman 2003). (5)

This concept of retrospective design decision-making is one of the most exciting aspects of doing qualitative research. Collecting data and reflecting on its meaning and then making decisions about what is actually being examined as a chaotic and nonlinear process is a key component of good qualitative research.

Authors in this text authors examine various approaches for research that have been utilized in music education (case study, ethnography, phenomenology, narrative inquiry, practitioner inquiry). However, Merriam (2009) suggests that some qualitative researchers do not chose a particular approach and instead complete what she terms a "basic qualitative research study" (22):

> A challenge to those new to qualitative research is trying to figure out what "kind" of qualitative research study they are doing and what their "theoretical framework" is. . . . In my experience, in applied fields of practice such as education, administration, health, social work, counseling, business, and so on, the most common "type" of qualitative research is a basic, interpretive study. One does a qualitative research study, not a phenomenological, grounded theory, narrative analysis, or critical or ethnographic study. Over the years I have struggled with how to label such a study, using words such as generic, basic, and interpretive. Since all qualitative research is interpretive, I have come around to preferring labeling this type of study as a basic qualitative study. (22)

I have been encouraging novice researchers to consider Merriam's notion of basic qualitative research as well as considering blended options so that no researcher is boxed in by qualitative research designs that at the root are meant to help researchers examine issues that are difficult to examine, messy, and often unwieldy.

Sampling

Regardless of the approach to qualitative research, all qualitative researchers employ purposeful sampling. Purposeful sampling allows the researcher to intentionally select information-rich, illuminative participants for in-depth study. Acknowledging the difficulty and ambiguity in selecting a sample size, Patton (2002) states in bold: **"there are no rules for sample size in qualitative inquiry"** (244). He writes about the difficulty in deciding the issue of sample size, likening it to the problem of a student who pesters her instructor about exactly how many pages a term paper should be, when the teacher has already said it should be long enough to cover the subject, no more, no less. To help the researcher, Patton suggests that validity of qualitative research depends more on the richness of the participants studied and the observation and analysis of the researcher than on the size of the sample.

Patton (2002) provides a comprehensive discussion of 16 variations of purposeful sampling strategies used in qualitative research including: extreme or deviant case, intensity, maximum variation, homogeneous, typical case, critical case, snowball or chain, criterion, theory-based sampling, confirming and disconfirming cases, stratified purposeful, opportunistic or emergent, purposeful random, sampling politically important cases, convenience, and combination or mixed purposeful sampling.

Common purposeful sampling strategies used in music education include: "typical case sampling" to "illustrate or highlight what is typical, normal, average" (243); "critical case sampling" which "permits logical generalization and maximum application of information to other cases because 'if it's true of this one case, it's likely to be true of all other cases'" (243); and "extreme or deviant case sampling," meaning "learning from unusual manifestations of the phenomenon intensely, but not extremely, for example, outstanding successes/notable failures" (243). Regardless of the sampling strategy used, researchers have a responsibility to justify why particular participants were chosen and how the reader should consider them in relation to others.

CONSIDERATION OF ISSUES NOT REPRESENTED IN THE BOOK

The challenge for any book Editor is often to define the scope of the volume. Authors for this text were instructed to focus their chapters on qualitative research in American music education. The decision to be exclusive to studies conducted in North America (Canada and the US) was made to help focus and contain the volume. Many authors struggled with this restriction, as there is a rich traditional of qualitative research within international contexts. Another delimitation aimed at focusing the scope of this book was that authors include only qualitative studies that appear in published journals or as dissertations; not conference presentations or unpublished manuscripts. In this section I think critically about additional decisions that were made with regard to inclusion and direct the reader in thinking about what might be missing.

In considering what might be missing or could have been considered for this book, it seems that a discussion of philosophical research or additional discussions of the use of philosophy in qualitative research might have been considered. Randall Allsup's chapter 3 offers the reader an introduction to epistemological issues with relation to qualitative research. However, philosophy is an area that might have received additional chapters.

An examination of research methods textbooks in education and music education reveals that some writers consider philosophical inquiry to be a separate research method (e.g., Phillips 2008) while others do not (e.g., Wiersma and Jurs 2009). Experienced scholars in music education take diverse positions on the issue. Heller, Edward, and O'Connor (2002), for example, do not consider philosophy a research method, although they do consider philosophical discourse an important scholarly activity and foundational in the research process (1090). Their definition of research focuses on knowledge acquisition that is supported by empirical evidence—that is, evidence that is observed through one of the senses—rather than systematic logic. In another chapter in the same volume, Elliott (2002) challenges that position, suggesting that Heller, Edward, and O'Connor's view is based on a particular ideology, empiricism, and represents a narrow perspective (1089).

John Scheib (chapter 4) was asked to author the chapter on theoretical frameworks that specifically grapples with the definition of theoretical framework, as well as includes a discussion of those frameworks and specific theories that have been explored in music education. His chapter includes a brief discussion of what he refers to as "methodological" frames, including phenomenology, interpretive interactionism, symbolic interactionism, and social constructionism. He also provides a comprehensive look at "theories" used in music education qualitative research, including theories of gender, teacher development, and role stress, among others. Scheib highlights that there is considerable confusion within the music education research community regarding theoretical frameworks and their use.

Patton (2002) provides a list 16 of what he considered the most common theoretical traditions, including: ethnography, autoethnography, reality testing (positivist and realist approaches), constructionism/constructivism, phenomenology, heuristic inquiry, ethnomethodology, symbolic interaction, semiotics, hermeneutics, narratology/narrative analysis, ecological psychology, systems theory, chaos theory (nonlinear dynamics), grounded theory, and orientational (feminist inquiry, critical theory, queer theory, among others). Complete chapters could have been written about any one of these traditions. However, few of them have been used extensively in music education.

Decisions regarding designs presented in this book (case study, narrative, phenomenology, ethnography, and practitioner inquiry) were made with regard to the common use of those approaches within music education. I had considered a chapter on the use of grounded theory. Although Creswell (2018) includes grounded theory as one of five specific approaches to qualitative research (his list includes case study, phenomenology, ethnography, narrative, and grounded theory), my initial sense was that there were not enough studies in music education that used the term "grounded theory" as an approach or design. In attending the Ethnographic and Qualitative Research conference in 2011 that I mentioned earlier, we noticed that the term "grounded theory" appeared in the abstract or handout of almost every presenter, but not as a design as much as an analysis procedure or as an overall term describing a characteristic of qualitative research.

In chapter 1 of this *Handbook* Matsunobu and Bresler mention grounded theory briefly and state:

> The idea of building a local or grounded theory is appealing to music education researchers, and grounded theory is sometimes noted as a main methodological tool in music education research. However, such research does not always utilize a theoretical sampling or gradual sampling method. Rather, the emphasis is placed upon category formation, reformation, and comparison as well as a constant shift between coding and analysis. Because of its positivist and postpositivist orientation (Denzin and Lincoln 2011), grounded theory is most frequently utilized in such fields as nursing and medical studies. Emphasis on grounded theory in music education research is less frequent, partly because its theory-building process with gradual sampling involves multiple cycles of case selection and takes longer than other types of case study. (10)

The 2011 edition of the *Sage Handbook of Qualitative Research* (Denzin and Lincoln 2011) includes a chapter entitled "Grounded Theory Methods in Social Justice Research" in which Kathy Charmaz[2] states:

> Grounded theory is a method of qualitative inquiry in which data collection and analysis reciprocally inform and shape each other through an emergent and iterative process. The term "grounded theory" refers to this method and its product, a theory developed from successive conceptual analysis of data. Researchers may adopt grounded theory strategies while using a variety of data collection methods. . . . It is often difficult, however, to discern the extent to which researchers have engaged grounded theory strategies (Charmaz 2007, 2010; Timmermans and Tavory 2007). (360)

I feel as if these sources support the notion that grounded theory may be used as a method, but may also be regularly combined with other approaches. Very few researchers in music education have stated grounded theory as their approach. No music education scholars have written extensively on the topic when compared to the other authors in this book, who have all published studies in music education using the approach they write about.

NOTES

1. This section of the Preface draws from Abeles and Conway (2010).
2. Charmaz is often referred to in the qualitative research scholarship as the author of "social constructivist grounded theory," which differs from the older version put forth by Glaser and Strauss (1967).

REFERENCES

Abeles, Harold, and Colleen M. Conway. 2010. "The Inquiring Music Teacher." In *Critical Issues in Music Education: Contemporary Theory and Practice*, edited by H. Abeles and L. Custodero, 276–302. New York: Oxford University Press.

Barrett, M. S., and S. L. Stauffer. 2009. "Narrative Inquiry: From Story to Method." In *Narrative Inquiry in Music Education: Troubling Certainty*, edited by M. S. Barrett and S. L. Stauffer, 7–17. Dordrecht, The Netherlands: Springer.

Barrett, M. S., and S. L. Stauffer. 2012. "Resonant Work: Toward an Ethic of Narrative Research." In *Narrative Soundings: An Anthology of Narrative Inquiry in Music Education*, edited by M. S. Barrett and S. L. Stauffer, 1–17. Dordrecht, The Netherlands: Springer.

Barone, Tom 2001. *Touching Eternity*. New York: Teachers College Press.

Bogden, Robert, and Sari K. Biklin. 2007. *Qualitative Research for Education: An Introduction to Theory and Methods*. 5th ed. Needham Heights, MA: Allyn and Bacon.

Bresler, Liora. 1995. "Ethnography, Phenomenology and Action Research in Music Education." *Quarterly Journal of Music Teaching and Learning* 6 (3): 4–16.

Bresler, Liora, and Robert E. Stake. 1992. "Qualitative Research Methodology in Music Education." In *Handbook of Research on Music Teaching and Learning*, edited by R. Colwell, 75–90. New York: Schirmer.

Charmaz, Kathryn. 2007. "Constructionism and Grounded Theory." In *Handbook of Constructionist Research*, edited by J. A. Holstein and J. F. Gubrium, 319–412. New York: Guilford.

Charmaz, Kathryn. 2010. "Studying the Experience of Chronic Illness through Grounded Theory." In *New Directions in the Sociology of Chronic and Disabling Conditions: Assaults on the Lifeworld*, edited by G. Scambler and S. Scambler, 8–36. London: Palgrave.

Charmaz, Kathryn, 2011. "Grounded Theory Methods in Socil Justice Research." In *The Sage Handbook of Qualitative Research*, edited by N. K. Denzin and Y. S. Lincoln, 4th ed., 359–80. Thousand Oaks, CA: Sage.

Creswell, John. 2018. *Qualitative Inquiry and Research Design: Choosing among Five Approaches*. 4th ed. Thousand Oaks, CA: Sage Publications.

Denzin, Norman K., and Yvonne S. Lincoln, eds. 1994. *Handbook of Qualitative Research*. Thousand Oaks, CA: Sage Publications.

Denzin, Norman K., and Yvonne S. Lincoln, eds. 2000. *Handbook of Qualitative Research*. 2nd ed. Thousand Oaks, CA: Sage Publications.

Denzin, Norman, and Yvonne S. Lincoln. 2005. *The Sage Handbook of Qualitative Research*. 3rd ed. Thousand Oaks, CA: Sage Publications.

Denzin, Norman, K., and Yvonne S. Lincoln. 2011. *The Sage Handbook of Qualitative Research*. 4th ed. Thousand Oaks, CA: Sage Publications.

Eisenhart, M. 1998. "On the Subject of Interpretive Reviews." *Review of Educational Research* 68 (4): 391–399.

Elliott, David. 2002. "Philosophical Perspectives on Research." In *The New Handbook of Research on Music Teaching and Learning*, edited by R. Colwell and C. P. Richardson, 85–103. New York: Oxford University Press.

Ethnographic and Qualitative Research Conference Program. 2011. Cedarville, OH.

Flinders, David J., and Carol P. Richardson. 2002. "Contemporary Issues in Qualitative Research and Music Education." In *The New Handbook of Research of Music Teaching and Learning*, edited by R. Colwell and C. P. Richardson, 1159–1176. New York: Oxford University Press.

Glaser, B. G., and A. L. Strauss. 1967. *The Discovery of Grounded Theory*. Chicago: Aldine.

Hammersley, M., and P. Atkinson. 2007. *Ethnography: Principles in Practice*. 3rd ed. New York: Routledge.

Heller, J. J., and Edward J. P. O'Connor. 2002. "Maintaining Quality in Research and Reporting." In *The New Handbook of Research on Music Teaching and Learning*, edited by R. Colwell and C. Richardson, 1089–107. New York: Oxford University Press.

Maxwell, Joseph A. 2013. *Qualitative Research Design: An Interactive Approach*. 3rd ed. Thousand Oaks, CA: Sage Publications.

Merriam, Sharon B. 1998. *Qualitative Research and Case Study Applications in Education*. San Francisco: Jossey-Bass.

Merriam, Sharon, B. 2009. *Qualitative Research: A Guide to Design and Implementation*. San Francisco: Jossey-Bass.

Merriam, Sharon B., and E. J. Tisdell. 2016. *Qualitative Research: A Guide to Design and Implementation*. 4th ed. San Francisco: Jossey-Bass Publications.

Patton, Michael Q. 2002. *Qualitative Research and Evaluation Methods*, 3rd ed. Thousand Oaks, CA: Sage Publications.

Patton, Michael Q. 2015. *Qualitative Research and Evaluation Methods*. 4th ed. Thousand Oaks, CA: Sage Publications.

Phillips, Kenneth H. 2008. *Exploring Research in Music Education and Music Therapy*. New York: Oxford University Press.

Seidman, Irving. 1990. *Interviewing as Qualitative Research*. New York: Teachers College Press.

Seidman, Irving. 1997. *Interviewing as Qualitative Research*. 2nd ed. New York: Teachers College Press.

Seidman, Irving. 2006. *Interviewing as Qualitative Research*. 3rd. ed. New York: Teachers College Press.

Stake, Robert E. 1995. *The Art of Case Study Research*. Thousand Oaks, CA: Sage Publications.

Stake, Robert E. 2010. *Qualitative Research: Studying How Things Work*. New York: Guilford Press.

Strauss, Anslum, and Juliet Corbin. 1998. *Basics of Qualitative Research: Techniques and Procedures for Developing Grounded Theory*. 2nd ed. Thousand Oaks, CA: Sage Publications.

Timmermans, S., and I. Tavory. 2007. "Advancing Ethnographic Research through Grounded Theory Practice." In *The Sage Handbook of Grounded Theory*, edited by A. Bryant and K. Charmaz, 493–512. London: Sage Publications.

Vidich, A. J., and S. M. Lyman. 2003. "Qualitative Methods: Their History in Sociology and Anthropology." In *The Landscape of Qualitative Research: Theories and Issues*, edited by N. K. Denzin and Y. S. Lincoln, 55–129. Thousand Oaks, CA: Sage Publications.

Wiersma, William, and Stephen G. Jurs. 2009. *Research Methods in Education*. 9th ed. Boston, MA: Pearson.

Contributors

Randall Everett Allsup, Associate Professor of Music Education, Teachers College, Columbia University

Janet R. Barrett, Professor of Music Education, University of Illinois

Liora Bresler, Professor of Curriculum and Instruction, University of Illinois

Colleen M. Conway, Professor of Music Education, University of Michigan

Scott N. Edgar, Associate Professor of Music, Lake Forest College

Kate R. Fitzpatrick, Associate Professor of Music Education, University of Michigan

Ryan M. Hourigan, Professor of Music Education and Director, School of Music, Ball State University

Patti J. Krueger, Professor of Music Education, University of Puget Sound

Koji Matsunobu, Honorary Research Fellow, University of Queensland, Australia

Janet Robbins, Professor of Music, West Virginia University (Emeritus)

John W. Scheib, Professor of Music Education and Dean of the College of Fine Arts, University of Utah

Sandra L. Stauffer, Professor of Music Education, Arizona State University

Chad West, Associate Professor of Music Education, Ithaca College

APPROACHES TO QUALITATIVE RESEARCH

CHAPTER 1

....

QUALITATIVE RESEARCH IN MUSIC EDUCATION

Concepts, Goals, and Characteristics

....

KOJI MATSUNOBU AND LIORA BRESLER

Sound is central to making sense, to knowing, to experiential truth.

(Feld 1996, 97)

THE past 20 years have been a coming of age for qualitative research in music education.[1] From a marginal, pariah methodology, qualitative research has become a legitimate, central methodology, with its own conferences, research journals, and venues. Mainstream qualitative genres such as case study and ethnography have proliferated (Lane 2011). New genres such as narrative and arts-based research have emerged (Barrett and Stauffer 2009, 2012; Bresler 2006; Barone and Eisner 2012; McCarthy 2004, 2007). From a methodologically conservative discipline in the late 1980s, inquiry in music education research has become fertile and cutting edge. A testimony to the richness, breadth, and depth of qualitative research in music education is this *Handbook*'s focus on qualitative inquiry.

The discipline has extended its foci to explore the processes of music teaching and learning, attending to the voices of teachers and learners at different ages, stages, and educational levels (Blair 2009; Bresler 1998; Conway et al. 2010; Powell 2003; Silvey 2005; Solomonson 2011). Research on the uses of technology in music education, corresponding to their dramatic increase in the past 30 years, has propagated (Bresler 1987; Ruthman 2006; Shin 2011; Thibeault 2007). Recognizing the educational power of music outside of schools, qualitative researchers have also examined the lived experience of listening to and making music in a broad range of settings, including instrumental studio teaching (Kedem 2009; Miller 2012), home schooling (Nichols 2012), musical interactions in playgrounds (Harwood 1998), performing arts centers (Bresler 2010), army bands (Cape and Nichols 2012), ensembles for elder musicians (Tsugawa 2009), and communities of ethnic music (Matsunobu 2011, 2012; Powell 2003; Veblen

1994). These experiences and educational practices of engaging in musical activities are not new (even when a specific technology may be). Performing and listening in diverse spaces, from the formal to the recreational, the mundane to the spiritual, have been with us for thousands of years. What is new is the application of disciplined, systematic inquiry toward an in-depth understanding of lived experience and processes of engagement, acknowledging the multiplicity of contexts and perspectives in shaping deeply held values, in learning, and in developing.

Qualitative research, which is by definition a social construct, is an umbrella term for a wide array of genres, including case study, ethnography, phenomenology, narrative inquiry, action, and formative research. Recognizing the differences in intellectual traditions, purposes, units of analysis, and foci, there are still common elements likely to be agreed upon. This chapter examines the shared assumptions within qualitative research—its broad goals, key concepts, general characteristics, and methods. We draw on some current research in music education that exemplifies these goals and concepts, at times extending the scope of qualitative research to draw on the powerful characteristics of music and sound. Our charge is to focus on research in the United States. We take this to refer to research that was conducted in US universities, reflecting the intellectual and structural traditions in North America. We leave out fine work conducted by colleagues in Australia, Europe, Asia, South America, and Africa.[2] However, it is important to remember that at all times, and particularly in the early twenty-first century, the disciplinary communities of research in music education are intensely globalized. American scholars, like their counterparts in other countries, travel around the world to present their work and publish in international journals and publications, with knowledge crossing both ways.

1.1. INTELLECTUAL ROOTS AND ASSUMPTIONS OF QUALITATIVE RESEARCH

As a scholarly discipline, music education has its inception in two parents: music and education. Shaped by postmodernist thinking (Denzin and Lincoln 2011), qualitative educational research can be traced to multiple traditions, primarily philosophy, anthropology, and action research. These represent two orientations (Bresler 1996): basic, with a primary goal of understanding (manifested, for example, in the traditions of anthropology and phenomenology); and applied, aimed toward a direct improvement of practice (manifested, for example, in action and formative research). Within philosophy, foundational to all research, phenomenology delves into uncovering the meaning and structure of lived experience and the inter-subjective world (van Manen 1990), with hermeneutics examining the theory and practice of interpretation (Gadamer 1988).

Qualitative research in music can be traced to ethnomusicology, itself the child of anthropology and musicology. Just as anthropologists seek to understand how a cultural system operates and shapes human interactions in a given society, ethnomusicologists explore the musical system of a culture and cultural system of music, focusing on the meanings and values of specific musical behaviors, processes, and products (Merriam 1964; Nettl 2005). The scope of ethnomusicology includes investigating the ways in which music is taught and learned in both formal and informal contexts.

These approaches, with their distinct emphases and intellectual traditions, provide an epistemological foundation of qualitative research methodology, generating specific methods to address goals in music education. The underlying assumption of hermeneutics and phenomenology that has influenced field-based inquiry is that social reality is constructed based on the specific perspective of the individual, evidenced, for example, in the diverse experiences by different people of the same musical performance, shaped by their personal and cultural contexts. Accordingly, social reality, unlike physical reality, is perspectival and multiple.

The situated nature of the researcher in relation to the social reality she studies marks a departure from the objectivist view that reality exists outside human consciousness. Qualitative research epistemologies presuppose that knowledge is neither inside a person nor outside in the world but exists in the relationship between them because humans are not mere repositories of knowledge but active constructors of meaning. In an interview setting, this suggests that the interviewee is seen as an active constructor of knowledge in collaboration with the interviewer rather than a vessel of answers (Holstein and Gubrium 2002). Whereas positivist research implicates fixed, objective distances, qualitative research involves the navigation of distances and movements among different perspectives, relying on the participants situated in diverse points, aiming to expand habitual forms of perceiving.

Researchers, like their participants, are situated within a specific context and perspective. Researchers' "subjectivities" (Peshkin 1988, 1994)—background, values, and lenses—shape their interpretation and, as such, must be acknowledged in the foreground. Rather than an enemy, subjectivity in research is a given, part of the human condition. Typically too close to discern, our subjectivities require acknowledgment and effort to cultivate a certain amount of distance (Bresler, chapter 12 of Volume 3 of this *Handbook*). Because of this nature, qualitative research can be conducive to self-awareness and the ability to perceive oneself. We are often unaware of our own values and frameworks of understanding until we face them in light of those of our informants. Positing that research is a journey and the researcher is a traveler, Kvale (1996, 4) observes,

> The journey may not only lead to new knowledge; the traveler might change as well. The journey might instigate a process of reflection that leads the interviewer to new ways of self-understanding, as well as uncovering previously taken-for-granted values and customs in the traveler's home country.

Emotions have an important role in helping identify subjectivity. From a feminist perspective, Jaggar (1989) argues against the view that emotions lead to errors or biases in research and claims that emotions and feelings are socially and culturally constructed and connected with cognition. Kleinman and Copp (1993) examine how emotions inform and support analysis. People in the same value system often share emotional responses and make similar judgments. Empathy, as Wilhelm Dilthey established more than a century ago, is a key goal of qualitative research (Stueber 2008). It is also its close partner (Bresler 2013). Empathy[3] involves "putting oneself in someone's shoes," in the specific context of the participant. Empathy helps us to understand the meaning of a person's action and experience "from within" but not in an attached manner.[4]

The relationships of the researcher with the setting differ, depending on the specific scholarly tradition. Anthropologists and ethnomusicologists have typically been cultural outsiders to the settings they study. Music educators are often insiders of the culture and values of their settings. Therefore, they are the experts and most knowledgeable of cultural knowledge (Eisner 1991). As insiders to the setting, they are likely to have better understanding and discernment of contents, pedagogies, and traditions. The pitfall is that they may have stronger convictions and persuasions, and may be prone to being more judgmental and less open to alternative views.

The forms through which interpretations are created and communicated shape the messages. The use of statistical measures and numbers emphasizes similarities across large samples and aims at reduction. Qualitative research, in contrast, aims at portraying the richness of individual cases through "thick descriptions" (Geertz 1973) and narrative, possibly incorporating visuals and sounds. The pursuit of depth and complexity and the attention to holistic, contextual reality rather than a priori variables require prolonged engagement. Prolonged engagement and immersion in the setting allow researchers to develop understanding through encounters and interactions with their participants, facilitating identification of additional foci and emerging relevant contexts. Data collection occurs simultaneously with preliminary data analysis, the latter shaping the next cycles of fieldwork. Research then is situational and emergent, recognizing and making explicit the interactive aspect between the researcher and the setting.

1.2. INTERPRETATION

Interpretation is required in any type of social research. In qualitative research, interpretation is ongoing and multiple: qualitative researchers aim to provide credible interpretations of the meanings, functions, and consequences of human actions, from the viewpoints of diverse participants. Interpretation starts from the very beginning of the research design and process—what to look at, where to start, whom to talk to, what issue to draw on; it continues throughout the stages of data gathering, analysis, and write-up of the study.

Researchers aim to be reflexive and open to new ways of looking, while seeking trustworthiness of their observations and interpretations. The concept of an "interpretive zone" originally referred to teamwork in research, where the group has multiple researchers[5] (Bresler et al. 1996; Wasser and Bresler 1996), and centers on contrapuntal interpretations as both process and product. The interactive voices of the different researchers—perspectives, commitments, and interpretations—create a polyphonic texture, with its consonances and dissonances. This zone forms a basis from which to further perceive, investigate, and negotiate understandings, striving to acknowledge multiple layers of meaning and achieve higher credibility. The practice of peer debriefing (one of the criteria suggested by Lincoln and Guba 1985) can be regarded as the creation of a (limited scope) zone to invite diverse etic perspectives, facilitating reflection on the gap between etic and emic perspectives in an effort to connect them.[6]

Qualitative research work often includes reflective anecdotes regarding the evolution of research perspectives, the trajectory of researchers' engagement in the field, and the expansion of self-understanding. All of these bring to light the interpretation process and offer essential information about the researcher. The fact that qualitative research can inform, reform, and transform self-understanding is part of the reason why qualitative research can be so rewarding.

1.3. REFLEXIVE PROCESSES OF RESEARCH DESIGNING, DATA COLLECTION, AND ANALYSIS

Qualitative researchers normally do not bring a fixed research design to fieldwork because they need to respond to the constraints and possibilities of each field. Research strategies are often emergent and subject to change in the research process (Hammersley and Atkinson 2007; Patton 2001). For example, initial research questions—often generated from etic points of view in the abstract context of scholarship rather than the realities of the settings—are refined over the course of research to make sense in the reality of each setting. Research is often guided by emergent questions. Some predetermined, a priori categories for data analysis and codes may be kept, while others will be generated in the process of data analysis. Similarly, literature review needs to respond to emerging issues (Eisenhart 1998). The researcher goes back and forth between theoretical and empirical data to refine understandings and interpretations. Because of this emergent process of qualitative research, methodological explanation is often provided in retrospect (Barone 2001; Vidich and Lyman 2003).

In the field, the researcher aims to meet diverse participants and observe all relevant events, to grasp a picture of what is going on, especially in the beginning phase of fieldwork. Fieldwork may start slowly as the researcher settles into a site. Data collection typically takes weeks and months. So does forming relationships in the field. It is often after the researcher leaves the field that a clearer idea of what he should have done emerges. This is why preliminary data analyses in the form of contact summary sheets and interim reports (Miles and Huberman 1984/1994) are extremely valuable. While the extent of fieldwork varies across genres—ethnographies are particularly long, with researchers commonly staying for a number of years, whereas evaluation case studies are characteristically short—the principle of collecting as much data as possible to facilitate an in-depth understanding of the field or phenomena applies to any genre of qualitative research.

Qualitative research is a collaborative endeavor, aiming to capture and incorporate different perspectives. Music educators writing within the traditions of ethnography and ethnomusicology collaborate with insiders to the culture. Support and assistance of these insiders for accessing the community, interviewing informants, and confirming research data are the conditions for successful research. Those operating in the traditions of action or formative research, typically key players in their settings, incorporate the voices of their collaborators in the settings. At the same time, they aim to draw on perspectives of outsiders for fresh perception of issues. In these processes, building relationships, including rapport and sociality, becomes a central part of the research experience. Qualitative researchers attend to what the informants feel, sense, and think, and become companions of the informants' lives for short (or longer) periods of time. Relations have to be established and identities co-constructed (Hammersley and Atkinson 2007, 4). Sometimes, the relationship fades out; at other times, it continues and evolves after the project. What makes relationships in qualitative research unusual (as compared not only with quantitative research but also with "ordinary" life) is the intensified transformation of researcher/participant relationships, a transformation that works in both directions (Bresler 1997, 20).

Qualitative research can be intensive in the forming of engagement and relationship. In his study, Matsunobu (2009) experienced such intensity while examining the lived experience of spirituality among adult music learners who participated in a musical pilgrimage from North America to Japan. As a researcher, language translator, and cultural insider, he shared 24 hours a day with the participants during the month of the pilgrimage. Drawing on the work of Victor Turner, he reported that the experiences of sharing sacredness and deepening spirituality brought him and his participants a sense of "communitas," making them deeply connected. This shared experience served as a point of reference for their subsequent reflections and understandings of musical and spiritual growth.

If the unit of analysis of phenomenology is the individual, emphasizing the uniqueness of the individual, the unit of analysis of anthropology and ethnomusicology is on the culture or sub-culture, highlighting shared values. The essence of ethnographic process is to make the strange familiar and to make the familiar strange. Emphasizing the former process, music education research has provided a wealth of knowledge about music teaching and learning. For instance, in his ethnography on Japanese brass bands, Hebert (2012) examined broader social, cultural, political, and historical contexts of music education, and revealed the system through which these contexts shape the current practice of school band and the culture of competition. Feay-Shaw (2002) explored the interface of Ghanaian and school cultures by examining how Ghanaian music was transmitted and taught in different settings, including higher education and secondary school contexts, by cultural bearers, foreign practitioners, and schoolteachers whose exposure to and expertise in Ghanaian drumming significantly varied. Powell (2003), while working with a group of taiko players in a community setting as a participatory observer, revealed a cultural pedagogy that helped them communicate their spirits and achieve body-mind and body-instrument integration.

Music education research also benefits from engaging in the process of making the familiar strange. For instance, Della Pietra and Campbell (1995) examined the culture of improvisation in American higher education using an ethnographic lens. Since improvisation is not a significant part of the musical training system in the United States, the researchers observed a music education methods course and examined the ways music education students developed an understanding of improvisation. Similarly, in her case study of a university vocal ensemble, Zaretti (1998) explored the processes and challenges of learning multicultural music through a combination of ethnomusicological and educational perspectives.

1.4. EXPLORATION OF AND THROUGH SENSES

We see the world as a noun and hear it as a verb.

—Burrows (1990, 21)

David Howes contends that anthropology's engagement with the sensory has shifted over the last century and a half from a concern with measuring bodies and recording sense data to an interest in sensing patterns, followed by an interest in reading texts, and finally to writing culture (Howes 2003, 3). In the course of these shifts, the content of anthropological knowledge has changed from being multisensory and social to being "spectacularly stylized" and centered on the individual ethnographer (Howes 2003, 3). The fundamental assumption of what came to be known as the "anthropology of the senses" is that sensory perception is a cultural as well as a physical act—that is, sight, hearing, touch, taste, and smell are not only means of apprehending physical phenomena, but also avenues for the transmission of cultural values (Classen 1997, 401). Given that perception is conditioned by culture, the ways in which people perceive the world may vary as cultures vary. Sensation, Howes suggests, is not just a matter of physiological response and personal experience, but is the most basic domain of cultural expression, the medium through which all the values and practices of society are enacted. Every domain of sensory experience, from music and sound through the scent of perfume to the savor of dinner, is a field of cultural elaboration, an arena for structuring social roles and interactions. We learn social divisions, as well as distinctions of gender, class, and race, through our senses. Sensual relations, Howes argues, are social relations (Howes 2003, xi).

If anthropology of the senses attends to embodiment as a tool of research and aims to expand what we investigate, arts-based research is a distinctive genre of social research that focuses on communicating multisensory dimensions of human experiences (Cahnmann-Taylor and Siegesmund 2008; Leavy 2009). The underlying belief of arts-based research is that artistic processes can inform educational research because the arts open up human sensibilities. Irwin and de Cosson claim that we as artists live "a life of awareness, a life that permits openness to the complexity around us, a life that intentionally sets out to perceive things differently" (2004, 33). Indeed, fundamental aspects of qualitative research, such as sense of space, meaning of silence, embodiment of relationship, ethics of mutual tuning-in, and nonverbal interactions, are what artists have explored through their work.

For musicians, sound is a medium of knowing, and music serves for them as an inspiration and process of research (Gouzouasis 2006; Leavy 2009). Sonic ethnography is a form of research to explore auditory dimensions of human experience as shaping and being shaped by the sound world (Powell 2012). Sonic ethnography of the school environment illuminates the uses, functions, and meanings of sound and music as part of the everyday construct of lived experience at school (Gershon 2011; Lum and Campbell 2007). The enculturation of musicians into the sound world heightens their perception of temporal dimensions such as sonic form, dynamics, rhythm, timbre, and orchestration (Bresler and Stake 1992; Bresler 2005). Aspects of musicianship, such as embodied connection and improvisation, are key to forming relationships with participants and settings (Bresler 2006).

1.5. CASE-SPECIFIC UNDERSTANDING

> Every person is like every other person but like no other person.
> —Denzin (2001, 39)

Qualitative research in education normally focuses on a few cases to facilitate in-depth study of educational phenomena. It is an inquiry of the particular rather than the general. The emphasis of the study is sometimes placed on understanding the case itself, other times on examining specific issues across cases (Stake 1995). Either way, the quality of the study depends on the richness of case(s) rather than the size of sample(s). Cases may be selected for different reasons: typicality, variety, balance of the cases, and representation of issues. Generalization in qualitative research can be made not to the population but to the issues and concepts that have been explored. The discussion of validity in qualitative research has less to do with the replicability of research than the plausibility of interpretation.

Qualitative scholars argue that case-specific understanding may transfer to other cases because every case represents its kind and thus shares with other cases a set of social, cultural, and historical contexts (Denzin 2001). Barone and Eisner observe, "In the particular resides the general," suggesting that one of the functions of qualitative research is "to locate what is general in what is particular" (2006, 101). As Jean-Paul Sartre has observed early on (in Denzin 2001), the universality of human reality can thus be understood through the singularity.

Context is background information that helps us understand the case. Contexts include the evolution of the case. In his *Touching Eternity*, depicting an art program in an Appalachian high school, Barone (2001) depicts the geographical context of the school, as well as the economics of the region, the culture and worldview of its inhabitants, and the artwork presented on walls of the schools.

Case studies in music education often opt for "typical" or non-atypical cases. For example, Silvey (2005) explored learning experiences of musical works through 13-year-old Ingrid. Silvey's case report begins: "There is nothing remarkable about Ingrid, one of three dozen young choral singers . . ." (11). Through this case, Silvey explains not only how Ingrid developed her relationships with musical pieces but also, without generalizing, what is possibly going on in the minds of many ordinary students. An in-depth understanding of a typical case helps the reader to understand the nature of other cases.

Stake, Bresler, and Mabry selected ordinary schools for their case studies of music and arts education. Mindful about "the hospitality of school district and teachers, and the complexity of the arts offering and community" (1991, 3–4), they aimed for a variety of demographics. In this multiple case project, each of the seven sites was unique. The researchers' interest was not in comparing the sites in terms of various criteria but in "giving each school a chance to tell its story of arts education."

Music education research targets not only typical cases but also exceptional and unusual cases, just as ethnomusicology research deals with both exceptional cases (e.g., gurus, leading performers, influential teachers) and ordinary cases (e.g., amateur players, beginning students) to draw a picture of a culture and its musical system. An example of an unusual case is that discussed by Carlow (2006), who explored immigrant students' musical experiences. In this particular work, she shed light on a Russian immigrant of Korean ancestry who was in the school choir; she depicted this student's experiences of cultural isolation, displacement, and also tension with a choral teacher. Among other participants, this student stood out, not because her parents come from distinctive cultural backgrounds, but rather, because she did not feel "American" she experienced being invisible in choral concerts at school. For a best-case example, Veblen (1994) observed and interviewed exemplary teachers to examine the changes and stability of the Irish music tradition. Here, the cases were selected by the reputation of teachers as well as their representation of diverse instruments, ages, and geographical locations.

Within the context of scientific expectation of generalizability, and knowing that generalizations are impossible, as lived experience is never context-free, qualitative researchers face the complex relationship between the singular and the universal, individual and collective experiences, particularization and generalization, micro-analysis and macro-analysis (Seale 1999; Stake 2010). Aware that generalization across cases is impossible, some researchers intend to build a theory through case studies. Grounded theory approach (Strauss and Corbin 1990) emerged from such aspirations, leading to the formulation of the "theoretical sampling" technique (Glaser and Strauss 1967). Theoretical sampling encourages a gradual sampling process of cases according to "their (expected) level of new insights for the developing theory, in relation to the state of theory elaboration so far" (Flick 1998, 65). This process involves teasing out patterns, themes, and concepts from data analysis, generating a hypothesis, and testing through purposefully selected cases to prove its applicability and also to rule out other explanations.

The idea of building a local or grounded theory is appealing to music education researchers, and grounded theory is sometimes noted as a main methodological tool in music education research. However, such research does not always utilize a theoretical sampling or gradual sampling method. Rather, the emphasis is placed upon category formation, reformation, and comparison, as well as a constant shift between coding and analysis. Because of its positivist and postpositivist orientation (Denzin and Lincoln 2011), grounded theory is most frequently utilized in such fields as nursing and medical studies. Emphasis on grounded theory in music education research is less frequent, partly because its theory-building process with gradual sampling involves multiple cycles of case selection and takes longer than other types of case study.

1.6. WRITING, REPRESENTATION OF DATA, AND CRITERIA

Differences among different genres of qualitative research have to do with goals, positionality of the researcher, emphases, units of analysis, and intellectual traditions (Bresler 1995; Jaeger 1997).

Terms for qualitative research sometimes overlap. Different descriptors refer to various aspects of the research. The term *case study* highlights a bounded system (Stake 1995). The term *interpretive inquiry* (Erickson 1986) highlights the centrality of interpretation. Naturalistic inquiry emphasizes observations as the non-interventionist nature of the research. Narrative inquiry refers to the centrality of first-person accounts (versus observations). Rather than being distinct genres, different terms underline different aspects of the research. The use of biographical and autobiographical materials, photographs and other visuals, poetry (Prendergast, Gouzouasis, Leggo, and Irwin 2009; Wiggins 2011), performance texts, and other cultural artifacts is often grouped under arts-based research.

The choice of terminology regarding what used to be "subjects" in positivism conveys values. Van Manen favors "persons" to refer to the uniqueness of each human being. He quotes Auden: "As persons, we are incomparable, uncountable, irreplaceable" (Auden 1967, cited in van Manen 1990). Many prefer the term "participants," highlighting the collaborative aspect of the research, whereas others use the term "informants" (Schwandt 2001).[7]

Key concepts travel across genres. Ryle's "thick description" made famous by Geertz (1973) is central to many genres. Thick description refers to the researcher's goal to report cultural meanings understood by the insiders and negotiated by the researcher. Geertz (1973) emphasizes that thick description is not the same as detailed description of the event but is rather an interpretive report of cultural meanings. Denzin (2001) comments that whereas "a thin description simply reports facts, independent of intentions or the circumstances that surround the action," a good thick description provides context-rich information—the history and evolution of the action, the intentions of the actors, and the meanings exchanged by them—all of which helps us understand the deep structures, presuppositions, and meanings of social and cultural practices. In thick description, the researcher seeks an emic understanding and describes meanings of behaviors, situations, and events as they unfold in the lives of—and in the eyes (and ears) of—the informants (De Munck 2009).

While in the field, the researcher seeks triangulation of data in order to increase trustworthiness of interpretation. Triangulation originally refers to the researcher's effort to converge data from multiple sources. For some scholars, triangulation is not a strategy for convergence, but a way to look at the phenomenon from different angles for richer understanding, which may result in contradicting observations (Flick 1998).

The researcher will practice "member check" or "respondent validation" of data in the field to ensure that collected data are reliable from the insiders' viewpoints. The text may include many and diverse voices representing each standpoint. "Prolonged engagement" is also central to making a credible explanation of data. Qualitative researchers try to maximize their involvement in the field because the phenomena they study are often "long and episodic and evolving" (Stake 2010, 29). Deep immersion in a culture or group over a long period of time does not necessarily ensure the resulting interpretation. However, longer involvement allows for the emergence of more natural understanding of the case, affording time and space to linger with the data, to scrutinize initial understanding, and to explore additional interpretations. Numbers are usually important. Quantitative ideas of enumeration and differences in size provide useful contextual information about the cases or phenomena under study in qualitative research. The distinction between quantitative and qualitative methods is more of a matter of emphasis on the particular or the general than a discrete boundary: if findings are drawn primarily from the aggregate of many individual observations, we call the study "quantitative," but the research still may emphasize either the particular or the general (Stake 2010, 19).

The criteria for high-quality inquiry and for high-quality reports are not the same (Bresler and Stake 1992). The former is controlled largely by the researcher, who is responsible for providing a credible account and interpretation of the phenomenon with accuracy of information and well-rounded discussion of the data. The latter appeals to the experience of the reader, asking to what extent the research facilitates inferences and vicarious experiences regarding the reader's own situations and responsibilities. The criteria for qualitative research (as well as quantitative research) reports are determined by both the researcher and the user of the research. Concerned about the impact of research, some postmodernist researchers extend the traditional view of credibility by promoting the use of fictionalized stories in the final report (Barone 2001; Barone and Eisner 2012; Denzin 2001). Still, many share the worry about misrepresentation and misappropriation of others. The acknowledgment of researchers' values, the transparency of the research process, the recognition of multiple perspectives, and the practice of member checks are meant to increase trustworthiness.

1.7. ETHICS

Ethics must be embedded throughout the research process (Bresler 1997). Ethical concerns are present at each stage of the research process: when forming the study, entering and being in the field, conducting interviews, analyzing and interpreting data, leaving the field, writing and disseminating the report. Like other aspects of qualitative research, ethical concerns are emergent and subject to change depending on the nature of each field. Qualitative researchers apply research ethics not only in the abstract (in terms of general rules, principles, IRB procedures, consent forms, etc.) but also in concrete situations, to respond to the particular needs and ethical standards of the researched people. Beyond matters of legislation through consent agreement for fieldwork and interviews, ethical conduct for qualitative researchers involves caring, imagination, sensitivity, and empathy.

Ethics, like the notions of privacy and confidentiality, is culture-specific. For instance, different cultures differ in their notions of separation between private and public spaces and the relationships between self and other (e.g., Hamid 2010; Katyal 2011). Formal ethical concerns must be negotiated in each case to protect informants' dignity and potential vulnerability. As practices of music education involve participants with diverse cultural backgrounds and forms of music, we need to pay attention to situation-specific ethical norms in the research process. As ethnomusicology has noted time and again, ownership of music is culturally determined: some music allows only limited or strict access and is not supposed to be documented.

Researchers need to be wary of the aftermath of their work. Published documents, even with anonymity, may reveal identities to insiders within the community. Insiders can easily figure out who said what based on their relationships with other members of the community and their relationships with the researcher. Thus, ethical concerns for within-group members must be extensive and carefully examined. Published documents may influence policymaking decisions, which can lead to disadvantageous results for the community, individual members, and future practitioners. Researchers should be mindful of these possible outcomes of their practice before embarking on a qualitative research project and writing a report.

1.8. Coda

This chapter has discussed qualitative research in music education, including its episte-mological, methodological, and ethical assumptions. In addition to the types of qualita-tive research discussed in music education research, including case study, narrative, and ethnographic methods, other forms of qualitative research, such as auto-ethnography (Bartleet and Ellis 2009; Manovski 2012), self-study (Conway et al. 2010), and perfor-mance ethnography (Denzin 2003), are relatively uncharted. One emerging setting of inquiry is the Internet. People are increasingly experiencing and sharing music through the Internet and digital media and developing a network and a sense of belonging through online communication. The instruction of music is now provided online, often via Skype or YouTube, reaching out to students of geographically isolated places. Qualitative research is extending its scope to capture the nature of music-making and meaning-making processes mediated by digital media. The examination of explicit ed-ucational practices (Schmidt-Jones 2012; White 2012) is at its beginning, and we antici-pate increasing research on the educational implications of online communication and sharing of meanings and values (Markham 2007).

If the Internet invites a global, transnational expansion of musical practices, local cultures are as important in shaping identities. Qualitative research can be a powerful tool to uncover cultural assumptions and meanings of education anywhere. This is espe-cially so when multiple cultures are compared (e.g., Tobin, Hsueh, and Karasawa 2009), either globally or locally. Brand made an apt observation regarding this matter through his cross-cultural work on music teacher education: "There is a need for understanding how music education students see their experiences. And the ethnographic interview provides a means of understanding through the eyes of music education students from both our culture and from another culture" (2002, 60–61). Qualitative research in cross-cultural contexts can bring an external gaze into our profession, making the "familiar strange" and raising critical questions; for instance, what is the nature of competition in our band world as compared to similar phenomena in other cultures (Hebert 2012)? Why do we have more band specialists than string specialists in our profession (Lo 2013)? Why do brass instrumentalists choose to teach general music rather than instrumental music (Robinson 2010)? Underlying the use of qualitative research conducted in cross-cultural, international settings is the expectation that the field of music education will be advanced further by examining our taken-for-granted assumptions (Bresler and Ardichvili 2002).

We began our chapter by referring to Feld on the centrality of sound as a modality of knowing and being in the world. Sound is a way of knowing, and soundscapes are in-tegral to social worlds. To understand the former is to know the latter. His concept of "acoustemology," a union of acoustics and epistemology, highlights the dynamic inter-play of sounds and sensuality in human emplacement in the world. As musicians and music educators engaged in the exploration of sonic sensibilities, we can contribute sig-nificantly to understanding the educational aspects of sound and music and the forms of knowledge and understanding that music education provides.

The most important criterion for any research is that it is about something important to researchers, with implications to theory and practice. Qualitative research requires full commitment, heightened perception, prolonged and intensified engagement, a willingness and ability to notice and examine one's fundamental assumptions, habits, and attachments. It requires openness to other ways of perceiving and understanding. These qualities are necessary (though not sufficient) to convey the "compellingness" of the research to readers, to allow them to understand new and different perspectives. Craft is crucial—the craft of disciplined observation, producing data records, preliminary and intensive analysis, and writing. In these and other aspects of research, we recognize the open-ended, improvised aspects that do not lend themselves to prescriptive recommendations, but require responsiveness to what we encounter (Bresler 2005). Precisely because the researcher is the main instrument, the commitment, skills, and abilities of the researcher are crucial. With pressure for quick products (impossible in a methodology that calls for prolonged engagement in data collection and analysis), qualitative research (like quantitative research) can be superficial, resulting in reporting and summarizing rather than expanding understandings. Cultivating qualitative research skills and sensitivities is a lifelong process, responding to new situations and contexts rather than importing "ready-made" categories. In this sense, the journey involved in qualitative research is similar to that of musicians and educators; it is a journey that leads to new encounters and opens up fresh insights into our understanding of the world.

NOTES

1. We are indebted to Betsy Hearne for her reading of this manuscript and helpful suggestions.
2. A wealth of research papers by researchers from all over the world can be found in such journals as the *International Journal of Music Education*, *Research Studies in Music Education*, the *British Journal of Music Education*, *Asia-Pacific Journal of Arts Education*, *Music Education Research*, the *International Journal of Community Music*, and the *International Journal of Research in Arts Education*. Sections attending to research in music education in these continents can also be found in the *Handbook of Research in Arts Education* (Bresler 2007).
3. Empathy is distinguished from sympathy, the latter characterized by emotional accord rather than cognitive perception, and as such lends itself to advocacy rather than inquiry.
4. Critical activists and scholars whose ultimate goal of research is to make social change may claim that all researchers take sides. They advocate one point of view or another. Value-free interpretive research is impossible (for instance, Denzin 2001).
5. But this concept can easily be applied in such a way as to include participants.
6. "Emic" refers to insider perspective and "etic" to outsider perspective. Emic theories are based on "native" explanations and predictions, while etic theories are based on the researcher's explanations and predictions. Etic is not simply an outsider perspective but an expert's explanation. Most ethnographers seek to present emic-derived, folk theories while addressing comparative, cross-cultural, etic theories. (De Munck 2009, 13).
7. Reflecting similar concerns, some critical scholars avoid the term "data" because human experiences and narratives are not to be chopped into parts for comparison and labeling.

REFERENCES

Barone, T. 2001. *Touching Eternity*. New York: Teachers College Press.

Barone, T., and E. Eisner. 2006. "Arts-Based Educational Research." In *Handbook of Complementary Methods in Education Research*, edited by J. Green, G. Camilli, and P. Elmore, 93–107. New York: Lawrence Erlbaum Associates.

Barone, T., and W. E. Eisner. 2012. *Arts Based Research*. Thousand Oaks, CA: Sage Publications.

Barrett, M., and S. L. Stauffer, eds. 2009. *Narrative Inquiry in Music Education: Troubling Certainty*. New York: Springer.

Barrett, M., and S. L. Stauffer, eds. 2012. *Narrative Sounding: An Anthology of Narrative Inquiry in Music Education*. New York: Springer.

Bartleet, B. L., and C. Ellis, eds. 2009. *Music Autoethnographies: Making Autoethnography Sing/ Making Music Personal*. Brisbane: Australian Academic Press.

Blair, D. V. 2009. "Fostering Wakefulness: Narrative as a Curricular Tool in Teacher Education." *International Journal of Education & the Arts* 10 (19). http://www.ijea.org/v10n19/.

Brand, M. 2002. "An Ethnographic Study of Hong Kong and American Music Education Students." *Contributions to Music Education* 29 (2): 47–65.

Bresler, L. 1987. "The Role of the Computer in a Music Theory Classroom: Integration, Barriers, and Learning." PhD diss., Stanford University.

Bresler, L. 1995. "Ethnography, Phenomenology, and Action Research in Music Education." *Quarterly Journal of Music Teaching and Learning* 6 (3): 6–18.

Bresler, L. 1996. "Basic and Applied Qualitative Research in Music Education." *Research Studies in Music Education* 6: 5–17.

Bresler, L. 1997. "Towards the Creation of a New Code of Ethics in Qualitative Research." *Council of Research in Music Education* 130: 17–29.

Bresler, L. 1998. "The Genre of School Music and Its Shaping by Meso, Micro and Macro Contexts." *Research Studies in Music Education* 1: 2–18.

Bresler, L. 2005. "What Musicianship Can Teach Educational Research." *Music Education Research* 7 (2): 169–83.

Bresler, L. 2006. "Embodied Narrative Inquiry: Methodology of Connection." *Research Studies in Music Education* 27: 21–43.

Bresler, L., ed. 2007. *International Handbook of Research in Arts Education*. New York: Springer.

Bresler, L. 2010. "Teachers as Audiences: Exploring Educational and Musical Values in Youth Performances." *Journal of New Music Research* 39 (2): 135–45.

Bresler, L. 2013. "Cultivating Empathic Understanding in Research and Teaching." In *Aesthetics, Empathy and Education*, edited by B. White and T. Costantino, 9–28. New York: Peter Lang.

Bresler, L., and A. Ardichvili, eds. 2002. *Research in International Education: Experience, Theory, and Practice*. New York: Peter Lang.

Bresler, L., and R. E. Stake. 1992. "Qualitative Research Methodology in Music Education." In *Handbook of Research on Music Teaching and Learning*, edited by R. Colwell, 75–90. Reston, VA: MENC, The National Association for Music Educators.

Bresler, L., J. Wasser, N. Hertzog, and M. Lemons. 1996. "Beyond the Lone Ranger Researcher: Teamwork in Qualitative Research." *Research Studies in Music Education* 7: 15–30.

Burrows, D. 1990. *Sound, Speech, and Music*. Amherst: University of Massachusetts Press.

Cahnmann-Taylor, M., and R. Siegesmund. 2008. *Arts-Based Research in Education: Foundations for Practice*. New York: Routledge.

Cape, J., and J. Nichols. 2012. "Engaging Stories: Co-Constructing Narratives of Women's Military Bands." In *Narrative Sounding: An Anthology of Narrative Inquiry in Music Education*, edited by M. Barrett and S. Stauffer, 23–36. Dordrecht, The Netherlands: Springer.

Carlow, R. 2006. "Diva Irina: An English Language Learner in High School Choir." *Bulletin of the Council for Research in Music Education* 170: 63–77.

Classen, C. 1997. "Foundations for an Anthropology of the Senses." *International Social Science Journal* 153: 401–412.

Conway, C. M., J. Eros, K. Pellegrino, and C. West. 2010a. "Life as an Instrumental Music Education Student: Tensions and Solutions." *Journal of Research in Music Education* 58 (3): 260–75.

Conway, C. M., J. Eros, K. Pellegrino, and C. West. 2010b. "The Role of Graduate and Undergraduate Interactions in the Development of Preservice Music Teachers and Music Teacher Educators: A Self-Study in Music Teacher Education." *Bulletin of the Council for Research in Music Education* 183: 49–64.

Della Pietra, C. J., and P. S. Campbell. 1995. "An Ethnography of Improvisation Training in a Music Methods Course." *Journal of Research in Music Education* 43 (2): 112–26.

De Munck, V. C. 2009. *Research Design and Methods for Studying Cultures*. Lanham, MD: Altamira Press.

Denzin, N. K. 2001. *Interpretive Interactionism*. 2nd ed. Thousand Oaks, CA: Sage Publications.

Denzin, N. K. 2003. *Performance Ethnography: Critical Pedagogy and the Politics of Culture*. Thousand Oaks, CA: Sage Publications.

Denzin, N. K., and Lincoln Y. 2011. *The Sage Handbook of Qualitative Research*. Thousand Oaks, CA: Sage Publications.

Eisenhart, M. 1998. "On the Subject of Interpretive Reviews." *Review of Educational Research* 68 (4): 391–99.

Eisner, E. 1991. *The Enlightened Eye: Qualitative Inquiry and the Enhancement of Educational Practice*. New York: Macmillan.

Erickson, F. 1986. "Qualitative Methods in Research on Teaching." In *Handbook of Research on Teaching*, 3rd edition, edited by Merlin C. Wittrock. New York: Macmillan.

Feay-Shaw, S. J. 2002. "The Transmission of Ghanaian Music by Culture-Bearers: From Master Musician to Music Teacher." PhD diss., University of Washington, Seattle.

Feld, S. 1996. "Waterfalls of Song: An Acoustemology of Place Resounding in Bosavi, Papua New Guinea." In *Senses of Place*, edited by S. Feld and K. H. Basso, 91–135. Santa Fe, NM: School of American Research Press.

Flick, U. 1998. *An Introduction to Qualitative Research*. London: Sage Publications.

Gadamer, H. 1988. *Truth and Method*. Edited and translated by G. Barden and J. Cumming. New York: Crossroad.

Geertz, C. 1973. *The Interpretation of Cultures: Selected Essays*. New York: Basic Books.

Gershon, S. W. 2011. "Embodied Knowledge: Sounds as Educational Systems." *Journal of Curriculum Theorizing* 27 (2): 66–81.

Glaser, B., and A. Strauss. 1967. *The Discovery of Grounded Theory*. Chicago: Aldine.

Gouzouasis, P. 2006. "A/r/t/ography in Music Research: A Reunification of Musician, Researcher, and Teacher." *Arts and Learning Journal* 22 (1): 23–42.

Hamid, M. O. 2010. "Fieldwork for Language Education Research in Rural Bangladesh: Ethical Issues and Dilemmas." *International Journal of Research and Method in Education* 33 (3): 259–71.

Hammersley, M., and P. Atkinson, P. 2007. *Ethnography: Principles in Practice*. 3rd ed. New York: Routledge.

Harwood, E. 1998. "Go on Girl: Improvisation in the Play of African-American Girls." In *In the Course of Performance: Studies in the World of Musical Improvisation*, edited by P. Bohlman and B. Nettl, 113–26. Chicago: University of Chicago Press.

Hebert, D. G. 2012. *Wind Bands and Cultural Identity in Japanese Schools*. New York: Springer.

Holstein, J. A., and J. F. Gubrium. 2002. "Active Interviewing." In *Qualitative Research Methods*, edited by D. Weinberg, 112–26. Oxford: Blackwell.

Howes, D. 2003. *Sensual Relations: Engaging the Senses in Culture and Social Theory*. Ann Arbor: University of Michigan Press.

Irwin, R., L., and A. F. De Cosson, eds. 2004. *A/r/tography: Rendering Self through Arts-Based Living Inquiry*. Vancouver, BC: Pacific Educational Press.

Jaeger, R. 1997. *Complementary Methods for Research in Education. American Education Research Association*. Washington, DC: American Educational Research Association.

Jaggar, A. M. 1989. "Love and Knowledge: Emotion in Feminist Epistemology." *Inquiry: An Interdisciplinary Journal of Philosophy* 32 (2): 151–76.

Katyal, K. R. 2011. "Gate-Keeping and the Ambiguities in the Nature of 'Informed Consent' in Confucian Societies." *International Journal of Research and Method in Education* 34 (2): 147–59.

Kedem, Y. 2009. "To Be Like Primrose: Understanding Tradition in a Viola Studio." *Music Education Research* 13 (2): 135–48.

Kleinman, S., and M. C. Copp. 1993. *Emotions and Fieldwork*. Thousand Oaks, CA: Sage Publications.

Kvale, S. 1996. *InterViews: An Introduction to Qualitative Research Interviewing*. Thousand Oaks, CA: Sage Publications.

Lane, J. 2011. "A Descriptive Analysis of Qualitative Research Published in Two Eminent Music Education Research Journals." *Bulletin of the Council for Research in Music Education* 188: 65–76.

Leavy, P. 2009. *Method Meets Art: Arts-Based Research Practice*. New York: Guilford Press.

Lincoln, Y. S., and E. G. Guba. 1985. *Naturalistic Inquiry*. Beverly Hills, CA: Sage Publications.

Lo, K. Y. 2013. "An Intercultural Study of Selected Aspects of String Educators' Beliefs and Practices in the United States and the United Kingdom." PhD diss., Indiana University, Bloomington.

Lum, C., and P. S. Campbell. 2007. "The Sonic Surrounds of an Elementary School." *Journal of Research in Music Education* 55 (1): 31–47.

Manovski, M. 2012. "Finding My Voice: [Re]living, [Re]learning, and [Re]searching: Becoming a Singer in a Culture of Marginalization." PhD diss., Oakland University, Rochester, MI.

Markham, A. N. 2007. "The Internet as Research Context." In *Qualitative Research Practice*, edited by C. Seale, G. Gobo, J. Gubrium, and D. Silverman, 328–44. Thousand Oaks, CA: Sage Publications.

Matsunobu, K. 2009. "Artful Encounters with Nature: Ecological and Spiritual Dimensions of Music Learning." PhD diss., University of Illinois at Urbana-Champaign.

Matsunobu, K. 2011. "Spirituality as a Universal Experience of Music: A Case Study of North Americans' Approaches to Japanese Music." *Journal of Research in Music Education* 59 (3): 273–89.

Matsunobu, K. 2012. "The Role of Spirituality in Learning Music: A Case of North American Students of Japanese Music." *British Journal of Music Education* 29 (2): 181–92.

McCarthy, M. 2004. "Using Story to Capture the Scholarship of Practice." In *Mountain Lake Reader: Conversations on the Study and Practice of Music Teaching*, 34–42. Project of a Consortium of Universities. The University of Tennessee.

McCarthy, M. 2007. "Narrative Inquiry as a Way of Knowing in Music Education." *Research Studies in Music Education* 29: 3–12.

Merriam, A. 1964. *The Anthropology of Music*. Evanston, IL: Northwestern University Press.

Miles, M. B., and Huberman, A. M. 1994. *Qualitative Data Analysis: An Expanded Source Book*. 2nd ed. Thousand Oaks, CA: Sage Publications.

Miller, B. A. 2012. "Student Composition in a Private Studio Setting: Rethinking Assumptions." In *Narrative Sounding: An Anthology of Narrative Inquiry in Music Education*, edited by M. Barrett and S. Stauffer, 305–27. New York: Springer.

Nettl, B. 2005. *The Study of Ethnomusicology: Thirty-one Issues and Concepts*. 2nd ed. Urbana: University of Illinois Press.

Nichols, J. 2012. "Music Education in Homeschooling: Jamie's Story." In *Narrative Sounding: An Anthology of Narrative Inquiry in Music Education*, edited by M. Barrett and S. Stauffer, 115–25. New York: Springer.

Patton, Q. M. 2001. *Qualitative Research and Evaluation Methods*. 3rd ed. Thousand Oaks, CA: Sage Publications.

Peshkin, A. 1988. "In Search of Subjectivity: One's Own." *Educational Researcher* 17 (7): 17–21.

Peshkin, A. 1994. "The Presence of Self: Subjectivity in the Conduct of Qualitative Research." *Bulletin of the Council for Research in Music Education* 122: 45–57.

Powell, K. 2003. "Learning Together: Practice, Pleasure and Identity in a Taiko Drumming World." PhD diss., Stanford University, Stanford, CA.

Powell, K. 2012. "Composing Sound Identity in Taiko Drumming." *Anthropology and Education Quarterly* 34 (1): 101–19.

Prendergast, M., P. Gouzouasis, C. Leggo, and R. Irwin. 2009. "A Haiku Suite: The Importance of Music Making in the Lives of Secondary School Students." *Music Education Research* 11 (3): 303–17.

Robinson, M. 2010. "From the Band Room to the General Music Classroom: Why Instrumentalists Choose to Teach General Music." *Bulletin of the Council for Research in Music Education* 185: 33–48.

Ruthman, S. A. 2006. "Negotiating Learning and Teaching in a Music Technology Lab: Curricular, Pedagogical, and Ecological Issues." PhD diss., Oakland University, Rochester, MI.

Schmidt-Jones, C. 2012. "An Open Education Resource Supports a Diversity of Inquiry-Based Learning." *International Review of Research in Open and Distance Learning* 13 (1): 1–16.

Schwandt, T. A. 2001. *Dictionary of Qualitative Inquiry*. 2nd ed. Thousand Oaks, CA: Sage Publications.

Seale, C. 1999. *Quality in Qualitative Research*. Thousand Oaks, CA: Sage Publications.

Shin, H. 2011. "Enabling Young Composers through the Vermont MIDI Project: Composition, Verbalization and Communication." PhD diss., University of Illinois at Urbana-Champaign.

Silvey, P. E. 2005. "Learning to Perform Benjamin Britten's Rejoice in the Lamb: The Perspectives of Three High School Choral Singers." *Journal of Research in Music Education* 53: 102–19.

Solomonson, G. T. 2011. "Segue: Entering into a Legacy." PhD diss., University of Illinois at Urbana-Champaign.

Stake, R. E. 1995. *The Art of Case Study Research*. Thousand Oaks, CA: Sage Publications.

Stake, R. 2010. *Qualitative Research: Studying How Things Work*. New York: Guilford Press.

Strauss, A., and Corbin, J. 1990. *Basics of Qualitative Research: Grounded Theory Procedures and Techniques*. Thousand Oaks, CA: Sage Publications.

Stueber, K. 2008. "Empathy." In *Stanford Encyclopedia of Philosophy*, edited by E. N. Zalta. Stanford, CA: Stanford University. http://plato.stanford.edu/archives/fall2008/entries/empathy.

Thibeault, M.D. 2007. "Music Making Lives: Score and Setting in the Musical Experiences of High School Students." PhD diss., Stanford University, CA.

Tobin, J., Y. Hsueh, and M. Karasawa. 2009. *Preschool in Three Cultures Revisited: China, Japan, and the United States*. Chicago: University of Chicago Press.

Tsugawa, S. 2009. "Senior Adult Music Learning, Motivation, and Meaning Construction in Two New Horizons Ensembles." PhD diss., Arizona State University.

Van Manen, M. 1990. *Researching Lived Experience*. Albany: State University of New York Press.

Veblen, K. K. 1994. "The Teacher's Role in the Transmission of Irish Traditional Music." *International Journal of Music Education* 24 (2): 1–30.

Vidich, A. J., and S. M. Lyman. 2003. "Qualitative Methods: Their History in Sociology and Anthropology." In *The Landscape of Qualitative Research: Theories and Issues*, edited by N. K. Denzin and Y. S. Lincoln, 55–129. Thousand Oaks, CA: Sage Publications.

Wasser, J., and L. Bresler. 1996. "Working in the Interpretive Zone: Conceptualizing Collaboration in Qualitative Research Teams." *Educational Researcher* 25 (5): 5–15.

White, P. 2012. "Thinking-in-Music-with-Music: Students' Musical Understanding and Learning in Two Interactive Online Music General Education Courses." PhD diss., Oakland University, Rochester, MI.

Wiggins, J. 2011. "Feeling It Is How I Understand It: Found Poetry as Analysis." *International Journal of Education and the Arts* 12 (LAI 3). http://www.ijea.org/v12lai3/.

Zaretti, J. L. 1998. "*Multicultural Music Education: An Ethnography of Process in Teaching and Learning*." Masters thesis, Indiana University, Bloomington.

·····································

CHAPTER 2

HISTORY OF QUALITATIVE RESEARCH IN AMERICAN MUSIC EDUCATION

·····································

COLLEEN M. CONWAY AND CHAD WEST

Just as music and education can be traced back across the centuries ultimately to the crude and custom-driven habits of primitive societies, qualitative inquiry has its roots in the intuitive and survivalist behavior of early peoples. For ages we have operated on hunches and emotions, increasingly using those that brought us safety and satisfaction. Gradually we saw the wisdom of what we already were doing by observing, questioning, keeping records and interpreting, respecting the experience and rumination of elders. Gradually we formed rules for study and names for our sciences. Music educators, too, increasingly drew from philosophers and social scientists to codify research problems.

(Bresler and Stake 1992, 76)

THIS chapter is intended to serve as a historical backdrop for qualitative research in American music education research publications.[1] After a brief discussion of the history of qualitative research within general education, we explore the following questions: How has qualitative research evolved in music education? What were the experiences of early qualitative researchers in music education? We begin to answer the first question with a presentation and discussion of what we call "qualitative sightings" in the 1992 *Handbook of Research on Music Teaching and Learning* and the 2002 *New Handbook of Research on Music Teaching and Learning*. In preparation for answering the second question, we interviewed several early qualitative researchers in the music education field. Insights from the interviews are presented within the following subheadings: (a) experiences of early qualitative journal article authors, (b) planning and implementation of University of Illinois Qualitative Research Conferences in 1994 and 1996, and (c) experiences of University of Illinois Qualitative Research Conference speakers and participants.

2.1. GENERAL HISTORY OF QUALITATIVE RESEARCH IN EDUCATION AND MUSIC EDUCATION

Merriam (2009) suggests that qualitative research in education derives from the work of anthropologists and sociologists asking research questions about "people's lives, the social and cultural contexts in which they lived, the ways in which they understood their worlds, and so on" (6). She quotes Bogdan and Biklen (2007) and traces qualitative research in education to Chicago sociologists in the 1920s and 1930s:

> In addition, especially in the life histories Chicago School sociologists produced, the importance of seeing the world from the perspective of those who were seldom listened to—the criminal, the vagrant, the immigrant—was emphasized. While not using the phrase, they knew they were "giving voice" to points of view of people marginalized in the society. (Bodgan and Biklin 2007, 10)

Wing (1993) points out that music education researchers have also argued the need for representing the "voice" of music teachers and music students through qualitative research.

Merriam suggests that research in professions such as education, law, and medicine has traditionally included a focus on understanding specific cases representing a phenomenon. She targets two seminal research publications from the mid-twentieth century as contributing to the emergence of qualitative research in education. The first is Glaser and Strauss's (1967) book *Discovery of Grounded Theory: Strategies for Qualitative Research*, and the other is Guba's (1978) monograph *Toward a Methodology of Naturalistic Inquiry in Educational Evaluation*. Guba and colleagues (i.e., Guba and Lincoln 1981; and more recently Denzin and Lincoln 2000, 2005, 2011) continue to serve as key resources for qualitative researchers.

Within music education, Bresler and Stake (1992) suggest that in addition to roots within education, philosophy, anthropology, and sociology, music education can look to biographical methods used in musicology and ethnomusicology. They suggest: "While sociology focuses on *interpretive biography* [italics theirs]—the creation of literary, narrative accounts and representations of lived experience (Denzin 1989)—the traditional use of biographies in music centers around life-events, especially family, patrons, and mentoring, a written account or history of an individual" (78).

2.2. QUALITATIVE SIGHTINGS IN 1992 AND 2002 *HANDBOOKS*

We present what we are calling "sightings" of qualitative research in both the *Handbook of Research in Music Education* (Colwell 1992) and the *New Handbook of Research on Music Teaching and Learning* (Colwell and Richardson 2002) in order as they appear in the *Handbooks*. There were only 13 qualitative dissertations in music education before 1992. Since the *Handbooks* are meant to report on published research in the field, it is helpful to know that up until 1990 (most likely the last publication date represented in the 1992 *Handbook*) there were five qualitative studies published in the *Journal of Research in Music Education* (JRME) and no studies in the *Bulletin of the Council for Research in Music Education* (CRME). The *Journal of Music Teacher Education* (JMTE) began in 1990.

2.2.1. *Handbook of Research in Music Education* (Colwell 1992)

The term "qualitative research" first appears in the 1992 *Handbook* in Reimer's "Toward a Philosophical Foundation for Music Education Research." Reimer suggested that qualitative research has "risen" in response to the "decline in the credibility of positivism" (29). He cited Eisner (1979) as well as Eisner and Peshkin (1990) and provided a paragraph defining qualitative research. His paragraph concluded:

> It is not just the simple matter that qualitative research provides another useful methodology, as sometimes assumed by music education researchers. It is that qualitative approaches construe human reality as being very different from the reality assumed by traditional science, raising the issue as to whether reality must continue to be conceived as unidimensional or whether it is possible for it to be multidimensional. (29)

His chapter went on to document the "paradigm wars" within qualitative and quantitative research in other fields, and Reimer cautioned music education researchers to not continue this trend, as it did not appear to be useful in other fields.

One chapter of the 55 chapters in the 1992 *Handbook* is devoted completely to qualitative research. Both authors of that chapter, Bresler and Stake, held faculty appointments within education, whereas the large majority of authors in the 1992 *Handbook* held faculty appointments within music education. Bresler and Stake presented their chapter according to the following sections: roots of qualitative methodology, characteristics of qualitative research, qualitative research in music education, and methods and criteria. They included discussion of 16 qualitative studies (including dissertations) within American music education at the time, most of which are described in various chapters in parts 3 and 4 of the 1992 *Handbook*.

In the chapter titled *Descriptive Research: Techniques and Procedures*, Casey (1992) mentioned the terms "naturalistic" (120) and "ethnographic" (121). He considered what he called "the newer *postpositivist* [italics his] paradigm [*sic*]" in his section on "obser-vational research" (120). He described this postpositivist qualitative research as an ap-proach that music educators should consider, as it may "hold great promise especially for observational research in music education" (120). Music education researchers today define "postpositivist" in very different ways from this 1992 usage. Casey also mentioned researchers Delorenzo (1989) and Krueger (1987), both of whom were interviewed as part of the preparation of this *Handbook* chapter. Their insights are reported later in this chapter.

In the Abeles (1992) chapter, meant to be an overview of all types of music edu-cation research, there was one short paragraph titled "ethnographic procedures," which began,

> Recently there has been growing interest among music educators in a research method primarily used by anthropologists and ethnomusicologists. The method is identified by several different labels, including ethnography, qualitative research, naturalistic research, and field research. (232)

There was one other short paragraph, later in the chapter, called "Interpreting Ethnographic Research," which mentioned Krueger (1987) again and suggested that it is difficult to generalize in ethnographic studies. The reader may wish to consult chapter 6 in this *Handbook* for an extended discussion of the history of the use of the term "gener-alizability" within qualitative research in music education.

The next mention of qualitative research in the 1992 *Handbook* did not appear until the "Research on Music in Early Childhood" chapter about 400 pages later. Scott-Kasner opened the qualitative section of her chapter by quoting Borg and Gall: "Though often viewed with suspicion by traditional, trained researchers, qualitative research has increasingly gained a place in educational settings (Borg and Gall 1989)" (634). She went on to suggest its value in studying young children and presented research within the headings of "ethnographic research," "naturalistic research," and "case study." These studies are presented and discussed in Volume 3, chapter 1 ("Early Childhood Music Education") of this *Handbook*.

The final mention of qualitative research in the 1992 *Handbook* occurred in the chapter "Music Teacher Education" (Verrastro and Leglar 1992) and presented findings from the teacher education studies by Krueger (1987) and Schleuter (1991) studies mentioned several times previously (685).

2.2.2. *The New Handbook of Research on Music Teaching and Learning* (Colwell and Richardson 2002)

Assuming that most 2002 *Handbook* authors had access only to studies with publication dates up to 2000, it is helpful to consider the changes in *Handbook* sightings over 10 years in relation to published qualitative research. During 1990–2000 there were eight qualitative studies that appeared in the *JRME* and 30 qualitative studies in the *CRME*. However, as *CRME* during these years was often several years behind in dissemination, it is possible that not all these studies were available to *Handbook* authors. The *CRME* also published 17 articles during this time period that discussed qualitative design, data collection, or analysis, but were not studies. Three qualitative studies appeared in the *JMTE* during 1990–2000. There were 38 qualitative dissertations in music education that appeared during the time period 1992–2002.

As was the case in the 1992 *Handbook,* the first mention of qualitative research in the 2002 *Handbook* occurred within a philosophy chapter. In a section focusing on "Educational Research in Context" within the chapter titled "Philosophical Perspectives on Research," Elliott (2002) wrote:

> Coincidentally, humanistic and postmodern scholars argued persuasively for more inclusive and socially sensitive ways of investigating educational issues. Indeed, the strict "cognitive" focus of much research in the 1960s and 1970s caused scholars (aware of postmodern thinking) to emphasize the paucity of research on human subjectivity, personal identity formation and gender issues. As part of the emphasis on the "whole person," educational research broadened to include Action Research, Ethnography, Narrative Inquiry, Critical Theory, Feminist Inquiry, and Postmodernism. (87)

Considering how qualitative research had been used in music education at the time, Elliott (like Reimer in the 1992 *Handbook*) referred to the paradigm debates and stated: ". . . contemporary research in education and music education includes a wide variety of complementary and competing forms of inquiry" (88).

Elliott devoted a complete section of his chapter to describing "Interpretivism" (92–93), but no music education studies were presented as exemplars. In the final mention of qualitative research in Elliott's chapter, he suggested "arts-informed" or "artistic scholarship" (99) may be in the future for music education research. Table 2.1 is a list of other qualitative "sightings" in the 2002 *Handbook.*

In a section of the Flinders and Richardson chapter titled "Exemplars of Qualitative Research in Music Education," the authors discussed two case studies, one "participant observation" study, one action research study, one ethnography, and one study using "verbal protocol analysis or "think alouds." Overall, the sense in the 2002 chapter is that there were still few examples of qualitative studies to be presented in the *Handbook.* Since 2002, case study [this volume chapter 5], ethnography [this volume chapter 6], and practitioner inquiry [this volume chapter 9] all emerged as common designs in

Table 2.1 Discussions of Qualitative Research in the 2002 *Handbook*

Author	Topic	Sighting
Hanley and Montgomery	Curriculum	Authors described how qualitative work might support curriculum work, and discussed several qualitative curriculum studies as examples.
Jordan-DeCarbo and Nelson	Early Childhood Music Education	Authors discussed the importance as well as the challenge of qualitative research. They mentioned that observation is a common strategy. They also provided references to sources that assist the qualitative researcher in early childhood settings.
Sink	Behavioral Research on Direct Music Instruction	"Qualitative techniques may complement, extend, and corroborate quantitative approaches for assessing the relative effectiveness of observed teacher-student interactions" (323).
Szego	Ethnography	"Although there are exceptions, music educators' ethnographies also tend to be characterized by enumerative rigor and an economy of cultural contextualization" (718).
Leglar and Collay	Teacher Education	"Music education researchers have been slow to adopt qualitative methods and even slower to turn these methods to the study of their own practice" (859). The authors encouraged teacher educators to examine their own teaching through qualitative approaches.
Pembrook and Craig	Teaching as a Profession	Authors devoted the first section of their chapter to studies that "focus on an insider, personal, narrative, experiential account of teaching as a profession" (786). However, none of the studies cited is a music education study; rather, they are all drawn from general teacher education.
Nierman, Zeichner, and Hobbel	Teacher Education	"There is a need for more case studies describing the 'how to' of music teacher education from a broad perspective" (833).
Rideout and Feldman	Music Student Teaching	Authors discussed action research as a suggested strategy in student teaching.
Hookey	Professional Development	Author discussed the need for teacher research as well as a focus on reflexive modes of research.
Heller and O'Connor	Maintaining Quality in Research and Reporting	Authors outlined three "types of research" in the following way: ". . . historical (mostly qualitative); descriptive (qualitative or quantitative), and experimental (mostly quantitative)" (1090).
Bartel and Radocy	Trends in Data Acquisition and Knowledge Development	Authors identified trends in data collection and argued that qualitative techniques have arisen as an alternative to the reductive nature of quantitative research and as a means toward explaining complex human constructs.
Flinders and Richardson	Contemporary Issues in Qualitative Research and Music Education	Authors began with a historical overview of qualitative research in education. They suggested that the earliest qualitative researchers were prepared for their work in colleges of education and not in schools of music (1168). They also discussed emerging changes in the use of the term "qualitative research" (1168–69).

music education (note that each has a complete chapter in this *Handbook*), while "participant observation" and "verbal protocol analysis" are now used more to describe a data collection procedure rather than to describe a design.

It is somewhat surprising that the 2002 *Handbook* did not include more qualitative studies. The primary focus was still on introducing the concepts of qualitative research. Looking ahead, from 2001–2011 there were 24 qualitative studies published in the *JRME*, 52 in the *CRME*, and 18 in the *JMTE*, while there were 94 qualitative dissertations in music education, suggesting a trend toward more qualitative research.

2.3. INTERVIEWEE SELECTION AND INTERVIEW PROCESS

2.3.1. *Journal of Research in Music Education*

We began our consideration of who to interview in music education with an examination of the earliest published qualitative research within the *JRME*. This examination uncovered the following qualitative studies: Krueger (1987); McGowan (1988); DeLorenzo (1989); Metz (1989); and Schleuter (1991). The first interview was held with Patti Krueger in the summer of 2011. I (Colleen) then interviewed both Lisa DeLorenzo and Lois Schleuter shortly afterward. In the context of these interviews it was mentioned that Rudy Radocy (who was *JRME* editor at the time of these early publications) had been particularly helpful to some of these early authors. Rudy was interviewed next. I was unable to find John J. McGowan but did eventually find Elayne Metz (now Elayne Achilles) and I interviewed her in the fall of 2011.

All interviews were conducted over the phone. I provided each interviewee with the Table of Contents for the *Oxford Handbook of Qualitative Research in Music Education* to give them some context for the work. I began each interview with specific questions about the published study in the *JRME*. I asked each researcher what led to the particular topic and research design. I also asked them to talk about what preparation they had for the use of qualitative research. I then asked them to speak about the *JRME* review process. Several were able to recall specific suggestions and comments from reviewers. Finally, I asked them to recall the reaction from the music education profession once the work was published. With Rudy Radocy, we also discussed his role as *JRME* editor at the time and his memory regarding acceptance of qualitative research. Rudy also had represented the *JRME* at the *CRME* Conferences (discussed in the next section of this chapter).

2.3.2. *Bulletin of the Council for Research in Music Education*

In examining the *Bulletin*, it became clear that the University of Illinois Qualitative Research Conferences in 1994 and 1996 were seminal events for qualitative research within music education; thus, we decided to interview conference planners, guest speakers, and conference participants. Four issues of the *Bulletin for the Council of Research in Music Education* (122, 123, 130, 131) were devoted to reporting Conference proceedings. Manuscripts in these issues included Conference session papers and reactions to the Conference. Using these manuscripts to develop interview questions, I (Chad) spoke with several of the Conference participants/authors (Liora Bresler, Eve Harwood, Cliff Madsen, Peter Webster, and Ed Asmus) regarding their articles, their memories of the Conference, and their experiences as qualitative researchers since then.

2.4. EXPERIENCES OF EARLY QUALITATIVE JOURNAL ARTICLE AUTHORS

2.4.1. Strong Connections to Colleges of Education

All of the early *JRME* authors had strong connections to College of Education faculty. Many of them continued to have strong College of Education connections throughout their careers. Krueger's (1987) work was the result of her dissertation in the School of Education at the University of Wisconsin where general education professor Michael Apple was a key figure in shaping Krueger's work. Lisa DeLorenzo (1989) stated: "I was really lucky that Teachers College supported my project, because I believe a lot of doctoral institutions would have preferred quantitative research."

Elaine Achiless (Metz 1989) was doing EdD dissertation work in a College of Education as well as a School of Music (half and half) and this early *JRME* article was a result of that work. She spent much of the rest of her career studying general education topics and working outside of music. Lois Schleuter (1991) did her doctoral work in the College of Education at Kent State. There were no music faculty on the committee and only the advisor and one committee member had a background in qualitative research. Her advisor was very interested in qualitative research and urged her to do a qualitative study. Flinders and Richardson (2002) contended that much of the qualitative research information we have in music education comes from Colleges of Education, and these interviews certainly support that statement.

2.4.2. Journal Review Process

When Krueger submitted to the *JRME*, the reviewers asked her to further verify generalizability, validity, and reliability. She noted, "I was asked to discuss ethnography using ideas and language that came from a more accepted experimental research framework." After her study was published in the *JRME*, it was introduced in the *Music Educators Journal*. Krueger reflected, "I hoped that there would be others waiting in the wings to see that ethnography and qualitative research would carry on in music education."

Schleuter (1991) said she found it difficult to pare down her 300+ page dissertation into a journal article, but Rudy Radocy allowed her to exceed the normal page limit. "Thank goodness for Rudy. If it had not been for him, I don't think it would have gotten in." "One of the reviewers said 'reject, because an N of three is totally inappropriate.'" Her response was, "These are three case studies—an appropriate N for a case study [N is no longer used in case study research] is one. Therefore, I have three times as much information as I need. I really didn't think I was going to get away with it, but that person said, 'OK, publish it.'" The third reviewer refused to accept any definition of qualitative research that she provided, even though the definitions were heavily cited. Radocy did not remember any particular effort on his part to help qualitative research move ahead in the *JRME*, but three of the four interviewees mentioned how helpful he had been in the process.

All four authors (Krueger, Delorenzo, Achilles, and Schleuter) had their dissertation articles published in the *JRME*, but none of them submitted future manuscripts to the *JRME*, instead sending to *UPDATE*, *JMTE*, *MEJ*, *CRME*, and other journals. Krueger said, "In retrospect, I made an unconscious decision to go to other journals. There were no obvious barriers, but the kinds of questions that were asked and the explanations one was asked to give at the time deterred me from submitting further works to the journal."

2.4.3. Changing Use of Terminology

It was clear in speaking with these early authors that the terms used to describe research have changed over the years. DeLorenzo reported that, at the time, she simply called her research "qualitative," whereas today, readers would expect a more concise categorization (e.g., case study, phenomenology, ethnographic, narrative). Schleuter's 1991 paper stated, ". . . the use of qualitative and ethnographic research has emerged as an insightful way to obtain these findings about teachers and their craft" (47). When asked if she wrote that because at the time she perceived qualitative and ethnographic to be exclusive of one another, she stated, "I probably was thinking about my target audience, statistical researchers, and that most people in music education who were reading the *JRME* would not be as familiar with the term 'qualitative.' I may have used the term 'ethnographic' as a means to relate qualitative research to the ethnographic research of those times."

Scheulter said she used the term "subjects" to describe what later qualitative researchers might call "participants." At the time, she did not recall anyone questioning her use of that term as being associated with quantitative research. Similarly, she does not recall any dispute regarding her use of the term "results," whereas later qualitative researchers would tend to use "findings." Both Krueger and Achilles agreed that terms have changed; both had used the term "ethnographic" back then. Achilles commented that more recent qualitative research has begun to better describe the concept of theoretical framework, which was not always addressed in the early qualitative studies.

2.5. PLANNING AND IMPLEMENTATION OF UNIVERSITY OF ILLINOIS QUALITATIVE RESEARCH CONFERENCES IN 1994 AND 1996

Many associate Cliff Madsen with the vast body of quantitative research conducted at Florida State University over five decades, and rightly so. However, his contribution to music education research extends also to qualitative studies. Though he conducted quantitative research through the 1960s, 1970s, and 1980s to, as he says, survive the tenure and promotion process, he began his career asking qualitative questions. When recalling his earliest qualitative work, Madsen described helping out at a local school in the 1960s:

> We just asked the teachers, "how may we help?" The teachers asked us to observe the students and themselves. So, that school became an observation magnet for over 10 years. Eventually we started developing things that could be counted. But all of this started from a qualitative perspective—instead of going out and saying to the teacher "you should be doing this," you say, "how may we help you?" And teachers themselves came up with ways to do that. The whole thing started for me by listening to K-6 teachers tell us what they thought was important.

Similarly, Eve Harwood began her qualitative research in the 1980s when qualitative research in music education was still relatively scarce. It was in the School of Education at the University of Illinois where she, along with contemporaries such as Carol Richardson and Nancy Whitaker, were introduced to qualitative research, since there was no model for such within the School of Music. At the time she was conducting her dissertation, most people referred to qualitative research as "naturalistic" research. She recalls what drew her to this type of inquiry:

> Back then more women were drawn to qualitative research. It was a narrative form; it used language rather than numbers; it involved fieldwork and prolonged engagement with students. For a variety of those reasons, it appealed to people like me who

were teachers who wanted to spend sustained periods of time with children they were teaching and for whom a narrative way of finding truth seemed more powerful and more natural.

2.5.1. Conference Planning and Implementation

Eve Harwood recalls how the idea for a conference on qualitative research in music education came about. The idea was conceived over dinner one evening with Liora Bresler, Eunice Boardman, Nancy Whitaker, and Carol Richardson at the 1993 MENC North Central Conference:

> I remember Eunice, Liora, and Nancy coming back from having had a meal together. They had been talking to Eunice about the lack of places to disseminate qualitative research in the music education journals as they were at the time. Someone tried to submit a case study and a reviewer came back and said, "what is this—an N of 1?" There were some conversations being had at AERA, but that was prior to a music SIG [Special Interest Group] being formed at AERA, which was where qualitative research subsequently got shared. And Eunice Boardman, who at the time was the editor of the *Bulletin*, said, "you all have been saying that there is no place to [disseminate] your research (and qualitative research was not Eunice's training either), so we're going to host a conference and the *Bulletin* will support it." So, that is how it started. I remember that Nancy Whitaker brought each of us a special bar of soap, which was the inauguration of this adventure.

In Eve's estimation, Illinois was the logical place to host the Conference, because they had in their school of education many experienced qualitative researchers such as Robert Stake, Norman Denzin, and Alan Peshkin.

The reasons for holding the Conference were to provide qualitative researchers a place to convene and also to make the case to the wider profession that qualitative inquiry was a legitimate form of research. John Grashel suggested that invitation be extended not only to qualitative researchers, but also to quantitative researchers like himself who wanted to know more about the topic. Eve explained:

> One person commented that "the women were doing all of the work and the men were taking all of the credit," but most looked at it as a wise political move. If this is going to become a legitimate respected form of research, then people like Cliff Madsen, Ed Asmus, and John Grashel have to buy in. And they have to be convinced that it is rigorous and systematic in different ways than they are accustomed. I think they did buy in. They spoke positively about this kind of research and that it was good for the field. They learned a lot at the conference and were glad to have come. They certainly were not dismissive. I also think it was wise that we had people like Norm Denzin, Alan Peshkin, and Bob Stake who were very highly respected within the field of education and had long publication records speaking at the beginning.

So, we had them at the beginning, then we had lots of presentations predominantly from women who were in music education, and then we had this sort of bookend at the end from the research authorities at the time.

Whereas the 1994 Conference was aimed at educating the music education research community about what qualitative research was, why it was important, and by what standards it should be judged, the 1996 Conference was more geared toward showcasing people in music education without relying so heavily on researchers from general education to make the transition. Elliott Eisner and Liora Bresler were both keynote speakers at the 1996 Conference.

2.5.2. Experiences of University of Illinois Qualitative Research Conference Speakers and Participants

Eve Harwood recalled that there was some defensiveness from the quantitative researchers regarding what they saw as denigrating or belittling quantitative research. They wanted to make the case that quantitative research had "come a long way from just running two batches of tests, running a few simple correlations and saying 'this one is better than that one.'" The quantitative world also was developing much more complex measures, more profound questions, and had more to offer than just simply counting things. Peter Webster recalls that he left the 1994 Conference "rejecting the notion that quantitative research was irrelevant in today's pluralistic and context-specific society" but that he "has since come to understand that that is not what most qualitative researchers believe." Ed Asmus recalls cautioning the profession to not simply move toward qualitative research as though it were easier: "I see qualitative [research] as much harder because you have to always be on your toes to assure that what you are doing is accurate and truly representative of the underlying things that are going on in human interactions." When asked about his response to the Conference, Cliff Madsen replied, "If there is an enemy out there, it is the misuse of numbers much more than lack of generalization."

Peter Webster recalls that after the 1994 Conference and subsequent American Educational Research Association (AERA) workshops, he began to understand that research is research.

When you start coding things, you start counting things—we naturally gravitate to numbers. Similarly, in quantitative work we are constantly interpreting what these things mean, and we are telling little side stories of outliers, so we often get into the qualitative massaging of some of this quantitative data. When you get down to it and try to make sense of something, you naturally are going to use both systems, it seems to me. There is a fallacy in the minds of some qualitative researchers who think they are going to do qualitative research so that they don't have to deal with numbers. I think you really do deal with some kind of numerical representation. You are looking at quantity. You are looking at tendencies, and you are making decisions about the magnitude of one thing or another.

2.5.3. How the Profession Has Evolved since the Conferences

The 1994 Conference was a landmark meeting for Peter Webster. He subsequently attended AERA workshops on qualitative research and began exploring it further.

> In 1994 I was a real neophyte in understanding how to look at something like trustworthiness or how to look at something like voice and how to deal with being clear as a researcher where your biases are. After the 1994 conference I understood inherently the value of it; I just had lots of questions about how these things would be written. Now I have come to a more nuanced understanding of how one deals with the mechanics of doing a good qualitative study. I've also become better as a reviewer when looking at qualitative research and understanding what is good and what is not. I think I have become an advocate of qualitative work because my standards have risen.

Eve Harwood noted that dissertations today "do not have to dedicate a whole chapter on defining case study and explaining why it is appropriate for this study. You just say that it is a case study or an ethnography, etc." While lengthy discussions about method are no longer warranted, attention to methodological rigor is still important. She feels that since the Conferences the profession has lost some rigor in qualitative methodology.

> Qualitative research has gone from being dubious or not respected to now being so respected that a lot of people want to claim that they are doing it who aren't, in fact. So, you get studies that collect open-ended responses on a survey and refer to that as qualitative data. What I see now are people who are missing prolonged engagement in the field. Three one-hour telephone conversations is not prolonged engagement in the field. A day is not prolonged engagement in the field. Triangulation is not achieved by one focus group, one interview, and a two-hour visit. People are missing being immersed in another environment in order to make meaning as a participant makes meaning. My reservation is that we may have gone too far in making it fashionable and acceptable and lost what was really important in those early conferences which was to say, "if you don't have statistical reliability, validity, and generalizability, then what do you have as criteria for judging the quality?" And we have those criteria. Prolonged engagement in the field and prolonged engagement with the data, and multiple levels of data analysis and triangulation and member checking—those things now get lip service, but when I look at what somebody actually says they did with member checking, it is often just, "we

ran a transcript past somebody." Well, they agreed that was what they said, but that is not the same as asking, "was what you said and what we wrote the most important thing you had to tell us?" for instance.

When asked how she thinks the profession has changed regarding journal acceptance of qualitative research, Liora Bresler noted that music seems to be behind the visual arts and that the profession is still slow to value publishing in the international journals as much as in American journals such as the *JRME* and *CRME*. Eve Harwood noted that although the *JRME* is "still pretty quantitative" there are more journals that now welcome qualitative research. Peter Webster, who currently serves on the *JRME* review board, was adamant that the relative lack of qualitative research in the *JRME* is not due to any overt bias, but notes that, "There aren't that many people on the board whose expertise is specifically in qualitative research."

> When you look at publications that accept large numbers of qualitative research, you see that the European journals are often more willing to publish qualitative work than some of the US journals. Some of the best qualitative work is not done in North America.

2.5.4. Predictions Regarding Future Directions for Qualitative Research in Music Education

When asked where she sees qualitative research heading in the future, Eve Harwood said that she views narrative inquiry as being in the same place now as qualitative research was in 1994. Liora Bresler believed that we will see more mixing of qualitative and quantitative techniques within the same studies. Cliff Madsen agreed:

> When we interviewed little children about their perceptions, it provided a richness of findings we just cannot get quantitatively. There are things that can be counted and things that ought not be counted. Mixed models are going to become more and more prevalent.

Peter Webster described how we have not yet come to a point in our field where we think of different methods as tools for pragmatically approaching problems:

> I really do not believe that we can build a profession by looking at qualitative evidence only. I really believe that we need to create ways where we can blend these things in ways that lead us to know where effectiveness lies. We're not going to move very far without that kind of marriage and that is why I think we have to get beyond the idea that you go to this school if you want to do qualitative work and go to this school if you want to do quantitative work.

2.6. CONCLUSION

While qualitative research has advanced in music education since the 1980s, there remain areas where clarity, definition, and argument are still needed. In the 1980s, in an attempt to define, justify, and defend qualitative research, authors argued that qualitative research was the epistemological antithesis of quantitative research and that the two could not and should not be combined. Has this worldview changed in the profession now that qualitative research is more accepted in our journals? Has qualitative research become so mainstream that standards for rigor have been relaxed? Whereas in the 1980s it was sufficient to label this type of inquiry as simply "qualitative," authors now are compelled to further classify their study. However, has our profession adequately defined such classifications as phenomenology, narrative inquiry, arts-based education research, grounded theory, case study, etc.? If so, do these classifications describe designs, lenses, data collection strategies, representations of findings, or some combination of all of these? What constitutes "data" in qualitative research? The remaining chapters in this *Handbook* are aimed at addressing these questions and serve as a guidepost for reference as well as discussion within our profession regarding qualitative research in music education.

NOTE

1. We wish to thank Matt Clauhs and Jared Rawlings for their help on drafts of this chapter.

REFERENCES

Abeles, H. F. 1992. "A Guide to Interpreting Research in Music Education." In *Handbook of Research in Music Education*," edited by R. Colwell, 227–46. New York: Schirmer Books.

Bartel, L. R., and R. Radocy. 2002. "Trends in Data Acquisition and Knowledge Development." In *The New Handbook of Research on Music Teaching and Learning*, edited by R. Colwell and C. P. Richardson, 1108–27. New York: Oxford University Press.

Bogdan, R. C., and S. K. Biklen. 2007. *Qualitative Research for Education: An Introduction to Theories and Methods*. Boston: Pearson.

Borg, W. R., and Gall, M. D. 1989. *Educational Research*. 5th ed. New York: Longman.

Bresler, L., and R. E. Stake. 1992. "Qualitative Research Methodology in Music Education." In *Handbook of Research in Music Education*, edited by R. Colwell, 75–90. New York: Schirmer Books.

Bulletin of the Council for Research in Music Education. 1994. Special issue: Qualitative Methodologies in Music Education Research Conference. Bulletin of the Council for Research in Music Education, 122.

Bulletin of the Council for Research in Music Education. 1995. Special issue: Qualitative Methodologies in Music Education Research Conference. Bulletin of the Council for Research in Music Education, 123.

Bulletin of the Council for Research in Music Education. 1996. Special issue: Qualitative Methodologies in Music Education Research Conference II. Bulletin of the Council for Research in Music Education, 130.

Bulletin of the Council for Research in Music Education. 1997. Special issue: Qualitative Methodologies in Music Education Research Conference II. Bulletin of the Council for Research in Music Education, 131.

Casey, D. E. 1992. "Descriptive Research: Techniques and Procedures." In *Handbook of Research in Music Education*, edited by R. Colwell, 115–34. New York: Schirmer Books.

Colwell, R., ed. 1992. *The Handbook of Research on Music Education.* New York: Schirmer.

Colwell, R., and C. P. Richardson, eds. 2002. *The New Handbook of Research on Music Teaching and Learning.* New York: Schirmer.

DeLorenzo, L. C. 1989. "A Field Study of Sixth-Grade Students' Creative Music Problem-Solving." *Journal of Research in Music Education* 37 (3): 188–200.

Denzin, N. 1989. *Interpretive Biography.* Beverly Hills, CA: Sage Publications.

Denzin, N., and Y. S. Lincoln. 2000. *Handbook of Qualitative Research.* 2nd ed. Thousand Oaks, CA: Sage Publications.

Denzin, N., and Y. S. Lincoln. 2005. *The Sage Handbook of Qualitative Research.* 3rd ed. Thousand Oaks, CA: Sage Publications.

Denzin, N., and Y. S. Lincoln. 2011. *The Sage Handbook of Qualitative Research.* 4th ed. Thousand Oaks, CA: Sage Publications.

Eisner, E. W. 1979. *The Educational Imagination.* New York: Macmillan.

Eisner, E. W., and A. Peshkin, eds. 1990. *Qualitative Inquiry in Education.* New York: Teachers College Press.

Elliott, D. 2002. "Philosophical Perspectives on Research." In *The New Handbook of Research on Music Teaching and Learning*, edited by R. Colwell and C. P. Richardson, 85–103. New York: Oxford University Press.

Flinders, D. J., and C. P. Richardson. 2002. "Contemporary Issues in Qualitative Research and Music Education." In *The New Handbook of Research of Music Teaching and Learning*, edited by R. Colwell and C. P. Richardson, 1159–76. New York: Oxford University Press.

Glaser, B. G., and A. Strauss. 1967. *The Discovery of Grounded Theory.* Chicago: Aldine.

Guba, E. 1978. "Toward a Methodology of Naturalistic Inquiry in Educational Evaluation." *CSE Monograph Series in Evaluation*, 8. Los Angeles: Center for the Study of Evaluation, University of California.

Guba, E. G., and Y. S. Lincoln. 1981. *Effective Evaluation: Improving the Usefulness of Evaluation Results through Responsive and Naturalistic Approaches.* San Francisco: Jossey-Bass.

Krueger, P. 1987. "Ethnographic Research Methodology in Music Education." *Journal of Research in Music Education* 35 (2): 69–77.

McGowan, J. J. 1988. "A Descriptive Study of an Arts-in-Education Project." *Journal of Research in Music Education* 36 (1): 47–57.

Merriam, S. M. 2009. *Qualitative Research: A Guide to Design and Implementation.* San Francisco: Jossey-Bass.

Metz, E. 1989. "Movement as a Musical Response among Preschool Children." *Journal of Research in Music Education* 37 (1): 48–60.

Reimer, B. 1992. "Toward a Philosophical Foundation for Music Education Research." In *Handbook of Research in Music Education*, edited by R. Colwell, 21–37. New York: Schirmer Book.

Schleuter, L. 1991. "Student Teachers' Preactive and Postactive Curricular Thinking." *Journal of Research in Music Education* 39 (1): 48–65.

Verrastro, R., and Leglar, M. 1992. "Music Teacher Education." In *Handbook of Research in Music Education*, edited by R. Colwell, 676–96. New York: Schirmer Books.

Wing, L. 1993. "Teachers in the Study of Music Teacher Education: Finding Voices." *The Quarterly Journal of Music Teaching and Learning* 4 (1): 5–12. (Reprinted with permission in *Visions of Research in Music Education* 16 (4), Autumn 2010, retrieved from http://www-usr.rider.edu/~vrme/.)

CHAPTER 3

....

EPISTEMOLOGY AND QUALITATIVE RESEARCH IN MUSIC EDUCATION

....

RANDALL EVERETT ALLSUP

THE twentieth century witnessed a profound epistemological turn in the field of social science research, particularly with regard to education and schooling. This paradigm shift—the so-called interpretive turn—is revealed in the gradual legitimation of qualitative research. Understanding this turn and how theories and beliefs about knowledge and the nature of what is known (e.g., epistemology) shape practices in classrooms and scholarly settings is of paramount importance for music education researchers. This chapter will define prevailing epistemological fields of thought as they relate to the questions researchers ask and the methods they use. I will tell a story of changing educational landscapes, shifting perspectives on learning, and new research methodologies (notice the use of first person; notice I did not say *the* story; notice the proposition that storytelling is a legitimate method of inquiry). The movement from a detached and "scientific" view of knowledge to paradigms that celebrate a diversity of viewpoints, even uncertainty in findings, announces new possibilities for twenty-first-century research in music and music education.

A brief word about my own methodology. One of the points I hope to make in this chapter is that beliefs about knowledge and mind must be congruent with the questions we ask and the methods of investigation we choose to employ. I will end by asserting that a system of values is likewise implicated in all forms of research, whether we acknowledge this assertion as true or not. I approach this account of epistemology and qualitative research as an embodied, culturally situated researcher. I will attempt to give readers an account that is rigorous and disciplined, while embracing a non-neutral subject position, one that is open, contingent, even fractured. Like many scholars and artists before me, I accept that the way we think is a highly complex and contradictory process. I am suspicious, for example, of research findings that are conclusive, or studies of learning that have rosy endings. Nor do I believe in a unified theory of mind, or forms of universal knowledge. To emphasize this claim, and to remain methodologically consistent with how I understand contemporary views of epistemology, the reader will find stories within my story, imaginary breaks that illustrate a particular point, and parenthetical asides that call attention to the subjective nature of knowledge and its nonlinear origins. Forgoing a notion of *Truth* with a capital "T" for *truths* with a small "t" and an "s," I hope to exemplify the very purpose of qualitative research as the study and contemplation of human reality in all its diversity and richness.

Isaac, in constructing the findings chapter of his doctoral dissertation, felt conflicted. His action research case study didn't really go the way he wanted it to. Some learning events could be seen as an unequivocal success, but many other events were failures—at least in his eyes. What should he write about? What quotes should he include? What field notes should he leave out? Torn by the perception that he needed an unambiguous conclusion, he felt ethically compromised. "Has anyone ever reached an unambiguous conclusion in a classroom of thirty students?" he asked himself. "Shouldn't my findings correspond to what I believe is real about teaching, what is real about the mind?"

3.1. CHANGING MINDS, CHANGING TIMES

Once upon a time, knowledge was seen as secure and permanent. For Plato and his followers, the particulars of life (say, a chair, a horse, or an ordinary man) were everyday manifestations of permanent concepts (Plato 2005). Knowledge-making was a normative activity that attempted to evaluate the correspondence between what is and what should be. A chair should correspond to its ideal form. A horse should look and act like a horse. A man should act in correspondence with the ideals that govern manhood. While few people today believe that forms and concepts exist independently of human construction (especially around constructs like gender), social convention gives knowledge the appearance of universality. The more a society agrees that four legs and a back make a chair (and a horse for that matter), the easier it is to create a shared body of knowledge and pass it on to others. But technological innovations, changing human values, and the increasingly multiple locations from which to see and examine the world have all cast uncertainty upon even the securest of categories. We know that chairs do not need legs and backs, and a horse can be understood as a pet in one context and food in another. The concept of manhood has undergone deconstruction and reconstruction across centuries. If epistemology is a theory of mind, then it is increasingly understood as a theory of changing minds, a plural and unstable positionality.

Applying knowledge-making to human contexts and human concerns is fraught with ambiguities and contradictions. Regarding education, we know that children do not learn in identical ways, regardless of the standardization of their learning method (Tyler 1949) or the developmental phase with which they are labeled (Piaget and Inhelder 1969). We know that a classroom of 30 children do not "see" Picasso's *Guernica* in exactly the same way (Eisner 2002); we know that certain musical instruments have gendered associations and that these associations cause problems for some children (Taylor 2009); we know that classical music is beautiful to some, but oppressive to others (Kingsbury 1998). These are some of the particulars, with their attendant contradictions, to which qualitative research is drawn. It is respect for the social and cultural dimensions of learning, and not merely the cognitive or universal, which expands and complicates a contemporary theory of knowledge.

3.1.1. Beliefs about Knowledge Shape Research

In this chapter we are talking about epistemology, research, and the environments of learning—specifically about changing notions of what counts as knowledge, how it is understood, and how it is explicated. To pose a research question in response to an educational problem is to operate from a particular belief system about knowledge and the mind, one that may or may not be articulated by the investigator. A music education researcher who wishes to study the effects of audiation (see Gordon 1997) on the performance outcome of an eighth-grade choir owes her intellectual inheritance to early twentieth-century behaviorists like E. L. Thorndike, B. F. Skinner, and John Watson. It is to view knowledge as caused behavior as determined by antecedent conditions (Thorndike 1932; Skinner 1953; Watson 1930). Disciplinary fields are likewise shaped by particular belief systems, favoring certain methods of operation and investigation over others. Not long ago, transcription was the hallmark of ethnomusicology. "Transcription told us what we could know about music and how we could know it. Music was objectified, collected, and recorded in order to . . . enable analysis and comparison" (Titon 1997, 87). We could peer into the musical mind of people who are vastly different from us, this theory goes, to extrapolate claims about who these people are and what they believe in (Merriam 1964).

A researcher who looks at the decision-making processes of young composers (see Webster 2002; Burnard and Younker 2004) sees knowledge as constructed by the individual and her community (Greene 2005). This researcher would be in epistemological agreement with the basic tenets of constructivism, as famously articulated in Dewey's *How We Think* (1910). In the constructivist theory of mind, students learn to observe and experiment "for the sake (i) of finding out what sort of perplexity confronts them; (ii) of inferring hypothetical explanations for the puzzling features that observation reveals; and (iii) of testing the ideas thus suggested" (196). The learner is a knowledge-maker, constantly readjusting the internal model that has given meaning and structure to the regularities in her life, which in turn provides the starting ground for further hypothesis-testing when past achievements meet new uncertainties (Dewey 1896).

Radical conceptions of mind and knowledge seek to capture the fractured and contingent aspects of lived experiences and their location within non-neutral settings (Lather 1986). Looking beyond classrooms and sub-cultures, and restless with traditional research paradigms that create linear or "tidy" concepts of reality, contemporary researchers are apt to consider the wider institutional structures and ideologies that shape young minds (Miller 2005). Writes Maxine Greene (1994),

> Some of the restiveness has been a response to the apparent uselessness of research in overcoming "savage inequalities" (Kozol 1991) that have plagued the schools and raised obstacles to achievement for so long. Some have been a response to a sense of powerlessness when it comes to the sufferings and violations of children and young people . . . [a good deal] is due to the separation of research or positive inquiry from moral considerations or the ethical perplexities troubling so many Americans today. (424)

Why, this cry goes out, are so many music researchers content to study intonation and nonverbal conducting gestures when a whole host of social problems are affecting all aspects of young adulthood? We are blinded by objectivity, and by neutrality, the story goes. Because all research is in point of fact *non*-neutral, and thus shaped by the gendered, racial, and political life-world of the researcher, no account—no finding, no interpretation—can be considered definitive, much less true (Lather 1993). Research that is content to produce objective findings that can be generalizable across genders, ethnicities, and cultures tells a falsehood about the changing human mind, its interconnection with others, and the role that culture plays in shaping individual narratives.

As noted, a theory of knowledge can be explicitly arrived at or intuitively felt, but is manifestly reflected in the shape of how and what we teach, as well as the conditioning environments of learning and our methods of instruction. This means that as researcher, teacher, or learner, we are never apart from an epistemological framework. A theory of knowledge is in part a theory of education, since education, which begins at birth, is the developmental effort to increase the power and sensibility of the socially constructed human mind. Education is larger than mere schooling, and encompasses all the conditions of knowledge-making throughout life. It is therefore of paramount importance to emphasize that an explicit or implicit theory of knowledge is implicated in all aspects of the research we design, from the problems we take notice of to the conclusions we arrive at.

Mr. Ortega uses a published diagnostic exam to determine who gets to play in band and what instrument they should start on. He believes that this test can predict musical readiness and talent. This is good for everyone, he reasons. Tests can help kids find out what they are good at.

3.1.2. The Quest for Certainty

Epistemological frames are always evolving. Even Plato knew that the conditions of knowledge-making change. His search for objective knowledge was in part a reaction to rapid change, a quest for certainty in an uncertain world. Dewey ([1929] 2008) would later famously critique this positionality as misguided. "The quest for certainty is a quest for a peace which is assured, an object which is unqualified by risk and the shadow of fear which action casts. For it is not uncertainty per se which men [*sic*] dislike, but the fact that uncertainty involves us in peril. . . . Quest for complete certainty can be fulfilled in pure knowing alone. Such is the verdict of our most enduring philosophic tradition" (7).

The Western "enlightened" tradition of finding solace in reason and objectivity that Dewey refers to in the preceding quote has been called into question by the aims of qualitative research, a mostly twentieth-century invention. Today's qualitative teacher-researcher might very well ask, what good is pure knowledge, what good are externally verified t-scores and isolated experimental variables when my music classroom never looks the same way twice? The uncertainty, risk, subjectivity, and change that Dewey speaks of—these are the conditions of schooling, out of which little that is immutable or "pure" can be found. To suggest that a music classroom in rural Oklahoma will encounter the same conditions and consequences as an urban school in Oakland is false assurance. Worse, objective measures of assessment too often blame the teacher and students for deficiencies when compared across mean scores, rather than looking at broader social phenomena. Consider the epistemological framework that currently rates New York City schools as A, B, C, D, or F.[1]

Qualitative research is designed for changing times (acknowledging that all eras of history have faced rapid change). As suggested in chapter 2, qualitative research methods are constantly evolving to meet the changing conditions of learning and teaching. Researchers must choose among multiple methods for the best way of answering the questions that emerge from the problem they wish to investigate. For example, there were no social networking sites only some years ago. A music education researcher today who wishes to study music-making and music-sharing in online communities will need to invent or reconstruct new ways of examining the questions that emerge from this social phenomenon. This hypothetical researcher might also wish to examine her assumptions about how knowledge or information is disseminated in such a setting, how learning takes place, and whether the epistemological frame she brings to the study is appropriate or needs mending. At the conclusion of this chapter, we will return to this idea, looking closely at the ways in which our beliefs about education and knowledge shape research design and analysis.

I move now to contextualize the changes that have taken place over the last century in North America regarding epistemological paradigms in social science research. As explicative, I point to the career of psychologist Jerome Bruner, a seminal thinker in the field of education and a role model for a life of scholarship and inquiry. In this story within a story of education and ideas, Bruner lived through and actively shaped many of the changes that are discussed within this *Handbook*. Just as importantly, Bruner has publicly amended many of his ideas about knowledge and education, famously moving from his spiral curriculum in the 1960s to a nuanced account of culture in the 1980s and 1990s, ending his career with a renewed passion for narrative research. This arc, I contend, is a good illustration of the shifting epistemological paradigms of the mid-twentieth century and early twenty-first. I point to Bruner as a firsthand observer and primary source (don't forget my role in this story as interpreter of his role), a public scholar whose writings on knowledge and the mind will serve to illuminate these turns.

3.2. AN EPISTEMOLOGICAL CASE STUDY: JEROME BRUNER

Few living education researchers have spent more time thinking about the mind and how we come to knowledge than Jerome Bruner. As one of the United States' major theorists and researchers, Bruner moved from a focus on the individual mind as the primary location of research interest to concern for the ways in which culture shapes and motivates how and what is learned. His mid-century foray into structuralism, a major intellectual paradigm that will be surveyed in the following, was a radical departure from the predominant school of behaviorist research, which narrowed purposeful or intended actions in favor of "caused" behavior. Decades later, in reaction to changing views on multiculturalism and education, Bruner expanded his earlier work to include more emphasis on culture and qualitative ways of knowing. In *Making Stories* (2002), he again readjusts his previous thinking and accepts a multifarious vision of knowledge, one where narratives complicate a unified theory of mind. The following section, "Scientific Thought, Positivism, and Behaviorism," describes the predominant epistemological framework that Bruner inherited as an early-career researcher in the 1950s, a time when qualitative research was located in the backwaters of anthropology and sociology.

3.2.1. Scientific Thought, Positivism, and Behaviorism

The Age of Enlightenment owes its name to a turning away from the dark, a principled move from myths and shadows and toward the bright light of reason. In this grand story of secular humanism, science replaced God sometime in the eighteenth century, and the result was social progress, technological innovation, and newer ever-escalating forms of knowledge based on observation, trial, and experiment. In the Western worlds, the scientific method became shorthand for rational thought. Paraphrasing a faculty discussion at Harvard University about the meaning of knowledge, Bruner ([1962] 1979) describes the aims of scientific thought:

> The intent of the scientist is to create rational structures and general laws that, in the mathematical sense, predict the observations one would be forced to make if one were without the general laws. To the degree that the rational structures of science are governed by principles of strict logical implication, to the degree that prediction becomes more and more complete, leading eventually to the derivation of possible

observations that one might not have made but for the existence of the general theory . . . science [then] increases the unity of our experiences in nature. This is the hallmark of the way of knowing called science. (74)

From the work of scientists both before and after Bruner came unified intellectual fields of general consensus called *foundational knowledge*, e.g., justifiable systems of belief governed by commensurability upon which entire frameworks of thought and research could depend. From this view, rational structures or general laws, constructed and reconstructed over centuries, have come to shape all aspects of human existence, even as these structures are often perceived to exist independently of lived experience. For music educators, foundational knowledge takes the form of Western common practice harmony, historical logic (Bach begat Haydn, Haydn begat Beethoven, Beethoven begat Brahms, etc.), notions of "mainstream" curricula or "mainstream" research, the sequential application of learning in lesson books, and the derivation of music into discrete elements. Without foundational knowledge, the argument goes, each generation would be buffeted by change, prey to conjecture or coincidence. Foundational knowledge—as elemental, as derivative, as unified—cuts across time, context, and culture.

As Bruner noted mid-century, foundational knowledge is arrived at through direct observation of the physical world, a primary doctrine of the umbrella concept referred to as *positivism*. For the architect of positivism, August Comte (1858), the most trustworthy (e.g., "valid") form of knowledge is that which is found in the description of sensory materials. Research into the facts of the world are confined to the "positively given," which has released—ostensibly—humankind from the shackles of superstition and inefficiency. Yet, "to engage effectively in the search for wisdom that led to such understanding, a person had to be able to transcend the lived world of transiency and imperfection. He (almost without exception 'he') had to move beyond opinion, impulse, experience and desire. . . . With such a model in mind, the person consulting a personal vantage point or preoccupation (or gender, social class, or race) can only be thought to be perpetually prey to illusion" (Greene 1994, 427).

Ms. Fairfax uses the same set of method books for all the learners in her piano studio. To remain in her studio, you must pass each exercise before going on to the next. She holds all her students to the same exacting standard, regardless of circumstance, ensuring consistent musical quality. Her no-excuses teaching method has been externally validated by the number of awards her piano students have won.

For the positivist, our mental states are inherently subjective, driven to ignore facts, or make excuses in the face of them. The data-driven No Child Left Behind Act of 2001 was a positivist effort to replace "the soft bigotry of low expectations" (George W. Bush) with a no-excuses curriculum, one that replaced the feelings and subjectivities (and judgment) of the teacher with assessment data in the form of cross-comparative standardized tests.[2] Pure data, in this view, keeps teachers from feeling sorry for their students, teachers who may be inclined to blame poor school performance on social forces like segregation, ethnicity, or poverty. It has been argued that much of secondary ensemble-based music education shares with positivism a data-driven no-excuses epistemology, where contests and competition make no excuses for the particularities of musical experiences and taste, or the varied desires of individuals (Allsup and Benedict 2008). Derivational structures, likewise, drive primary music curricula, conceiving of all musics everywhere as reducible to the elementals of pitch, duration, timbre, texture, and dynamics.

By the mid-twentieth century, the logic of positivism reached its apex in the radical work of North American behaviorists like E. L. Thorndike, B. F. Skinner, and John Watson. *Behaviorism* as a sub-theory of positivism holds that human or animal psychology is to be entirely concerned with the examination of objectively observable external behavior and nothing else. In a nod to the earlier writings of Compte, Watson writes, "the behaviorist began his own formation of the problems of psychology [mind, knowledge] by sweeping aside all medieval conceptions. He dropped from his scientific vocabulary all subjective terms such as sensation, perception, image, desire, purpose, and even thinking and emotion, as they were subjectively defined" (Watson 1930, 5–6; Anderson 2005, 8–9). Extrapolating theories of mind through the isolation of highly controlled variables, learning was reduced to stimulus and response. Teaching was reduced to reinforcement.

Chiding the discipline of cognitive psychology for being "champions of reductionism" (175), Bruner (1979) criticized what he saw as a theory of mind that was preoccupied with small things:

> The modest successes [of cognitive behaviorism] have all been, in a special way, in vitro, treating chunks of behavior out of the controlling contexts in which they ordinarily occur, even though the contexts have a massive influence over the chunks. The more rigorously isolated from context and the more tightly controlled the conditions of experiment, the more precise and the more modest the results have been. . . . This brave and bold approach doubtless worked in physics, where the connection between controlled experiment and nature had become clear. (170)

According to this critique, the behaviorist/quantitative approach fails to address richer notions of mind. What of the larger "controlling contexts" that shape the individual chunks of human experience? Bruner was less dissatisfied with the scientific method of observation, trial, and experiment than he was of the epistemological frame that precluded behaviorists from asking better questions. A different epistemological framework was needed, one that could nudge the science of knowledge closer to qualitative accounts of human experience.

3.2.2. Structuralism and Educational Research

In reducing the effects of learning to ever-smaller design constructs, often through quantitative methods, a logical question arose. What if a behavioral psychologist's tightly controlled experimental variables were not actually independent of each other? What if the variables were implicated in a larger cultural system? What if the so-called isolates were in fact "part of a *structure*, a structure whose existence was in the head or mind of the subject, like his language and its rules" (Bruner 1979, 173, emphasis added)? Calling upon the work of linguist Noam Chomsky (1968) and anthropologists like Claude Lévi-Strauss (1963), Bruner hypothesized that a reaction to a stimulus or a reaction to any aspect of one's environment is never isolated. Instead, reaction—or more accurately, human experience—is always *structure dependent*. In other words, "the significance of any feature is determined by its position in a structure" (Claude Lévi-Strauss 1963, 183).

In this view, the individual mind is implanted with internalized references and rules that are coded by language, culture, context, and emotion. Thus, even the smallest reaction to a variable is never entirely predictable and requires interpretation. Whether we are a cognitive psychologist or an everyday interlocutor, to find out the meaning of a wink or a grin requires an interpretation of the cultural conventions that give meaning to the act (Geertz 1973). A wink can be conspiratorial in one setting or flirtatious in another. A grin can be malicious or spry. Cultural structures taint even the loneliest utterance with multiple meanings. For educational researchers, this was a critical advance: the doctrine of structuralism effectively opened the door to alternative ways of doing and knowing.

In this chapter, I have narrowed my survey of structuralism to its impact on education. It is important to note that structuralism in educational psychology was adopted from larger, more complex disciplinary fields like semiotics (Peirce 1931–1936), linguistics (Bloomfield 1914), and anthropology (Lévi-Strauss 1963). For progressive leaders in the field of education research, structuralism was viewed in relief as a radical departure from behaviorism. Finding the stimulus/response paradigm old-fashioned, they moved to this newer theory of knowledge in which "abiding structures" give form and function to persons, cultures, and domains of inquiry. "Underlying a discipline's 'way of thought,' there is a set of connected, varyingly implicit, generative propositions" (Bruner 1966, 154).

For example, generative propositions in math and physics include universal theorems and rules of association and distribution upon which people (say) build bridges or design homes (Bruner [1960] 1996). In music, deep structures include rules for voice leading, harmonic progressions, the tempered scale, or acoustics. According to this theory, musical genres and styles may differ on a surface level, just as bridges and homes differ across neighborhoods and nation-states, but they all adhere to universal internal structures or essential elements (Elliott 1995, 43–45). Such a concept of derivative knowledge (not breaking with the Western tradition of foundational knowledge) allowed educational researchers to ask more dynamic questions about the ways in which persons and cultures interact—mathematically, musically, or otherwise. "The different activities of a society are interconnected in such a way that if you know something about the technological response of a society to an environment [to its structural elements], you will be able to make some shrewd guesses about its myths or about the things it values" (Bruner [1960] 1996, 154).

Ms. Garrett's high school choir programs works from a diverse repertoire, annually featuring folk arrangements, canonic classical work, show tunes, and gospel songs in end-of-year concerts. Garrett believes that you can learn the same fundamental elements of music regardless of genre or style. "Music is a universal language," she tells her students, "though it is found in many different forms. The basics of musicianship come first, then a singer can sing anything."

Anticipating of the work of later theorists, it is important to state that future critics will take a hard aim at this proposition (Allsup 2013; Butler 1992). *Post*-structuralists will argue that these structures are neither universal nor politically neutral. Nor are they basic, or transferable. Worse, what Bruner identifies as a deep disciplinary structure can be equally understood as various forms of prejudice disguised in universal terms (Lyotard 1979; Miller 2005). For example, the deep structural complexity of Western classical music can often operate as an ideology, not a benign unifying structure, one that effectively keeps non-Western musics and youth music off limits in schools and Schools of Music (Nettl 1995). However, before returning to this critique in the following section, it is important to emphasize that structuralism was a progressive stance for two reasons. First, it brought mid-century psychology closer to the humanities, and to acts of interpretation. Secondly, it re-signaled interest in generative concepts of mind and human intentionality.

Regarding the practice of public schooling, this was a profound epistemological turn by troubling commonly held concepts of teaching and learning that were based on stimulus-and-response-type settings. Instead of drill-and-kill and rote memorization, curricular emphasis was placed on holistic concepts and reflective thinking (see, for example, the Manhattanville Music Curriculum Project of 1970). Bruner's *spiral curriculum* became the most famous educational manifestation of this new theory of knowledge. The premise begins with the idea that all "intellectual activity anywhere is the same, whether at the frontier of knowledge or in a third-grade classroom. What a scientist does at his desk or in his laboratory, what a literary critic does in reading a poem, are of the same order as what anybody else does when he is engaged in like activities—*if he is to achieve understanding*" (Bruner 1960/1996, 14, emphasis added). Thus, "to understand something is to sense the simpler structure that underlies a range of instances" (Bruner 1966, 106). By asking young mathematicians to think like "real" mathematicians and young musicians to think like "real" musicians, students could grasp profound concepts at an age far earlier than common wisdom previously imagined.

The basic concepts of a discipline, according to this theory, are necessarily interrelated, so that understanding the place and purpose of music in human society means exploring the relationships of (say) duration, form, and pitch in the construction of a song—*any* song. Even more radically, "the foundations of any subject may be taught to anybody at any age in some [intellectually honest] form" (Bruner 1960, 12). In evoking the concept of a spiral, each time a learner returns to a basic concept, the knowledge acquired grows in complexity and interest.

Through a relentless focus on the fundamentals of aural skills training, Dr. Bryce believes that he is "teaching for transfer." By understanding the specifics of a larger general rule—in this case through instances of chord recognition and sight singing—the music majors in his charge will become better musicians; e.g., they will play better in tune, improvise what they hear in their head, and conduct better from scores. Dr. Bryce believes there is no such thing as a good musician without a foundation in aural skills.

As author of this historical survey of knowledge and the mind, I step outside my role as documentarian to suggest that the structuralist doctrine of the 1950s and 1960s is alive and well in contemporary music education practice, even as alternative epistemological conceptions—*post-structural* or *postmodern* conceptions that we will soon explore—have blossomed meanwhile. I would argue that most formally trained musicians, the classical and jazz musicians who graduate from today's conservatories and Schools of Music, are the product of decades of step-by-step instruction, all based on the commonsense "ideology" of structuralism. Delving ever deeper into the sonic fundamentals of our art form, we may too easily accept the notion that all music is reducible to its elements—a Western art construct that is not shared universally (Frith 2003). To subscribe to this theory of mind, I contend, is to delimit curricular and research possibilities. It is a tidy view of learning—one that Bruner came to suspect was inadequate as well.

3.2.3. First-Person Singular: Qualitative Research Emerges

Notice for a moment the construction of this chapter. Notice the ways in which I resist the voice of grand narrator, the voice of objectivity and disinterested analysis. Notice the nonlinear pauses for critique. Notice the italicized interruptions, the indented fictions that attempt to illuminate a particular truth (Barone 2000). Notice the use of gender-inclusive language. Notice, above all, the unapologetic use of first-person singular, the "I" that automatically qualifies any statement or claim as contingent. Not long ago, researchers in music education were expected to refer to themselves in the third person singular. *"This researcher sought to explore the effects of . . ."* Or, *"this survey was designed by the researcher to investigate . . ."* As a kind of Truth claim, third-person references in research writing signaled that the trouble of subjectivity could be effectively stanched by adopting the outward appearance of an unemotional objective observer—the white-coated social scientist who assures readers that research design and findings are valid, and (especially) unpolluted by a particular "point of view." It is important to look at what counts as validity or trustworthiness in qualitative research and how the declaration of one's positionality is an acknowledgement of one's partiality (meaning both the partiality of what can be observed and then communicated as a finding, and the partiality of inherent bias). The point I call attention to is the qualitative embrace of what Mikhail Bakhtin ([1975] 1986) famously called the *heteroglossia* of language and lived experience, the multiple, contradictory, and interrelated flux of discourses and discursive practices that constitute the individual and make language and communication incapable of neutrality.

Subject and subjectivity are the defining terms of qualitative research, viewed here as

> a situated activity that locates the observers in the world. It consists of a set of interpretive, material practices that make the world visible. These practices transform the world. They turn the world into a series of representations, including field notes, interviews, conversations, photographs, recordings, and memos to the self. At this level, qualitative research involves an interpretive, naturalistic approach to the world. This means that qualitative researchers study things in their natural settings, attempting to make sense of, or interpret, phenomena in terms of the meanings people bring to them. (Denzin and Lincoln 2008, 4)

Culture constitutes the observer. Culture shapes the observed. Any correspondence between a phenomenon and its interpretation is just that—*an interpretation*.

> A clear epistemological trend began with a view of knowledge that stressed its absolute, permanent character. The result has been a clear focus on normative approaches to identifying the needs and abilities of learners through standards and measures of change. The alternative form is a focus on the social and contextual and acknowledges issues of temporality, relativity, and situation dependence—from a static, passive view of knowledge toward a more adaptive and active one. (Gadsden 2008, 41)

This is the epistemological turn that *required* qualitative methods of trial, observation, and analysis. It is a turn away from abstract theories of derivative structures and their effect on the individual mind. A turn from the laboratory inside toward the "natural world"—the schools, the playgrounds, the garages, and sidewalks—outside.

3.2.4. Cultural Views of Mind

Culture is commonly thought of as the shared practices, laws, customs, institutions, and artifacts that give shape to the social behaviors of a particular nation or group of people. But culture shapes minds as well as behaviors; it is more than an overlay upon the constraints of biological life. Rather, culture "provides us with the toolkit by which we construct not only our worlds but our very conceptions of our selves and our powers" (Bruner 1996, x). Culture is the medium through which theories of knowledge are made. "It is a way of construing the world, the universe, society, and men and women. It is, at the same time, a matrix of meaning, a framework for understanding, and a plan for action. It defines desirable goals, appropriate means, and the broader values to be honored in human action. By so doing . . . culture is a force in human action, a sculptor of society, a major influence on human events" (Salzman 2008, 3). Culture, thus, is "constitutive of mind. By virtue of this actualization in culture, meaning achieves a form that is public and communal rather than private and autistic" (Bruner 1990, 33).

This notion was a sea change for social science, moving educational research away from an individualistic conception of mind toward visions of learning that are situated and nongeneralizable. "Some years after I first became actively engaged with education, I set down what seemed to me some reasonable conclusions in *The Process of Education*. It seems to me in retrospect, some three decades later, that I was then much too preoccupied with solo, intrapsychic processes of knowing and how these might be assisted by appropriate pedagogies" (Bruner 1996, xi). Bruner doesn't say exactly what precipitated his turn, but the 1980s and 1990s were witness to growing demographic changes within and outside the research university. Second- and third-wave feminism, the politics of racial identity, ACT UP and gay rights, organized conservative pushback—these events and others made the process of education highly political, non-neutral, and definitively *post*-structural. "A theory of education that was to serve all could no longer take for granted the supporting assistance of a benign, even neutral culture" (xiii). The how-to teaching plans that were built on foundational or derivative knowledge like Bruner's spiral curriculum or the Manhattanville Music Curriculum Project (Thomas 1970) had to concern themselves with new questions in the shaping of the multicultural mind, like why this and not that? For whom is this appropriate and why? And, who is being heard and who is being silenced?

A new insistence on the plurality of circumstance and the particularity of individual ways of knowing made it more difficult than ever to subscribe to the idea that all human experiences are tied together by deep and abiding structures. Recall Bruner's (1962) structuralist position, "to understand something is to sense the simpler structure that underlies a range of instances" (106). Rather than speak of transfer between simple truths or elements, today there is a much closer examination of the manner in which certain domains of knowledge came to claim dominance, how they legitimize or privilege certain ways of knowing, and how especially (and importantly for researchers) they are wrapped in a "master narrative," the logic of historical truth that effectively silences discussions on value (Lyotard 1979). For example, as long as nineteenth-century Western classical art music and its complex structural elements are the norm against which other musics are measured, the value that youth musics or folk musics serve will remain unseen or unheard, or in the case of research, unlooked for.

A debate is taking place in Jarrett's state. Do so-called popular musicians have the appropriate musical skills and knowledge base to teach music in public schools? Should popular musicians be allowed to apply for state teaching certification? What training would be expected of them? What kind of "pre-clinical" teaching practicum could they be placed in? What remediation would be required? Jarrett is skeptical of this notion of remediation, sensing that such a framework privileges one cultural practice over another.

Skepticism, uncertainty, and deconstruction are the starting points for a postmodern or post-structural theory of knowledge.[3]

> The core of postmodernism is the *doubt* that any method or theory, discourse or genre, tradition or novelty, has a universal and general claim as the "right" or the privileged form of authoritative knowledge. Postmodernism *suspects* all truth claims of masking and serving particular interests in local, political, and cultural struggles. But it does not automatically reject conventional methods of knowing and telling as false or archaic. Rather, it opens those standard methods to inquiry and introduces new methods, which are also, then, subject to critique. (Richardson 2000, 928)

This is the interpretive turn in education research, where the conventions of hypothesis, trial, and experiment take on new cultural or *qualitative* dimensions. Talk of rationality and reason, the computational brain of inputs and outputs, gives way to notions of mind that are contextually situated, full of feelings and desire, sometimes contradictory and fractured (Damásio 1994; Harding 1986). For Bruner and others, methods of research and inquiry that take culture into account must now open up. To accept the notion that knowledge is constructed and reconstructed in public with others, that *reality is an interpreted experience and not objectively verifiable*, gives scholarly inquiry more perspectives from which to see, hear, listen, observe, and reflect.

The rest of this *Handbook* will deal with the various research paradigms that have flourished in this post-positivist landscape. Case study research, as surveyed by Janet R. Barrett chapter 5 of this volume, will explore knowledge as context-governed and context-bound. Qualitative analysis in teacher research, as described in chapter 9, will be understood as framed by the beliefs that govern learning in particular education environments. I move now to briefly survey a recent development in education research where the practical/personal knowledge of the teacher-researcher is highlighted through first-person accounts (for a fuller account, see chapter 8 in this volume, "Narrative Inquiry and the Uses of Narrative in Music Education Research").

3.2.5. Narrative Trends in Education Research

As I close this overview of the major turning points in research, epistemology, and education in the twentieth and early twenty-first centuries, I take note of the emerging role of storytelling as a way of getting at mind, truth, and subjectivity. The social construction of ourselves as we interact with and alongside others is the starting point for narrative research (Barrett and Stauffer 2009). Pluralistic notions of mind and knowledge-making—conflicting, unfolding, relational, unstable—gesture toward the very situatedness of life and the limits to which observation can be put (Clandinin and Connelly 2000). "Our mental states," writes Bruner (1996), "seem not to be bound even by the canon of non-contradiction: we love and hate simultaneously and are often not sure whether this is really a contradiction. And the measures we formulate for the physical world seem to fit poorly to those that characterize our subjectivity: subjective time and space do not neatly correspond with Newtonian clocks and meter sticks" (161). In writing about the function of autobiography in narrative research, Janet Miller writes, "many of us grow up with Western cultural norms that reinforced notions of an 'I' that was an always 'accessible self,' one completely open to observation, rational analysis, and even 'correction' by self and others rather than an 'I' that is performative, that comes into provisional being through social construction" (51–52).

What does it mean to accept the provisional nature of being and knowing, and to embrace this positionality as an educational researcher? What does it mean to remember intimately the feelings of an event, though not its details; to tell a story of learning that has no rosy ending, or even sequential logic? What does this mean as it relates to issues of truth, subjectivity, what is known and what is knowable? As author of this chapter, I think of my own internal confusions and contradictions regarding the research I have chosen to conduct, and how these inherent contradictions led me to ask particular questions in particular ways. For example, I have been deeply shaped by my experiences in high school band, a long-ago place of extrinsic musical success and fellowship, but a space I had trouble recreating for others (Allsup 1997). Recalling the formative contradictions that Bruner describes in the preceding, band was a diversity-affirming and a diversity-phobic place; a mono-cultural and multi-cultural environment—one that introduced me to music I could not find on my own, but had no room for the music I listened to at home or in the car (Allsup 2003). In my research some decades later, I explore the contradictions that come with examining a phenomenon that has revealed itself as simultaneously transformational and limiting (Allsup 2012; Allsup and Benedict 2008).

As "temptations to reconsider the obvious," stories can subvert the normative nature of "typical" educational experiences (Bruner 2002, 10–11). Stories are likewise invitations to inquiry and interpretation. Looking at the world as if it could be otherwise, new positions are staked imaginatively. Questions arise. Common wisdom is challenged. *Band creates community—maybe, but not inherently. Who feels represented? Whose voice is heard? Who gets left out? What role does pedagogy play in inhibiting or enhancing community?* Facts give way to multiple meanings and multiple conditions. *My high school band won multiple state competitions. But what was experienced along the way? What was learned, what wasn't learned? What was the official curriculum? What was the hidden curriculum?* Research informed by way of reflexive acts—the circular folding-back process whereby assumptions and claims are examined and re-examined, often through narrative processes—can pry open those categories that resist examination the most, categories through which conventional wisdom has silenced or devalued alternative educational practices. *Winning speaks for itself. The ends justify the means. Seeing is believing.* When narrative accounts are understood as inquiry into multi-contextual ways of knowing the world, they assist us in all stages of research. As invitations to uncertainty, we make the qualitative turn toward greater complexity, richness, and diversity.

Saewon teaches general music in a multicultural urban environment. Her high school students become highly engaged when they are afforded the opportunity to talk about the music they like. Saewon is often surprised by how unpredictable this exercise can be. Stories of friendship, loss, dislocation, and pleasure remind her that music is never heard the same way twice. *These narratives are often accompanied by personal breakthroughs, turning points in life that are given form and structure through the art of storytelling. She reminds herself that as constructions (some might say fictions), these musical autobiographies are revelations of mind and culture. There are many truths to attend to, and she is always left with new questions, new fascinations.*

3.3. IMPLICATIONS FOR QUALITATIVE RESEARCH

Understanding the place of epistemology in music education research begins by examining our beliefs about teaching and the nature of learning. We were teachers before we were researchers. We were learners before we were teachers. It is therefore critical to remind ourselves that the research questions we ask, the problems we locate to study, and the conclusions we arrive at are *epistemological expressions of what we believe is true or justifiable* based on our past experiences as teachers and learners.

As an exercise, consider the following claims. What would I be committing myself to if I believe they are true?

- Intonation is pure.
- All children are different.
- Music is reducible to its elements.
- Excellence is measurable.
- Culture affects musical preference.
- Fictions reveal truth.
- Musical auditions are predictors of teaching ability.
- There is one right way to play jazz.

The point of this exercise is to reinforce the following admonition: the relationship between one's epistemological view of education must be consistent with the design of one's research. If through my experiences as a teacher I have come to the justifiable belief that all children are unique and endowed with the right to express their uniqueness through music, then I am likely to consider them as co-participants or co-inquirers in the study I design, and not subjects to observe behind mirrored glass. If through my experiences as a learner, I have come to believe that audition results are predictors of future teaching success, then I am committing myself to an epistemological framework that is built upon a linear construct of causal relationships. Being aware of one's epistemological stance matters because some research designs are incommensurable with particular beliefs about education. Likewise, the epistemological stance that one has adopted—whether consciously arrived at or not—effectively limits the methodological approaches that are available for investigating a problem. I cannot believe in case study design and the generalizability of knowledge all at once. I cannot believe in elemental or derivative knowledge and at the same time examine the generative meaning-making processes of a culturally diverse music classroom.

This awareness makes clear my final point: that all theories of knowledge are implicated in a system of values. It is for this reason that music education researchers are morally obliged to examine their beliefs about the human mind, how and where growth occurs, and the purposes to which an education in music is designed by one for the sake of another. Consider once again the list of claims in the preceding. What *values* would I be committing myself to if I believe they are true? How are these values expressed in the research I design? A researcher who believes that all children deserve a voice in the construction of their music classroom is exhibiting a very different set of values from the researcher who videotapes the intonation challenges of third-graders when they sing alone in front of others. The researcher who matches music education audition scores to success in student teaching *practicums* is looking very differently at education from the researcher who studies the autobiographies of music teacher aspirants.

It was this awareness of the relationship between a vision of mind, a research domain, and an expression of human values that propelled Jerome Bruner through 70 years of active and ever-changing scholarship. His career portrait suggests that it is our values that drive innovation, not the other way around. Consider the scholars in our field whose vision of learning was guided by their epistemological values, whose research was animated by a larger public good—Eunice Boardman, Marilyn Zimmerman, and James Mursell are just a few. Concerned as we are with the minds of the children we study and the young lives we hope to improve, we are now moved to ask: What do students deserve, and how does my study help them? Who benefits from the results of my work? How can my values point to new lines of inquiry?

NOTES

1. New York City public schools are rated with grades A–F on the basis of four factors derived from numerical data about each "cohort" (grade level) in the school. This data includes metrics about (i) student progress, (ii) student performance, (iii) school environment, and (iv) ability in closing the achievement gap (Educator Guide: New York City Progress Report High School November 28, 2011).
2. "George W. Bush's Speech Delivered at the NAACP's 91st Annual Convention." *Washington Post*, July 10, 2000.
3. The umbrella term "postmodern" describes the break with enlightened humanism that took place in ideas and the arts in the 1970s, under which various disciplines and doctrines like post-structuralism, post-humanism, feminism, queer theory, and critical race theory adhere.

REFERENCES

Allsup, R. E. 1997. "From Herscher to Harlem: A Subjective Account." *Music Educators Journal* 83 (5): 33–36.

Allsup, R. E. 2003. "Mutual Learning and Democratic Action in Instrumental Music Education." *Journal of Research in Music Education* 51 (1): 24–37.

Allsup, R. E. 2012. "The Moral Ends of Band." *Theory into Practice* 51 (3): 179–87.

Allsup, R. E. 2013. "The Compositional Turn in Music Education: From Closed Forms to Open Texts." In *Composing Our Future: Preparing Music Educators to Teach Composition*, edited by Michele Kaschub and Janice Smith, 57–70. Oxford & New York: Oxford University Press.

Allsup, R. E., and C. Benedict. 2008. "The Problems of Band: An Inquiry into the Future of Instrumental Music Education." *Philosophy of Music Education Review* 16 (2): 156–73.

Anderson, J. R. 2005. *Cognitive Psychology and Its Implications*. 6th ed. New York: Worth.

Bakhtin, M. M. (1975) 1986. *The Dialogic Imagination: Four Essays*. Translated by Kenneth Brostrom. Austin, TX: University of Texas Press Slavic Series.

Barone, T. 2000. *Aesthetics, Politics and Educational Inquiry: Essays and Examples*. New York: Peter Lang.

Barrett, M. S., and S. L. Stauffer, eds. 2009. *Narrative Inquiry in Music Education: Troubling Certainty*. New York: Springer.

Bloomfield, L. 1914. *An Introduction to the Study of Knowledge*. New York: Henry Holt.

Burnard, P., and A. Younker. 2004. "Problem-Solving and Creativity: Insights from Students' Individual Composition Pathways." *International Journal of Music Education* 22: 59–76.

Bruner, J. (1960) 1996. *The Process of Education*. Cambridge, MA: Harvard University Press.

Bruner, J. 1966. *Toward a Theory of Instruction*. Cambridge, MA: Harvard University Press.

Bruner, J. 1979. *On Knowing: Essays for the Left Hand*. 2nd ed. Cambridge, MA: Harvard University Press.

Bruner, J. 1990. *Acts of Meaning*. Cambridge, MA: Harvard University Press.

Bruner, J. 1996. *The Culture of Education*. Cambridge, MA: Harvard University Press.

Bruner, J. 2002. *Making Stories: Law, Literature, Life*. New York: Farrar, Straus and Giroux.

Butler, J. 1992. "Contingent Foundations. Feminism and the Question of 'Postmodernism.' " In *Feminists Theorize the Political*, edited by Judith Butler and Joan Scott, 3–21. New York: Routledge.

Chomsky, N. 1968. *Language and Mind*. New York: Harcourt, Brace and World.

Clandinin, D. J., and F. W. Connelly. 2000. *Narrative Inquiry: Experience and Story in Qualitative Research*. San Francisco, CA: Jossey-Bass.

Comte, A. 1858. *The Positive Philosophy of Auguste Comte*. New York: Calvin Blanchard.

Damásio, A. 1994. *Descartes' Error: Emotion, Reason, and the Human Brain*. New York: Putnam.

Denzin, N. K., and Y. S. Lincoln. 2008. *The Landscape of Qualitative Research*. 3rd ed. Thousand Oaks, CA: Sage Publications.

Dewey, J. 1896. "The Reflex Arc Concept in Psychology." *The Psychological Review* 3 (4): 357–70.

Dewey, J. 1910. *How We Think*. New York: D. C. Heath.

Dewey, J. (1929) 2008. *The Quest for Certainty*. Vol. 4 of *Later Works, 19251953*, edited by Jo Ann Boydston. Carbondale: Southern Illinois University Press.

Eisner, E. 2002. *The Arts and the Creation of Mind*. New Haven, CT: Yale University Press.

Elliott, D. J. 1995. *Music Matters: A New Philosophy of Music Education*. New York: Oxford University Press.

Frith, S. 2003. "Music and Everyday Life." In *The Cultural Study of Music: A Critical Introduction*, edited by Martin Clayton, Trevor Herbert, and Richard Middleton, 92–101. New York: Routledge.

Gadsden, V. L. 2008. "The Arts and Education: Knowledge Generation, Pedagogy, and the Discourse of Learning." *American Educational Research Association* 32: 29–60.

Geertz, C. 1973. *The Interpretation of Cultures*. New York: Basic Books.

Gordon, E. E. 1997. *Learning Sequence in Music: Skill, Content and Patterns: A Music Learning Theory*. Chicago: GIA.

Greene, M. 1994. "Epistemology and Educational Research: The Influence of Recent Approaches to Knowledge." *Review of Research in Education* 20: 423–64.

Greene, M. 2005. "A Constructivist Perspective on Teaching and Learning in the Arts." In *Constructivism: Theory, Perspectives, and Practice*, edited by Catherine Twomey Fosnot, 2nd ed., 110–29. New York: Teachers College Press.

Harding, S. 1986. *The Science Question in Feminism*. Ithaca, NY: Cornell University Press.

Kingsbury, H. 1998. *Music, Talent and Performance: A Conservatory Cultural System*. Philadelphia: Temple University Press.

Kozol, J. 1991. *Savage Inequities*. New York: Crown.

Lather, P 1986. "Issues of Validity in Openly Ideological Research: Between a Rock and a Soft Place." *Interchange* 17 (4): 65–84.

Lather, P. 1993. "Fertile Obsession: Validity after Poststructuralism." *Sociological Quarterly* 34 (4): 673–93.

Lévi-Strauss, C. 1963. *Structural Anthropology*. Translated by Claire Jacobson and Brooke Grundfest Schoepf. New York: Basic Books.

Lyotard, J. 1979. *The Postmodern Condition: A Report on Knowledge*. Translated by Geoff Bennington and Brian Massumi. Minneapolis: University of Minnesota Press.

Merriam, A. P. 1964. *The Anthropology of Music*. Evanston, IL: Northwestern University Press.

Miller, J. L. 2005. *Sounds of Silence Breaking: Women, Autobiography, Curriculum*. New York: Peter Lang.

Nettl, B. 1995. *Heartland Excursions: Ethnomusicological Reflections on Schools of Music*. Chicago: University of Illinois Press.

No Child Left Behind Act of 2001. P.L. 107–110 § 115. Stat. 1425.

Peirce, C. S. 1931–36. *The Collected Papers*. 6 vols., edited by Charles Hartshorne and Paul Weiss. Cambridge, MA: Harvard University Press.

Plato. 2005. *Protagoras and Meno*. Translated by Adam Beresford. London: Penguin Classics.

Piaget, J., and B. Inhelder. 1969. *The Psychology of the Child*. New York: Basic.

Richardson, L. 2000. "Writing: A Method of Inquiry." In *Handbook of Qualitative Research*, 2nd ed., edited by Norman K. Denzen and Yvonna S. Lincoln, 923–48. Thousand Oaks, CA: Sage Publications.

Salzman, P. C. 2008. *Culture and Conflict in the Middle East*. Amherst, NY: Humanity Books.

Skinner, B. F. 1953. *Science and Human Behavior*. New York: Free Press.

Taylor, D. M. 2009. "Support Structures Contributing to Instrumental Choice and Achievement among Texas All-State Male Flutists." *Bulletin for the Council for Research in Music Education* 179: 45–60.

Thomas, R. 1970. *MMCP Synthesis: A Structure for Music Education*. Bardonia, NY: Media Materials.

Thorndike, E. L. 1932. *The Fundamentals of Learning*. New York: Teachers College Press.

Titon, J. T. 1997. "Knowing Fieldwork." In *Shadows in the Field: New Perspectives for Fieldwork in Ethnomusicology*, edited by Gregory F. Barz and Timothy J. Cooley, 87–100. New York: Oxford University Press.

Tyler, R. W. 1949. *Basic Principles of Curriculum and Instruction*. Chicago: University of Chicago Press.

Watson, J. B. 1930. *Behaviorism*. New York: Norton Publishers.

Webster, P. R. 2002. "Creative Thinking in Music: Advancing a Model." In *Creativity and Music Education: Research to Practice*, edited by Timothy Sullivan and Lee Willingham, 1–18. Edmonton: Canadian Music Educators' Association.

CHAPTER 4

....

PARADIGMS AND THEORIES

Framing Qualitative Research in Music Education

....

JOHN W. SCHEIB

RATHER than testing hypotheses, qualitative researchers often seek to produce "descriptions and explanations of particular phenomena" (Hammersley and Atkinson 1995, 25). Qualitative inquiry begins with a topic of concern out of which the researcher poses what Malinowski (1984) refers to as "foreshadowed problems" (see Hammersley and Atkinson 1995; Stake 2000). From these foreshadowed problem(s), the researcher develops questions to guide his/her research. These questions further inform and guide the study and evolve throughout the course of the research. Due to this evolution, there are often no clear and set stages to traverse in carrying out research (Stake 2000). The researcher needs to have a plan of action, design, strategy, and methods to carry out the research, but many of the different stages (e.g., data generation, write-up, question posing, hypothesizing) overlap. Stake (2000) remarks, "Issue development continues to the end of the study; write-up begins with preliminary observations" (445).

Several scholars address the dichotomy of the open-ended yet prescribed procedures of qualitative research as improvisation (Graue and Walsh 1998; Janesick 2000). Janesick (2000) likens qualitative research to improvisatory dance—structured yet free-form. Graue and Walsh (1998) describe qualitative research design being similar to music improvisation; to improvise you first need well-developed skills and a good plan, then you can concentrate on the song (fieldwork) without focusing on the technique.

Theory can play an important part in providing structure to this improvisation by serving as both a *guide* and *ballast* (Ravitch and Riggan 2012). Likening qualitative research to a fine cloth, Creswell (2007) identifies the theoretical framework as the "loom on which fabric is woven" (35). The use of theory in qualitative research also provides lenses to help focus the investigator and bring into focus (or magnify) the researcher's intent for the reader.

However, confusion appears to permeate understandings on the use and role of theory in qualitative research—even the very definition of *theoretical framework*. In their text, *Reason and Rigor: How Conceptual Frameworks Guide Research*, Ravitch and Riggan (2012) assert:

> there is considerable confusion and even disagreement about both the content and role of conceptual frameworks in social science research. The ambiguity around the substance, form, and terminology of conceptual frameworks . . . leads to an array of terms—*theoretical framework, conceptual framework, conceptual model, theory,* and *literature review*—being used imprecisely or even interchangeably, as well as to amorphous expectations and directives for the conceptual framing of empirical research (135).

In making a distinction between *conceptual frameworks* and *theoretical frameworks*, they define the former to be more inclusive and holistic than the latter, with the conceptual encapsulating the theoretical and being composed of three separate but related parts:

(1) *Personal interests*—"curiosities, biases, and ideological commitments . . . theories of action . . . and epistemological assumptions" (10);
(2) *Topical research*—"work (most often empirical) that has focused on the subject" (11);
(3) *Theoretical frameworks*—"*formal* theories; those that emerge from and have been explored using empirical work" (12).

Equally perplexed, Anfara and Mertz (2006) perused the canon of leading textbooks in qualitative research methods and found similarly divergent ideas and directives regarding the role and place of theory in qualitative research. Their analysis yielded three somewhat distinct understandings of theory and theoretical frameworks:

(1) Theory has little (or no) role in qualitative research.
(2) Theory relates primarily to methodology/epistemology (e.g., paradigm, orientation).
(3) Theory relates to "empirical or quasi-empirical theory of social and/or psychological processes . . . that can be applied to the understanding of phenomena" (xxvii).

Although Ravitch and Riggan (2012) provide a distinction between conceptual frameworks and theoretical frameworks, there are similarities in how the latter has been defined and often used in qualitative research. What they refer to as *personal interests* appears to be somewhat synonymous with Anfara and Mertz's (2006) description of theory relating to methodology and/or epistemology. As well, Ravitch and Riggan's (2012) description and definition of *theoretical framework* appears to be more congruent with Anfara and Mertz's (2006) third level of theory as an empirical/quasi-empirical model. In a review of qualitative research published in the *Journal of Music Teacher Education* (*JMTE*) and what has been determined as the eminent music education research journals published in the United States (see Lane 2011), the *Journal of Research in Music Education* (*JRME*) and the *Bulletin of the Council for Research in Music Education* (*CRME*), the predominance of studies identified as utilizing a *theoretical* or *conceptual* framework can similarly be grouped into theory defined as either methodologically/epistemologically based, or empirically/quasi-empirically based.

This chapter further explores these two conceptions through examining widely used qualitative research method texts as well as qualitative studies completed in the United States and published in music education research journals. Because of the confusion and ambiguity that surround scholarly discussions on the role, use, and definitions of theoretical frameworks in qualitative research, and perhaps quite fitting for a discussion of theoretical frameworks, I use as a theoretical frame for this chapter a model based on the somewhat congruent arguments provided by Anfara and Mertz (2006) as well as Ravitch and Raggan (2012). The purpose of this chapter is not only to try to clear away the silt from the murky waters surrounding understandings of what constitutes a theoretical framework, but also, equally important, to provide readers with potentially useful theories, frameworks, and applications toward helping them in their own scholarly pursuits. Toward these efforts (and also due to the nature of such a piece on both published research and the theories that framed them), a somewhat lengthy list of sources is included at the end of the chapter, referencing all that has been discussed. I also provide several direct quotes in hopes of giving the reader a better sense of the particular perspective and to further frame sections of this chapter. It is important to note that due to space limitations I will primarily only engage in a pragmatic (and perhaps utilitarian) discussion, leaving debates and commentary of a more philosophical and/or epistemological nature to others.

4.1. PARADIGMS AND ORIENTATIONS

A research design describes a flexible set of guidelines that connect theoretical paradigms first to strategies of inquiry and second to methods for collecting empirical material.

(Denzin and Lincoln 2000a, 22)

[A paradigm is] a filter or grid through which the world is understood. It is not a theory or set of rules governing thought so much as an orientation of mind that determines how one thinks about the world.

(Kohl 1992, 117).

Qualitative research is an interpretive endeavor. As such, the researcher's worldview shapes the entire investigation—the design of the study, research questions, data generation, and findings. Identifying and disclosing this worldview are therefore critical to sufficiently presenting, understanding, and contextualizing the research for both the investigator and the consumer. An individual's worldview can be referred to as a *paradigm*. Denzin and Lincoln (2000a) state that a paradigm takes into account ethics, epistemology, ontology, and methodology. Ethical questions center on moral principles; epistemological questions investigate how a person knows what he or she knows; ontological questions focus on the nature of being; and methodological questions ask how best to gain understandings about the world.

In addition to qualitative methods materials authored or edited by Denzin and Lincoln (e.g., 2000a, 2000b, 2011), often-cited sources for those framing their research by identifying a theoretical lens centered more exclusively in the domains of methodological, epistemological, ontological, or philosophical realms also include those by Creswell (2003, 2007) and Patton (2002). Denzin and Lincoln (2000a) outline the research process in five phases, the second considering the ontological, epistemological, and methodological questions the researcher should examine in understanding and identifying his or her beliefs that shape not only the researcher but also the research itself. To this they warn, "Each interpretive paradigm makes particular demands on the researcher, including the questions he or she asks and the interpretations the researcher brings to them" (19), and they identify four general interpretive paradigms: positivist and post-positivist, constructivist-interpretive, critical, and feminist-post-structural. Similarly, Creswell identifies the four *worldviews* of post-positivism, constructivism, advocacy/participatory, and pragmatism (2003, 2007), as well as five *interpretive communities*: postmodern perspectives, feminist theories, critical theory and critical race theory, queer theory, and disability theories (2007). Patton (2002) provides an even more comprehensive list of no less than 16 of the most common *theoretical traditions* (which he also refers to as conceptual frameworks): ethnography, auto-ethnography, reality testing (positivist and realist approaches), constructionism/constructivism, phenomenology, heuristic inquiry, ethnomethodology, symbolic interaction, semiotics, hermeneutics, narratology/narrative analysis, ecological psychology, systems theory, chaos theory (nonlinear dynamics), grounded theory, and orientational (feminist inquiry, critical theory, queer theory, among others).

Although these sources (and others) are well-known and substantive works commonly consulted in qualitative research methods instruction, only a handful of music education qualitative researchers appear to exclusively rely on this methodological/epistemological understanding when disclosing a theoretical or conceptual framework in their studies—most either do not explicitly mention a theoretical framework or provide what Anfara and Mertz (2006) would identify as an empirically based theory of social/psychological processes (and what Ravitch and Riggan [2012] would classify as a theoretical framework). To avoid inadvertent confusion between what Creswell (2003, 2007), Denzin and Lincoln (2000a, 2000b, 2011), and Patton (2002) describe as theoretical frameworks, and those provided by Ravitch and Riggan (2012) (which are more consistent with Anfara and Mertz's [2006] empirical-based model), for the purposes of this chapter the term *paradigm* might better differentiate the former interpretation from the latter, even considering this term as well holds a considerable amount of debate as to its working definition in qualitative research (see Lincoln and Guba 2000).

4.1.1. Phenomenology

Among music education qualitative research studies reviewed for this chapter that state a theoretical framework relating more to a paradigm, the most commonly utilized appears to be *phenomenology*, with Patton (2002) cited as the source. Patton defines phenomenological approaches as focusing on "exploring how human beings make sense of experience and transform experience into consciousness, both individually and as shared meaning" (104).

Hourigan (2009) framed his study of preservice music teachers working with special needs children utilizing a phenomenological approach to data generation through immersing himself, as researcher, along with seven participants in a long-term field experience. Through journals, interviews, observations, and regular discussions, he sought to capture their constructed perceptions, both individually and collectively, as well as gauge their growth and evolution of understandings as they collaborated and interacted with each other and the special needs children.

In an earlier phenomenological study, Hourigan was also part of a team of investigators who examined the phenomena of preservice brass and woodwind instrument technique course delivery from the perspective of four early career instrumental music teachers and the researchers, themselves, as instructors of the techniques courses (Conway et al. 2007). Data were generated through observations, individual and group interviews, surveys, and self-study logs completed by the teacher-researchers. Designed, in part, to serve as a program evaluation, the phenomenological design helped yield profound insight into the perceived roles these courses played in teacher preparation.

Combining a phenomenological approach further framed by heuristic inquiry, Conway engaged in two additional co-investigator studies (see Conway and Holcomb 2008; Conway and Hodgman 2008). A type of phenomenological exploration, heuristics more deliberately highlights the researcher's role as active participant and focus of study in the investigation (Patton 2002). This heuristic frame helped structure and guide amplified inquiry into the needs of mentors (Conway and Holcomb 2008) and the experience of leading a collaborative intergenerational performance project (Conway and Hodgman 2008).

4.1.2. Theoretical Models
from Methodological Perspectives

An example of moving a methodological/epistemological framework toward a more concrete theoretical/conceptual model can be found in Gromko's (1996) study of children's understandings of compositional techniques. Utilizing interpretive interactionism, a methodological approach based on a synthesis of symbolic interactionism, hermeneutics, and ethnography (Denzin 1989), Gromko further *operationalized* the study by incorporating concepts found in the related literature, including tasks by

Bamberger (1991) and providing a theoretical foundation steeped in the theories of Piaget, Bruner, and Howard Gardner.

Conway (1999) also framed her development of teaching cases using a post-positivist symbolic interactionist paradigm. Without utilizing an empirically based theoretical construct, the aim was to remain more reflexive in her inquiry toward focusing on building rather than supporting theory.

Dobbs (2010) completed an introspective study returning to a discourse analysis and critical examination of her doctoral dissertation in order to uncover the study's limitations. Further shaping the investigation through the theoretical lens of *speech act theory* (see Austin 1962), Dobbs was able to reach deeper levels of analysis by focusing more intently on illocutionary acts (those that, in themselves, solicit intended action or effect).

In studying the combined development and community of preservice music teachers and music teacher educators, Conway and others (2010) provided a conceptual framework that focused on material mostly gleaned from literature that discussed concepts related to communities of learning. Without overtly citing a specific theory to frame their study (and also using the term *conceptual* rather than *theoretical*, likely to further illustrate the point), the framework could be categorized as an *orientation* (but perhaps is more similar to Ravitch and Raggan's *topical research* component of their three-legged conceptual framework design); however, the stated conceptual framework provided the study with an appropriate foundation for enhanced clarity and direction. One could argue that the implicit theoretical underpinnings of the study venture into the realm of social constructionism, which can be either theoretical or empirical (Graue and Walsh 1998). The former (without the latter) might allow for a more open frame providing increased flexibility toward building theory, the latter more narrowly focusing the study with additional opportunity to engage in theory testing. For example, Kruse and Taylor (2012) cited social constructivism as a foundational element in the design of their study of preservice teachers involved in a mentored research experience in order to highlight the need for this level of reflexivity.

Carter (2013) framed his investigation into the identity formation of four African American gay college band students through the multiple lenses of post-structural theory, critical race theory, and critical theory. The study was further structured through the use of a form of participative inquiry prescribed by Kemmis and Wilkinson (1998).

4.2. BEYOND METHODOLOGY AND EPISTEMOLOGY

. . . formal theory emerges from empirical work, and empirical research is frequently used to test or apply formal theory.

(Ravitch and Riggan 2012, 13).

Returning to the earlier discussion involving the different and often confusing conceptions, descriptions, definitions, and explanations surrounding what constitutes *theory* in a purported theoretical framework, a rift appears among qualitative research scholars, notably those that author method texts for purposes of guiding investigators in designing their research. Up until this point I have focused on understandings of and music education research utilizing *theory as paradigm*, with foundations in "the methodology the researcher chooses to use and the epistemologies underlying that methodology" (Anfara and Mertz 2006, xix). In the context of forming a more comprehensive conceptual framework, these "ideological commitments" and "epistemological assumptions" have also been referred to as *personal interests*, separate from a *theoretical framework* (Ravitch and Riggan 2012, 10). Theory, as presented through the ensuing discussion, becomes more specific and directly related to the topic under investigation—a more focused frame, or lens, to guide both the researcher and reader.

Theoretical frameworks providing this more tapered perspective are as plentiful as they are varied, coming not only from the field of social science research but also from many others particularly relevant to music education, including (but certainly not limited to) sociology, psychology, and anthropology. A wide variety of teaching/learning theories are found among qualitative studies published in music education research journals reviewed for this chapter, including theories centered on reflective thinking, shared understandings, reasoned action, mutual learning and democratic action, constructivism and constructionism, gender association, and multiple intelligences. In addition and pertaining to studies involving preservice and in-service music teachers, theories related to career phases, professional roles, intellectual development, knowledge construction, and appropriate practice are also prominent. As Anfara and Mertz (2006) proclaim, "it is, indeed, this diversity and richness of theoretical frameworks that allow us to see in new and different ways what seems to be ordinary and familiar" (xxvii).

4.2.1. The Music-Makers

In examining the musical lives and understandings of children, studies often provided theoretical frameworks based not entirely on any one empirical theory but rather frames formed from ideas gleaned from several. For example, Richardson (1996) and Whitaker (1996) employed frameworks informed by protocol analysis in examining the critical thinking of both seasoned and neophyte musicians, and Allsup (2003) and Wiggins (1999/2000) explored the shared experience of music learning through the theoretical perspectives of several renowned theorists (e.g., John Dewey, Paulo Freire, Maxine Greene, Mikhail Bakhtin). As well, Wayman (2004) combined Gardner's (1983) *Theory of Multiple Intelligences* and Ajzen and Fishbein's (1980) *Theory of Reasoned Action* to frame an inquiry into the perceptions of middle school students enrolled in a general music class, and Beegle (2010) utilized constructivist learning theory in designing improvisational tasks for fifth-grade students, acknowledging the works of Bruner, Dewey, Montessori, Piaget, and Vygotsky (and others) as being influential.

In a phenomenological inquiry into the perceptions of high school students regarding gender stereotypes and instrument choice, Conway's (2000) theoretical framework was also informed by several related theories pertaining to the social construction of gender, citing works by Green (1997), Shepard and Hess (1975), and Tibbetts (1975), in particular. Also investigating gender differences in the musical lives of high school students, Abramo (2011) used understandings from social constructionism and pointedly referred to West and Zimmerman's (1987) argument that gender identity is formed by the individuals in their day-to-day routines and actions—they *do gender*.

4.2.2. Learning to Be a Teacher

Studies that centered on preservice music teachers transitioning to professionals appeared to be framed a bit more concretely than studies focusing on music teaching/ learning. Several investigators more pointedly referred to specific theories that shaped their inquiry. Among them, theoretical frameworks were found notably steeped in the works of Belenky and others (1986/1997), Carper (1970), Dewey (1933), Feiman-Nemser (1983), Fuller (1969), Fuller and Bown (1975), Schwab (1969, 1971, 1973, 1983), Shulman (1987), and Perry (1999).

Barrett and Rasmussen (1996) utilized Schwab's (1983) *four commonplaces of the curriculum* (teacher, learners, subject matter, and milieu) to frame an investigation into preservice teachers' perceptions of teaching music to third-grade general music students through the use of videotaped cases. Further investigating how apprentice teachers comprehend teaching elementary general music students, Campbell (1999) developed a multilevel framework in his ethnographical exploration of 43 music education students involved in fieldwork. Campbell also utilized ideas from Schwab (1969, 1971, 1973), using his theories of educational experiences as interactions, further categorized into *content, pedagogical*, and *practical* domains (Shulman 1987). Teacher development in this study was framed by both *teacher concerns* as presented by Fuller and Bown (1975) and Feiman-Nemser (1983), and Dewey's (1933) model of effective *reflective thinking* in practice.

Fuller's teacher concerns model (Fuller 1969; Fuller and Bown 1975) was also prevalent in other studies that examined the professional development of preservice teachers (see Paul 1998; Berg and Miksza 2010; Miksza and Berg 2013). Fuller's model consists of three levels, moving from concerns centered on the teacher him- or herself, to the task of teaching, and finally to the students and the impact of instruction. In addition to utilizing this model, Paul (1998) also incorporated Carper's (1970) four categories of professional role development, which provided another layer and added dimension toward investigating the participants' sense of *ownership of occupational title and identity, commitment to professional tasks and knowledge, institutional position and reference group identification*, and *recognition of social position*.

Theoretical models of knowledge and intellectual development have also been useful in framing studies that sought to view and gauge the transformations that preservice teachers undergo on their journey from pupil to professional. In a study of student teachers reflecting on the value and usefulness of curricular and co-curricular experiences in preparing them to be teachers, a colleague and I used Perry's (1999) ethical and intellectual development model as a theoretical framework to gauge if their perceptions were influenced by their intellectual development (Hourigan and Scheib 2009). Perry identified nine linear sequential intellectual positions through which undergraduate students at Harvard University progressed from dualistic, through multiplistic, to relativistic thinking. Although Perry's model is frequently cited in the music education research literature, ours was found to be the only study that incorporated it as a theoretical framework (Palmer 2012); however, Kerchner (2006) earlier utilized a related theoretical frame provided by Belenky and others (1986/1997) that was developed through interviewing women (in opposition to Perry's model, which was based on research involving predominantly male students). This women-specific theoretical model provides five developmental *perspectives*, specific to the ways in which women acquire knowledge. The first perspective, *silence*, describes women who feel disconnected from knowledge, believing they have no independent voice. The second perspective, *received knowledge*, is somewhat similar to Perry's dualistic position where truths are absolute and transmitted by authority. At the third level, the *subjective knower* recognizes herself as an authority and source of knowledge. *Procedural knowers* at the fourth level tend to focus on evaluating the accuracy and merit of truths through dialogue and critique. The final *constructed knowledge* perspective describes the knower as realizing that knowledge and truth are ultimately mutable, constructed in part through experience and bound by context.

4.2.3. Professional Lives

Moving from the development of preservice teachers to studies focusing on the professional lives and instructional strategies of in-service music teachers, concrete and specific theoretical frameworks were equally (if not increasingly) found to shape investigations. Included among these were theories centered on occupational roles and related stress (Beehr 1987; Kahn et al. 1964), career stages of the teacher (Steffy et al. 2000), teacher knowledge construction (Clandinin and Connelly 1995; Louden 1991; Noddings 1999; Shulman and Shulman 2004; Zeichner and Liston 1987), preference for and suitability of work environment (Boyd et al. 2005; Young et al. 1997), and developmentally appropriate practice (Bredekamp and Copple 1997).

I found a useful theoretical framework in studying the professional lives of teachers in the area of *role theory* (Parsons 1954) and *occupational role stress* (Beehr 1987; Kahn et al. 1964). In a collective case study of four music teachers and the combined experience they shared, I used the lens of role theory to focus my investigation of music teacher job (dis) satisfaction (Scheib 2003). In particular, six role stressors (*role conflict, role ambiguity, role overload, underutilization of skills, resource inadequacy, non-participation*) provided the framework to explore sources of discontent as well as the underlying foundational psychological manifestations. As a theoretical framework, these six role stressors also guided the development of interview questions, helped focus observations, and aided in the coding and analysis of interview and field note transcripts.

The *Life Cycle of the Career Teacher* model (Steffy et al. 2000) was used as a theoretical frame in studies examining perceptions of both experienced teachers (Conway 2008) as well as student teachers and first-year teachers (Conway, C. Micheel-Mays, and L. Micheel-Mays 2005); the former investigated perceptions of professional development throughout one's career, the latter compared perceptions between early career stages and the model itself. This life cycle model is comprised of six progressive and sequential phases (*novice, apprentice, professional, expert, distinguished, emeritus*), each with distinct characteristics, focusing on the process of professional growth along the continuum (Steffy et al. 2000).

In studies exploring teacher knowledge construction, Barrett (2007) developed a conceptual framework based on theories and research findings gleaned from an extensive review of literature, building notably on ideas of *knowledge landscapes* (Clandinin and Connelly 1995) and *latitudinal knowledge* (Noddings 1999) to frame her investigation into the construction and utilization of interdisciplinary knowledge. Stegman (2007) also developed a conceptual framework to aid in her analysis of transcriptions of interviews and reflective dialogue between student teachers and their cooperating teachers. Primarily informed by the works of Zeichner and Liston (1987) and Louden (1991), four areas of reflection (*technical, clinical, personal, critical*) were used to frame her study.

In her investigation of why newly inducted music teachers opted to (or opted not to) seek employment in urban school districts, Bruenger (2010) developed interview questions and data comparison criteria to help guide analysis through developing a theoretical framework based on employment inducement studies found in the literature, notably referencing findings related to issues of work environment suitability (Young et al. 1997) and proximity (Boyd et al. 2005). In a related commentary, the National Association for the Education of Young Children (NAEYC)'s position statement on Developmentally Appropriate Practice (DAP), comprising *five key areas of practice* (see http://www.naeyc.org/DAP), provided the external codes to categorize data generated in an ethnographic exploration of three kindergarten general music classrooms (see Miranda 2004).

4.3. ABSENCE OF THEORY?

Glaser and Strauss (1967) are credited with the first use of grounded theory in their research on dying (Charmaz 2000). They coined the term *grounded theory* as the "discovery of theory from data systematically obtained from social research" (Glaser and Strauss 1967, 2). Glaser and Strauss's use of grounded theory was innovative because it contested the belief that qualitative research was merely descriptive and could not build theory (Charmaz 1995). By coding and looking for thematic strands, grounded theorists build theory based on data. However, many argue that the researcher can never really go into a study without a preconceived theoretical base, whether it be explicit or not. To emphasize this point, Graue and Walsh (1998) assert,

> Our view, however, is that the notion has been vulgarized in daily practice into a naïve empiricism, as though each researcher goes into the field without theory and there in the amassed data discovers theory, like a jewel hidden in the rubble. . . . Should theory be grounded? Eventually, it should be well grounded, but theory does not grow on trees, waiting to be plucked by the careful observer. It does not leap out of one's data record. It is constructed, and it has its origins in many places. (28)

An absence of a clearly stated and/or defined theoretical framework is not uncommon among qualitative research studies published in music education journals in the United States. Some authors rather deliberately proclaim that this is due to their desire to remain reflexive and less prescriptive in their approach, and some remind that the methodology/paradigm requires theory to play a lesser or more nonexistent role (see Conway's [2003] discussion of narrative inquiry). In many other studies, various theoretical constructs and/or paradigms are discussed in the context of the literature review, indicating the formation of a lens (or lenses) that can profoundly shape and influence research questions, methods, and analysis (e.g., Bergee, Eason, and Johnson 2010; Carlow 2006; Conkling 2003; Dammers 2010; Mills 2010). Although involving research that was conducted outside the United States, in her study centered on the area of social justice Griffin (2011) more overtly describes this approach as *theoretical threads leading to inquiry*.

Establishing a clear representation of the structure, framework, and theoretical lens(s) through which the study is bound (even loosely) is important. Likened to a road map, it helps guide the researcher and reader on course toward arriving at a destination—even if, by design, the destination is unknown at the onset. As Graue and Walsh (1998) argue, "One cannot not have theory. Everyone has views about how the world and some of its various parts work. The researcher needs to make these views explicit" (28). Clearly identifying and deliberately providing the theories that inform one's work is also important toward simply disclosing particular perspectives and inherent biases. One does not need to be vacant of theory in order to build it; processes of assessing, supporting, and building theory can coexist.

4.4. A CALL FOR CLARITY

> . . . theory cannot simply emerge from or reflect data, because interpretation and analysis is [*sic*] always conducted within some preexisting conceptual framework brought to the task by the analyst.
>
> (Henwood and Pidgeon 2003, 134)

In considering all that has been discussed, in particular the often incongruent and ambiguous descriptions, explanations, definitions, and use of the term "theoretical framework" and what constitutes theory within a framework, I propose considering as a default model clearly identifying the broader conceptual framework in our work as qualitative researchers, consistent with Ravitch and Riggan's (2012) description, which prescribes the researcher more comprehensively identifying both paradigm/orientation (personal interests) as well as empirical/quasi-empirical theory (theoretical framework), in addition to findings from empirical research located in the literature (topical research).

At present, relatively few qualitative research studies published in music education in the United States provide such a comprehensive and clearly defined structure (at least in the published versions of these studies). In addition to this more holistic approach, this conceptual model provides the researcher with a framework, in itself, to guide research design, leaving less room for the investigator to inadvertently sidestep important elements of and questions pertaining to the research. As well, this framework might better align the efforts and findings of qualitative research to other research published in and outside the field of music education. I contend that as more uniformly contextualized information is identified, disclosed, and discussed within a given study (especially within this context), the greater chance the inherently profound thoughtfulness and rigor of the inquiry will be better recognized. This enhanced level of clarity and uniformity might in turn not only help research journal editorial review committees in their work reviewing qualitative studies submitted for publication consideration, but also potentially help attract new audiences to the field of qualitative research in music education.

Using the framework-as-lens metaphor, a more comprehensive conceptual framework could be likened to a multifocal progressive prescription lens, smoothly transitioning from various focal lengths, enhancing vision at a variety of distances, moving from wide (e.g., *theory related to methodology/epistemology* [Anfara and Mertz 2006]; *personal interests* [Ravitch and Riggan 2012]) to more narrow (e.g., *empirical/quasi-empirical theories of social/psychological processes* [Anfara and Mertz 2006]; *theoretical framework* [Ravitch and Riggan 2012]) fields of view, and further shaped and constructed throughout to provide relief from any other correctable cause for blurred vision (e.g., *topical research* [Ravitch and Riggan 2012]). All parts of the lens are designed to seamlessly function together toward providing clear vision at all angles and distances.

4.5. FINDING THEORY

In addition to and in support of many of the theoretical frameworks discussed in this chapter, social and cultural theories steeped in social constructionism, Vygotskian models (e.g., activity theory), post-Piagetian perspectives, and systems theory have been found to be useful in studying children and their worlds (Graue and Walsh 1998).

Resulting from a review of the literature in the area of music teacher identity construction and the professional lives of teachers, Pellegrino (2009) suggests that theoretical frameworks informed by the sociocultural works of Gee (1996, 2000/2001), Rogoff (1995), and Wenger (1998), and the life narratives and histories of Ayers (1989), Goodson (1980/1981, 2008), and Goodson and Sikes (2001) could be useful in studying preservice and in-service music teachers. Further widening our view, Yin (1994) provides a coherent categorization of the common theories often found in social science research—which Anfara and Mertz (2006, xviii) help clarify with the following concise descriptions:

1. *Individual theories* focus on the individual's development, cognitive behavior, personality, learning, and interpersonal interactions.
2. *Organizational theories* focus on bureaucracies, institutions, organizational structures and functions, and effectiveness or excellence in organizational performance.
3. *Group theories* deal with family issues, work teams, employer-employee relations, and interpersonal networks.
4. *Social theories* focus on group behavior, cultural institutions, urban development, and marketplace functions.

As I alluded to earlier, theories abound that could potentially be useful for informing or framing qualitative research in music education. As I mentor novice qualitative researchers over the years I have found it particularly helpful to recommend they continually investigate how other disciplines outside of music education have pursued the crux of their research topic, looking for theories that may help explain the phenomena, context, or problem, or help move them in other directions previously not considered. As a community of scholars (and particularly among those of us relatively new to scholarly inquiry), we tend to restrict our understandings to theories and theoretical constructs from those used within the limited sphere of our discipline and others closely aligned. The best piece of advice I was given when I myself was an apprentice researcher was to broaden my perspective through reading and engaging in coursework outside this sphere—particularly in areas that I believed might hold valuable (and possibly alternative) insight related to my preliminary thoughts on the core issues under investigation.

REFERENCES

Abramo, J. M. 2011. "Gender Differences of Popular Music Production in Secondary Schools." *Journal of Research in Music Education* 59 (1): 21–43.

Ajzen, I., and M. Fishbein. 1980. *Understanding Attitudes and Predicting Social Behavior.* Englewood Cliffs, NJ: Prentice-Hall.

Allsup, R. E. 2003. "Mutual Learning and Democratic Action in Instrumental Music Education." *Journal of Research in Music Education* 51 (1): 24–37.

Anfara, V. A., and N. T. Mertz. 2006. *Theoretical Frameworks in Qualitative Research*. Thousand Oaks, CA: Sage Publications.

Austin, J. 1962. *How to Do Things with Words*. London: Oxford University Press.

Ayers, W. 1989. *The Good Preschool Teacher: Six Teachers Reflect on Their Lives*. New York: Teachers College Press.

Barrett, J. R. 2007. "Music Teachers' Lateral Knowledge." *Bulletin of the Council for Research in Music Education* 174: 7–23.

Barrett, J. R., and N. S. Rasmussen. 1996. "What Observation Reveals: Videotaped Cases as Windows to Preservice Teachers' Beliefs about Music Teaching and Learning." *Bulletin of the Council for Research in Music Education* 130: 75–88.

Bamberger, J. 1991. *The Mind Behind the Musical Ear: How Children Develop Musical Intelligence*. Cambridge: Harvard University Press.

Beegle, A. C. 2010. "A Classroom-Based Study of Small-Group Planned Improvisation with Fifth-Grade Children." *Journal of Research in Music Education* 58 (3): 219–39.

Beehr, T. A. 1987. "The Themes of Social Psychological Stress in Work Organizations: From Roles to Goals." In *Occupational Stress and Organizational Effectiveness*, edited by A. W. Riley and S. J. Zaccara, 71–101. New York: Praeger.

Belenky, M., B. Clinchy, N. Goldberger, and J. Tarule. 1986/1997. *Women's Ways of Knowing: The Development of Self, Voice, and Mind*. New York: Basic Books.

Berg, M. H., and P. Miksza. 2010. "An Investigation of Preservice Music Teacher Development and Concerns." *Journal of Music Teacher Education* 20 (1): 39–55.

Bergee, M. J., B. J. A. Eason, and C. M. Johnson. 2010. "Galvanizing Factors of Communities Applying to Become One of the 'Best 100 Communities for Music Education.'" *Bulletin of the Council for Research in Music Education* 186: 27–42.

Boyd, D., H. Lankford, S. Loeb, and J. Wyckoff. 2005. "The Draw of Home: How Teachers' Preferences for Proximity Disadvantage Urban Schools." *Journal of Policy Analysis and Management* 24 (1): 113–32.

Bredekamp, S., and C. Copple, eds. 1997. *Developmentally Appropriate Practice in Early Childhood Programs*. Rev. ed. Washington, DC: National Association for the Education of Young Children.

Bruenger, S. D. 2010. "Why Select New Music Teachers Chose to, or Chose Not to, Apply to Teach in an Urban School District." *Journal of Music Teacher Education* 19 (2): 25–40.

Campbell, M. R. 1999. "Learning to Teach Music: A Collaborative Ethnography." *Bulletin of the Council for Research in Music Education* 139: 12–36.

Carlow, R. 2006. "Diva Irina: An English Language Learner in High School Choir." *Bulletin of the Council for Research in Music Education* 170: 63–77.

Carper, J. 1970. "The Elements of Identification with an Occupation." In *Sociological Work*, edited by H. S. Becker, 177–88. Chicago: Aldine Publications.

Carter, B. A. 2013. "'Nothing Better or Worse Than Being Black, Gay, and in the Band': A Qualitative Examination of Gay Undergraduates Participating in Historically Black College or University Marching Bands." *Journal of Research in Music Education* 61 (1): 26–43.

Charmaz, K. 1995. "Grounded Theory." In *Rethinking Methods in Psychology*, edited by J. A. Smith, R. Harre, and L. V. Langenhove, 27–49. London: Sage Publications.

Charmaz, K. 2000. "Grounded Theory: Objectivist and Constructivist Methods." In *Handbook of Qualitative Research*, 2nd ed., edited by N. K. Denzin and Y. S. Lincoln, 509–35. Thousand Oaks, CA: Sage Publications.

Clandinin, D. J., and F. M. Connelly. 1995. *Teachers' Professional Knowledge Landscapes.* New York: Teachers College Press.

Conkling, S. W. 2003. "Uncovering Preservice Music Teachers' Reflective Thinking: Making Sense of Learning to Teach." *Bulletin of the Council for Research in Music Education* 155: 11–23.

Conway, C. M. 1999. "The Development of Teaching Cases for Instrumental Music Methods Courses." *Journal of Research in Music Education* 47 (4): 343–356.

Conway, C. M. 2000. "Gender and Musical Instrument Choice: A Phenomenological Investigation." *Bulletin of the Council for Research in Music Education* 146: 1–17.

Conway, C. M. 2003. "Story and Narrative Inquiry in Music Teacher Education Research." *Journal of Music Teacher Education* 12 (2): 29–39.

Conway, C. M. 2008. "Experienced Music Teacher Perceptions of Professional Development throughout Their Careers." *Bulletin of the Council for Research in Music Education* 176: 7–18.

Conway, C. M., J. Eros, R. Hourigan, and A. M. Stanley. 2007. "Perceptions of Beginning Teachers Regarding Brass and Woodwind Instrument Techniques Classes in Preservice Education." *Bulletin of the Council for Research in Music Education* 173: 39–54.

Conway, C. M., J. Eros, K. Pellegrino, and C. West. 2010. "The Role of Graduate and Undergraduate Interactions in the Development of Preservice Music Teachers and Music Teacher Educators: A Self-Study in Music Teacher Education." *Bulletin of the Council for Research in Music Education* 183: 49–64.

Conway, C. M., and T. M. Hodgman. 2008. "College and Community Choir Member Experiences in a Collaborative Intergenerational Performance Project." *Journal of Research in Music Education* 56 (3): 220–37.

Conway, C. M., and A. Holcomb. 2008. "Perceptions of Experienced Music Teachers Regarding Their Work as Music Mentors." *Journal of Research in Music Education* 56 (1): 55–67.

Conway, C. M., C. Micheel-Mays, and L. Micheel-Mays. 2005. "A Narrative Study of Student Teaching and the First Year of Teaching: Common Issues and Struggles." *Bulletin of the Council for Research in Music Education* 165: 65–77.

Creswell, J. W. 2003. *Research Design: Qualitative, Quantitative, and Mixed Methods Approaches.* 2nd ed. Thousand Oaks, CA: Sage Publications.

Creswell, J. W. 2007. *Qualitative Inquiry and Research Design: Choosing among Five Approaches.* 2nd ed. Thousand Oaks, CA: Sage Publications.

Dammers, J. 2010. "A Case Study of the Creation of a Technology-Based Music Course." *Bulletin of the Council for Research in Music Education* 186: 55–65.

Denzin, N. K. 1989. *Interpretive Interactionism.* Newbury Park, CA: Sage Publications.

Denzin, N. K., and Y. S. Lincoln. 2000a. "The Discipline and Practice of Qualitative Research." In *Handbook of Qualitative Research*, 2nd ed., edited by N. K. Denzin and Y. S. Lincoln, 1–28. Thousand Oaks, CA: Sage Publications.

Denzin, N. K., and Y. S. Lincoln, eds. 2000b. *Handbook of Qualitative Research.* 2nd ed. Thousand Oaks, CA: Sage Publications.

Denzin, N. K., and Y. S. Lincoln. 2011. *The SAGE Handbook of Qualitative Research.* 4th ed. Thousand Oaks, CA: Sage Publications.

Dewey, J. 1933. *How We Think: A Restatement of the Relation of Reflective Thinking to the Educative Process.* Boston: D. C. Heath.

Dobbs, T. 2010. "Talking to Myself: Re-framing Music Classroom Discourse." *Bulletin of the Council for Research in Music Education* 183: 7–24.

Feiman-Nemser, S. 1983. "Learning to Teach." In *Handbook of Teaching and Policy*, edited by L. S. Shulman and G. Sykes, 150–70. New York: Longman.

Fuller, F. F. 1969. "Concerns of Teachers: A Development Conceptualization." *American Educational Research Journal* 6 (2): 207–26.

Fuller, F. F., and O. H. Bown. 1975. "Becoming a Teacher." In *74th Yearbook of the National Society for the Study of Education, Part II*, edited by K. Ryan, 25–52. Chicago: University of Chicago Press.

Gardner, H. 1983. *Frames of Mind: The Theory of Multiple Intelligences*. New York: Basic Books.

Gee, J. P. 1996. *Social Linguistics and Literacies: Ideology in Discourse*. 2nd ed. London: Taylor and Francis.

Gee, J. P. 2000/2001. "Identity as an Analytic Lens for Research in Education." *Review of Research in Education* 25: 99–125.

Glaser, B. G., and A. L. Strauss. 1967. *The Discovery of Grounded Theory: Strategies for Qualitative Research*. Chicago: Aldine.

Goodson, I. F. 1980/1981. "Life Histories and the Study of Schooling." *Interchange* 11 (4): 62–76.

Goodson, I. F. 2008. *Investigating the Teacher's Life and Work*. Rotterdam, Netherlands: Sense.

Goodson, I. F., and P. Sikes. 2001. *Life History Research in Educational Settings: Learning from Lives (Doing Qualitative Research in Educational Settings)*. Buckingham, UK: Open University Press.

Graue, M. E., and D. J. Walsh. 1998. *Studying Children in Context: Theories, Methods, and Ethics*. Thousand Oaks, CA: Sage Publications.

Green, L. 1997. *Music, Gender, Education*. Cambridge: Cambridge University Press.

Griffin, S. M. 2011. "Reflection on the Social Justice Behind Children's Tales of in- and out-of-School Music Experiences." *Bulletin of the Council for Research in Music Education* 188: 77–92.

Gromko, J. E. 1996. "In a Child's Voice: An Interpretive Interaction with Young Composers." *Bulletin of the Council for Research in Music Education* 128: 37–58.

Hammersley, M., and P. Atkinson. 1995. *Ethnography: Principles in Practice*. 2nd ed. New York: Routledge.

Henwood, K., and N. Pidgeon. 2003. "Grounded Theory in Psychological Research." In *Qualitative Research in Psychology: Expanding Perspectives in Methodology and Design*, edited by P. M. Camic, J. E. Rhodes, and L. Yardley, 131–55. Washington, DC: American Psychological Association.

Hourigan, R. M. 2009. "Preservice Music Teachers' Perceptions of Fieldwork Experiences in a Special Needs Classroom." *Journal of Research in Music Education* 57 (2): 152–68.

Hourigan, R. M., and J. W. Scheib. 2009. "Inside and outside the Undergraduate Music Education Curriculum." *Journal of Music Teacher Education* 18 (2): 48–61.

Janesick, V. J. 2000. "The Choreography of Qualitative Research Design." In *Handbook of Qualitative Research*, 2nd ed., edited by N. K. Denzin and Y. S. Lincoln, 379–99. Thousand Oaks, CA: Sage Publications.

Kahn, R. L., D. M. Wolfe, R. P. Quinn, and J. D. Snoek. 1964. *Organizational Stress: Studies in Role Conflict and Ambiguity*. New York: Wiley.

Kemmis, S., and M. Wilkinson. 1998. "Participatory Action Research and the Study of Practice." In *Action Research in Practice: Partnership for Social Justice in Education*, edited by B. Atweh, S. Kemmis, and P. Weeks, 21–36. New York: Routledge.

Kerchner, J. L. 2006. "Collegiate Metamorphosis: Tracking the Cognitive and Social Transformation of Female Music Education Students." *Bulletin of the Council for Research in Music Education* 169: 7–24.

Kohl, H. 1992. *From Archetype to Zeitgeist: A Compendium of Definitions of Intriguing and Important Words Used to Discuss Ideas in the Humanities, Literature and the Arts, and the Social Sciences*. New York: Little, Brown.

Kruse, N. B., and D. M. Taylor. 2012. "Preservice Music Teachers' Perceptions of a Mentored Research Experience: A Study within a Study." *Journal of Music Teacher Education* 22 (1): 35–49.

Lane, J. 2011. "A Descriptive Analysis of Qualitative Research Published in Two Eminent Music Education Research Journals." *Bulletin of the Council for Research in Music Education* 188: 65–76.

Lincoln, Y. S., and E. G. Guba. 2000. "Paradigmatic Controversies, Contradictions, and Emerging Confluences." In *Handbook of Qualitative Research*, 2nd ed., edited by N. K. Denzin and Y. S. Lincoln, 163–88. Thousand Oaks, CA: Sage Publications.

Louden, W. 1991. *Understanding Teaching: Continuity and Change in Teachers' Knowledge*. New York: Teachers College Press.

Malinowski, B. 1984. *Argonauts of the Western Pacific*. Prospect Heights, IL: Waveland.

Miksza, P., and M. H. Berg. 2013. "A Longitudinal Study of Preservice Music Teacher Development: Application and Advancement of the Fuller and Bown Teacher-Concerns Model." *Journal of Research in Music Education* 61 (1): 44–62.

Mills, M. 2010. "Being a Musician: Musical Identity and the Adolescent Singer." *Bulletin of the Council for Research in Music Education* 186: 43–54.

Miranda, M. L. 2004. "The Implications of Developmentally Appropriate Practice for the Kindergarten General Music Classroom." *Journal of Research in Music Education* 52 (1): 43–63.

Noddings, N. 1999. "Caring and Competence." In *The Education of Teachers*, edited by G. A. Griffin, 210–20. National Society of the Study of Education.

Palmer, C. M. 2012. "Intellectual Development of Preservice and Novice Music Educators: A Review of Two Models and Their Use in the Literature." *Journal of Music Teacher Education* 22 (1): 50–62.

Parsons, T. 1954. *Essays in Sociological Theory*. Rev. ed. Glencoe, IL: Free Press.

Patton, M. Q. 2002. *Qualitative Research and Evaluation Methods*. 3rd ed. Thousand Oaks, CA: Sage Publications.

Paul, S. J. 1998. "The Effects of Peer Teaching Experiences on the Professional Teacher Role Development of Undergraduate Instrumental Music Education Majors." *Bulletin of the Council for Research in Music Education* 137: 73–92.

Pellegrino, K. 2009. "Connections between Performer and Teacher Identities in Music Teachers: Setting an Agenda for Research." *Journal of Music Teacher Education* 19 (1): 39–55.

Perry, W. G. 1999. *Forms of Ethical and Intellectual Development in the College Years*. San Francisco: Jossey-Bass. (Orig. pub. 1968/1970, New York: Holt, Rinehart and Winston.)

Ravitch, S. M., and M. Riggan. 2012. *Reason and Rigor: How Conceptual Frameworks Guide Research*. Thousand Oaks, CA: Sage Publications.

Richardson, C. R. 1996. "A Theoretical Model of the Connoisseur's Musical Thought." *Bulletin of the Council for Research in Music Education* 128: 15–24.

Rogoff, B. 1995. "Observing Sociocultural Activity on Three Planes: Participatory Appropriation, Guided Participation, and Apprenticeship." In *Sociocultural Studies of Mind*, edited by J. V. Wertsch, P. del Rio, and A. Alvarez, 139–64. Cambridge, UK: Cambridge University Press.

Scheib, J. W. 2003. "Role Stress in the Professional Life of the School Music Teacher: A Collective Case Study." *Journal of Research in Music Education* 51 (2): 124–36.

Schwab, J. J. 1969. "The Practical: A Language for Curriculum." *School Review* 78: 1–23.

Schwab, J. J. 1973. "The Practical 3: Translation into Curriculum." *School Review* 81: 501–22.

Schwab, J. J. 1983. "The Practical 4: Something for Curriculum Professors to Do." *Curriculum Inquiry* 75 (3): 239–65.

Shepard, W. O., and D. T. Hess. 1975. "Attitudes in Four Age Groups toward Sex Role Division in Adult Occupations and Activities." *Journal of Vocational Behavior* 6: 27–39.

Shulman, L. 1987. "Knowledge and Teaching: Foundations of the New Reform." *Harvard Educational Review* 57 (1): 1–22.

Shulman, L. S., and J. H. Shulman. 2004. "How and What Teachers Learn: A Shifting Perspective." *Journal of Curriculum Studies* 36 (2): 257–71.

Stake, R. E. 2000. "Case Studies." In *Handbook of Qualitative Research*, 2nd ed., edited by N. K. Denzin and Y. S. Lincoln, 435–54. Thousand Oaks, CA: Sage Publications.

Steffy, B. E., M. P. Wolfe, S. H. Pasch, and B. J. Enz. 2000. *Life Cycle of the Career Teacher*. Thousand Oaks, CA: Corwin Press.

Stegman, S. F. 2007. "An Exploration of Reflective Dialogue between Student Teachers in Music and Their Cooperating Teachers." *Journal of Research in Music Education* 55 (1): 65–82.

Tibbetts, S. L. 1975. "Sex-Role Stereotyping in The Lower Grades: Part of the Solution." *Journal of Vocational Behavior* 6: 255–61.

Wayman, V. E. 2004. "An Exploratory Investigation of Three Middle School General Music Students' Beliefs about Music Education." *Bulletin of the Council for Research in Music Education* 160: 26–37.

Wenger, E. 1998. *Communities of Practice: Learning, Meaning, and Identity*. New York: Cambridge University Press.

West, C., and D. H. Zimmerman. 1987. "Doing Gender." *Gender and Society* 1 (2): 125–51.

Whitaker, N. L. 1996. "A Theoretical Model of the Musical Problem Solving and Decision Making of Performers, Arrangers, Conductors, and Composers." *Bulletin of the Council for Research in Music Education* 128: 1–14.

Wiggins, J. H. 1999/2000. "The Nature of Shared Musical Understanding and Its Role in Empowering Independent Musical Thinking." *Bulletin of the Council for Research in Music Education* 143: 65–90.

Yin, R. K. 1994. *Case Study Research*. 2nd ed. Thousand Oaks, CA: Sage Publications.

Young, I. P., A. W. Place, J. S. Rinehart, J. C. Jury, and D. F. Baits. 1997. "Teacher Recruitment: A Test of the Similarity-Attraction Hypothesis for Race and Sex." *Educational Administration Quarterly* 33 (1): 86–106.

Zeichner, K. M., and D. P. Liston. 1987. "Teaching Student Teachers to Reflect." *Harvard Educational Review* 57 (1): 23–48.

CHAPTER 5

....

CASE STUDY IN MUSIC EDUCATION

....

JANET R. BARRETT

CASE studies are frequently employed in music education research, in education at large, and across the social sciences, and for good reason. A scan of scholarly journals confirms their widespread use, which is further substantiated in content analyses of qualitative articles and dissertations (Kantorski and Stegman 2006; Lane 2011). The ubiquity of case study as a form of inquiry can be attributed to many factors, related to the adaptability of its design and process, compatibility with educational research, transparency for readers, and pedagogical utility in research education. Accompanying their widespread use is widespread criticism as well. Case studies are often critiqued for lack of methodological rigor, irregularity in design, and limited utility. VanWynsberghe and Khan, for example, pose the challenge: "Why is [case study] so regularly invoked in educational and other social science research and yet so irregularly, randomly, and poorly defined?" (2007, 80). Merriam observes that case studies in education have come to serve as a "catch-all" category for studies that cannot easily be identified as another type (1998, 18).

The purpose of this chapter is to (a) address divergent definitions of case study; (b) represent key dimensions of case studies drawn from these definitions in a diagram; (c) relate this diagram to common criticisms and misconceptions surrounding case studies; (d) apply resulting analytical insights to select case studies drawn from music education journals; and (e) propose avenues for improving the overall impact and utility of case studies within music education.

5.1. ON THE PREVALENCE OF CASE STUDY IN MUSIC EDUCATION

It may be useful to elaborate further on the appeal and prevalence of case studies in music education. One primary reason is their affinity to related fields within the social sciences. The roots of case study lie in the fields of anthropology, sociology, and psychology, which have historically informed education as an especially synthetic field. In turn, music education research is a hybrid of an arts discipline infused with modes of inquiry freely adapted from the social sciences. Accordingly, case studies lend themselves to central issues of teaching and learning, schools, and subject matters. Their highly *contextual nature* lends itself well to educational settings, in which there is likely to be considerable entanglement of phenomenon and context (Yin 2009, 18).

The focus of the case is infinitely variable—a person, an event, a program, a group, or multiple entities—depending upon how the researcher defines, or binds, the territory of what is to be studied. Cases can be single or multiple, oriented toward a single holistic unity, or pointed toward various embedded instances within a context (Yin 2009). They can be oriented in historical frames as well as grounded in contemporary issues. The researcher's process of defining and articulating a bounded system worthy of study is what Ragin calls "casing" (1992, 218). The process affords *flexibility of focus* in broadly defining the phenomenon of interest; as researchers subsequently draw boundaries more closely, the scope of the case comes into sharp view. The leeway afforded in the selection and binding of the case tailors the case study to the myriad musical issues related to persons, programs, processes, and contexts.

Of special interest in this chapter is the capacity of case studies to convey the *particularity and complexity* that attend a phenomenon of interest. Aspects of the lived experience of music teaching and learning are often too nuanced, contextualized, and interdependent to be reduced to discrete variables. The dynamic intersections of subject matter, learners, teacher, and educational milieu are vital to our professional understanding; case study reports can aptly convey the multifaceted ecologies of life in music classrooms.

Multiplicity is another hallmark. Case studies lend themselves to *multiple scholarly orientations* such as ethnography, phenomenology, social constructivism, and critical perspectives, where the types of questions and the stances toward inquiry are steeped in interdependent networks of thought and practice. The case study approach (if indeed, there is any uniformity of approach, a question to be addressed later) employs *multiple methods* of data collection, drawing generously from related traditions within qualitative research. Fieldwork, observation, interviews, document analysis, and other items of material culture are commonly utilized.

A layperson who seldom reads research accounts has an implicit sense that a case study involves keen scrutiny of a topic requiring careful investigation, lasting duration, and clear purpose. This *transparency of intent* broadens their appeal. Case study reports, which build on narrative, literary, and other authorial conventions, allow for *broad readership*. Compared to some other forms of inquiry, case studies generally pose fewer barriers to reading and interpretation. Rich description, for example, allows the reader to come close to lived situations, feel their pulse and tensions, and weigh how they might extend to other settings and situations. Verisimilitude, when achieved, extends the immediacy, impact, and practical significance of cases.

Pedagogical applications to research education are of considerable interest. For those who teach qualitative research methods, case studies provide *meaningful and manageable* frameworks for students taking their first forays into systematic interpretive inquiry. Case studies can be delimited in such a way (by making thoughtful decisions about binding the case, the duration of the study, the availability of participants for purposeful sampling, etc.) to allow novice qualitative researchers to experience all of the phases of conducting a qualitative study in a relatively concise and timely fashion. Conducting a condensed version of a case study as a collective exercise in a methods class has proven fruitful in teaching qualitative analysis and interpretation (J. Barrett 2007), in addition to the common practice of conducting individual pilot projects within the supportive structures of a research methods course.

5.2. DIVERGENT CONCEPTIONS OF CASE STUDY

Definitions matter in that they often encapsulate the essential components of a methodological design or approach. In case study research, such definitions abound. Many influential texts address this proliferation, addressed by VanWynsberghe and Khan: "The past three decades of scholarship on case study research have produced more than 25 different definitions of case study, each with its own particular emphasis and direction for research" (VanWynsberghe and Khan 2007, 81). Repeatedly, the question emerges: Is case study a method, an approach, or a research design? To address this persistent dilemma, I have chosen key examples for commentary, drawing from commonly cited methodologists associated with case study, such as Robert E. Stake, Robert K. Yin, and Sharan B. Merriam, as well as scholars who are less frequently cited in music education (Helen Simons, Gary Thomas, Rob VanWynsberghe, and Samia Khan) but whose thinking is germane. Each of these researchers emphasizes or accentuates various components of case study; when studied together, key attributes and their relationships emerge.

Stake's definition is one of the most frequently cited:

> Case study is the study of the particularity and complexity of a single case, coming to understand its activity within important circumstances. (1995, xi)

Here, Stake emphasizes both the focal center, the single case, and its concomitant circumstances or context. The implied purpose is understanding through multidimensional elaboration of the specific features of the case and their interrelations, the "particularity and complexity." Stake elaborates that in education and social sciences, researchers concentrate on persons and programs to understand them "for both their uniqueness and commonality" (1). Many researchers, however, looking for guidance in constructing and carrying out a case study have been puzzled by this oft-quoted passage from Stake's later writing:

> Case study is not a methodological choice but a choice of what is to be studied. . . . By whatever methods, we choose to study *the case*. We could study it analytically or holistically, entirely by repeated measures or hermeneutically, organically or culturally, and by mixed methods—but we concentrate, at least for the time being, on the case. (Stake 2005, 443)

This passage unambiguously centers on the subject of interest for the case study while conveying both broad possibility and considerable ambiguity regarding the design and conduct of the study.

Robert K. Yin, also known for his series of texts on case study research, emphasizes rigor in design, while also embracing the complementary nature of quantitative and qualitative approaches. Yin forwards a two-pronged definition that moves into the methodological. The first installment of the definition aligns with Stake's, stressing the interactions of the focal subject of the case and its naturalistic setting:

A case study   is an empirical inquiry that
- Investigates a contemporary phenomenon in depth and within its real-life context, especially when
- The boundaries between phenomenon and context are not clearly evident. (Yin 2009, 18)

In the second part of the definition, Yin addresses methodological aspects of design to guide the logical conduct of the study:

The case study inquiry
- Copes with the technically distinctive situation in which there will be many more variables of interest than data points, and as one result
- Relies on multiple sources of evidence, with data needing to converge in a triangulating fashion, and as another result
- Benefits from the prior development of theoretical propositions to guide data collection and analysis. (Yin 2009, 18)

This further elaboration of the case study emphasizes the *process* of conducting the case study by drawing attention to multiple variables, sources of evidence, need for triangulation, and use of theoretical constructs to inform data generation and analysis. Merriam (1998) points out these distinctions in her discussion of Stake and Yin's definitions, bridging both emphases while also drawing attention to the final outcome of inquiry:

> Case studies can be defined in terms of the process of conducting the inquiry, the bounded system or unit of analysis selected for study, or the product, the end report of a case investigation. (43)

An especially productive conception of the case study is forwarded by Thomas, who recasts the way the unit of analysis is considered while simultaneously giving weight to the analytical frame that gives a case shape and purpose. Thomas suggests that a case study comprises two elements:

1. A "practical, historical unity," which I shall call the *subject* of the case study, and
2. An analytical or theoretical frame, which I shall call the *object* of the study. (2011b, 513)

The *subject* of the case study (by which he means the focal center, rather than participants) maps onto previous delineations of the bounded case in context. Thomas gives equal balance, however, to the *object*. His concept of the analytical or theoretical frame is well worth pursuing, as the underdevelopment of this frame fuels many criticisms of case studies, and often plagues work in music education particularly. As he explains, cases are always instances of a larger class; they are cases *of* something. Potential explanations or thinking tools (here drawing from Bourdieu), drawn from theory or developed to scaffold the emerging constructs, are constructed to illuminate the phenomenon of interest. The object is the "analytical focus that crystallizes, thickens, or develops as the study proceeds" (2011a, 514). In Thomas's view, a clear articulation of the object, even in its dramatic unfolding, is essential in grounding the assumptions that relate to the selection of the case and justify its purposes, as well as in the process of relating the findings to larger issues that arise *from* the study of the case. Thus—and this is a crucial distinction for those who maintain that case studies are not generalizable—the particularistic nature of case studies can extend to instances of the phenomenon beyond the case itself. Thomas combines these two elements in the following definition:

> Case studies are analyses of persons, events, decisions, periods, projects, policies, or other systems that are studied holistically by one or more methods. The case that is the subject of the inquiry will be an instance of a class or phenomena that provides an analytical frame—an object—within which the study is conducted and which the case illuminates and explicates. (Thomas 2011b, 513)

Thomas's critique of underdeveloped or under-theorized studies goes to the heart of the matter, addressing the problem of extendability, or use of the case study findings outside the direct case itself, head-on:

The ostensible looseness of the case study as a form of inquiry and the conspic-
uous primacy given to the case (the subject) is perhaps a reason for inexperienced
social inquirers, especially students, to neglect to establish any kind of *object* (liter-
ally and technically) for their inquiries. Identifying only a *subject,* they fail to seek
to explain anything, providing instead, therefore, a simple description in place of a
piece of research. For the study to constitute research, there has to be something to be
explained (an object) and something potentially to offer explanation (the analysis of
the circumstances of the subject). (513)

One final excerpt will draw attention to a final element of case study research, that of the
purpose of the inquiry, taken to mean the broad uses to which the case study can be put
(rather than the specific purpose statement within the study itself). Simons's definition
aligns with many dimensions already noted, but goes beyond the description of the inquiry as product, process, subject, or object, to articulate powerful outcomes:

> Case study is an in-depth exploration from multiple perspectives of the complexity and
> uniqueness of a particular project, policy, institution, programme or system in a "real
> life" context. It is research-based, inclusive of different methods and is evidence-led. The
> primary purpose is to generate an in-depth understanding of a specific topic (as in a
> thesis), programme, policy, institution, or system to generate knowledge and/or inform
> policy development, professional practice and civil or community action. (2009, 21)

Each research methodologist emphasizes various components of case studies. Notably,
however, the definitions do not, as a whole, restrict the researcher to a fixed set of methodological procedures, analytic moves, or representational forms. These remain open-
ended and flexible. Thus, learning to conduct, guide, or evaluate case studies in music
education depends on keen decisions for selecting and binding the case (the *subject*),
articulating its conceptual or analytical frameworks (the *object*), employing appropriate
and multiple strategies for data generation, addressing clear purposes, and providing a
detailed report of the case that is particularistic and complex. The actual strategies for
data generation and analysis, however, may be borrowed from other qualitative forms
of inquiry, as may the analytical techniques used to draw meanings from the data, and
the verification strategies (Creswell 2007) employed to lend credence to the findings.
Reading multiple research texts and examples has led me to conclude that there is
little that is fixed in case studies regarding data collection, analysis, and validation beyond the guidelines and heuristics that guide most qualitative inquiries. Thus, in this
chapter, I will not articulate a method for case study, since the procedures and criteria
for conducting a case study overlap or mirror other designs.

I have drawn from these conceptual definitions to represent these components
in Figure 5.1. This diagram attempts a synthesis of the definitions discussed in the
preceding and their corresponding emphases. It conveys the interdependent nature of
the case itself as a bounded system in context (Stake, Yin, Merriam), in complementary balance with the object of the case, the phenomenon situated within an analytical
frame (Thomas). The use of the arrow between the subject and object is especially important to denote the dynamic nature of the theoretical frame as it intersects with the

bounded system delineating the case. Ragin notes the interdependence of "ideas and evidence" (1992, 218) as each implicates the other. The extended purposes of the case (Simons) are addressed through the particularized and detailed presentation of the case (Merriam) to illuminate and explain the phenomenon. The processes of data generation and collection, analysis, and interpretation are more open-ended and variable, allowing researchers to structure the design and conduct of a study in ways that meet other criteria for qualitative research processes. In the final research report, these dimensions are communicated through the skillful, scholarly, and occasionally artful, presentation of the study.

5.3. MISUNDERSTANDINGS AND CRITICISMS

Researchers conducting or learning to conduct qualitative research often encounter predictable criticisms that make up what Flyvbjerg calls the "conventional view, or orthodoxy, of the case study" (2011, 302). He takes on the paradox that case studies seem to be ubiquitous but generally held in very low esteem within academe. Flyvbjerg presents five misunderstandings about case study that, when confronted, could ameliorate this status problem (Table 5.1).

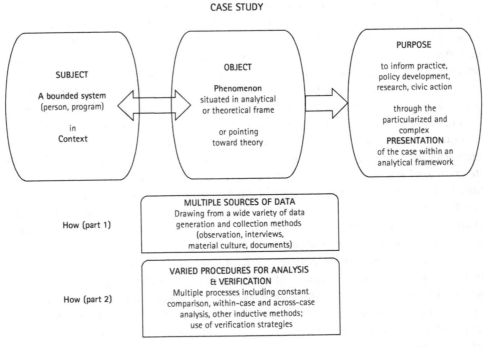

FIGURE 5.1. Dimensions of a case study.

In this section, I will trace and comment upon Flyvbjerg's analysis. The first misconception—stemming from the valuation of general theoretical knowledge over concrete case knowledge—is critical for educational researchers to address explicitly. At heart, explains Flyvbjerg, is a fundamental misalignment in epistemic underpinnings. General, rule-bound knowledge systems, a hallmark of disciplined inquiry in the natural sciences, facilitate explanation and prediction. In contrast, research on the nature of human learning emphasizes concrete context-dependent knowledge, which when constructed allows learners to progress from novice to more expert levels of understanding. Case studies, then, are central to the development of expertise founded on the nuanced and refined examination of concrete cases. As an example of this epistemological contrast, Flyvbjerg cites Donald Campbell, probably the most well-known methodologist in social science, who initially dismissed context-based studies as having little to contribute to context-independent and predictive theory. Later, he came to revise his view that naturalistic observation, "noisy, fallible, and biased though it be" (1975, 179), is valuable in social inquiry. Music education looks to case studies for multiple accounts of concrete, context-based knowledge, crucial in forming collective expertise and professional knowledge to inform teaching and learning.

Flyvbjerg's second misconception raises the thorny question of generalizability, a frequently sounded alarm when it comes to the applicability and overall significance of case studies. Many efforts in qualitative research have been devoted to either rejecting the possibility of generalization as fundamentally incommensurable with idiographic inquiry ("based on the particular individual") when placed at odds with nomothetic research ("based on laws"),[1] or reconceptualizing different types of generalization in order to find reasonable justifications for case studies to point beyond the particular. Flyvbjerg's position is that in certain instances case study findings can be useful in "testing theory in a 'soft sense,' that is for testing propositions and hypotheses" (2011, 305). One instance in particular is in falsification, wherein carefully documented

Table 5.1 Five Misunderstandings about Case Study (Flyvbjerg 2011)	
Misunderstanding No. 1	General, theoretical knowledge is more valuable than concrete case knowledge.
Misunderstanding No. 2	One cannot generalize on the basis of an individual case; therefore, the case study cannot contribute to scientific development.
Misunderstanding No. 3	The case study is most useful for generating hypotheses, that is, in the first stage of a total research process, while other methods are more suitable for hypotheses testing and theory building.
Misunderstanding No. 4	The case study contains a bias toward verification, that is, a tendency to confirm the researcher's preconceived notions.
Misunderstanding No. 5	It is often difficult to summarize and develop general propositions and theories on the basis of specific case studies.

Flyvbjerg (2011, 302).

observations can result in the revision or rejection of theoretical propositions. Aligning with the reconceptualists, many researchers distinguish other types of generalizability from more positivist or "scientific" assumptions, such as Yin's concept of *analytic generalization*, which "depend(s) on using a study's theoretical framework to establish a logic that might be applicable to other situations" enabling researchers to claim that findings "are generalizable to theoretical propositions and not to populations or universes" (2012, 18). A related reconceptualization is *transferability*, involving "generalizations from one case to another (similar) case" (Onwuegbuzie and Leech 2010, 883).

The issue of generalizability has considerable import for researchers in music education. Taking the latter notion of transferability first, this implies that researchers describe the particularities of their cases and contexts to such a degree that readers can determine the extent to which findings from the case study can be deemed relevant to settings outside the case. Transferability, then, rests on the thick description of the case and its complexities. The other aspect of transferability has to do with the reader's capacities to extend the findings to other instances and settings. In other words, the responsibility for transferability rests with both the researcher and the reader.

Analytic generalizability has much to do with the framework of concepts, assertions, and assumptions that undergird the case and the way this framework is expanded, revised, streamlined, and made more complex and tangible as a result of the analysis. Literature reviews, for example, often provide a scaffolding of related constructs that are used by the researcher in building a more nuanced conception of the case. These a priori concepts, however, need not constrict the case; instead, they inform data generation, analysis, and interpretation. When the theoretical frame of the case is subsequently redrawn, then, the insights that permit new understandings inform the use, interpretation, and even the extendability of the findings to new studies or situations. Thus, in analytic generalization, the principles—in their redrawn form—carry across from the case to situations outside the case, not the specific instances.

Flyvbjerg's third misconception relates to both the intended use of case studies in theory building and generation and also their relationships to other forms of inquiry. Case studies are sometimes viewed as initial steps within an overall line of inquiry in order to generate hypotheses that can subsequently be examined through other approaches. Flyvbjerg counters that case studies are useful in examining all sorts of knowledge dependent upon the researcher's information-oriented selection of the case. For example, extreme or deviant cases are warranted to test the "limits of existing theories and to develop new concepts, variables, and theories" related to these extreme cases. Maximum variation cases can demonstrate the "significance of various circumstances" for cases "that are very different on one dimension." Critical cases are those that have "strategic importance in relation to the general problem." They describe instances in which more typical positive instances occur, as well as "least likely" or negative cases. Finally, Flyvbjerg mentions paradigmatic cases, purposefully chosen because they are likely to contribute to the development of "a metaphor or [to] establish a school for the domain that the case concerns" (2011, 307). Of course, researchers may not be able to determine a priori how the case will fall into a categorical type, and in fact, there may be overlap.

Flyvbjerg's fourth misconception is tied intrinsically to the researcher's position, stemming from concern that researchers will show bias as preconceived notions crowd out alternate observations and explanations. Claims to rigor are suspect when the researcher's observations, professional experience, and immersion in related literature inhibit perception and critical thought rather than enabling them. Yet subjectivity is also seen as positive rather than detrimental. Since the researcher serves as the instrument, this entanglement is not only necessary but also unavoidable. Again, Flyvbjerg claims that through observation, interviewing, document analysis, and other methods, researchers often question their prior assumptions and revise them as new data are generated through fieldwork. He maintains that

> the case study contains no greater bias toward verification of the researcher's preconceived notions than other methods of inquiry. On the contrary, experience indicates that the case study contains a greater bias toward falsification of preconceived notions than toward verification. (2011, 311)

A particularly useful account of the interplay of observation and interpretation in a music teaching and learning setting can be found in M. Barrett and Mills (2009), who describe how they subjected their data-generation methods and findings to critical analysis while jointly conducting an ethnographic case study of an English cathedral choir school.

Finally, the fifth misunderstanding has to do with the reporting of the findings of case studies related to the difficulty of summarizing and developing theory on the basis of their conduct. Case studies are replete with data and interpretation in order to fulfill their primary goal of particularizing and complexifying the case under scrutiny. Dense case material cannot be easily reduced to a tidy set of principles, executive summaries, or tight conclusions. The solution, recommends Flyvbjerg, is to keep case studies open, rather than closing them up. This requires that the researcher present the complex, multidimensional narrative of the case without reverting to facile encapsulations and superficial overviews. "Something essential may be lost by summarizing," he cautions (2011, 312). At the same time, researchers may link the findings of the study to one or more theoretical orientations while leaving the readers to decide on the goodness of fit from their perspectives. In this way, the "case study . . . can contribute to the cumulative development of knowledge . . . in using the principles and propositions" (313) that lead to analytical generalization or transferability.

Other conceptual and methodological problems mentioned in the literature include insufficient framing of the study (lack of conceptual structure); lack of transparency in conducting the study; insufficient analysis or interpretation of data; failure to address alternate explanations; shallow rather than detailed description; and ambiguity such that it is difficult to build a line of inquiry stemming from the substantive contributions of a case. Much methodological rigor rests on the explicit "trail" of decisions, which Stake suggests as a first line of defense against common critiques of case studies as:

> subjective, arbitrary, nonrepresentative, and inconclusive. Which is probably true, but the study is not thus invalidated. The counter to these charges, if strong efforts to produce a valid study have occurred, is a good description of the methodological and conceptual reasoning that took place, including efforts at verification and disconfirmation. (1988, 273)

Methodological rigor is often the clarion call for improving the quality of research; Stake's admonition rings loudly for those conducting, reviewing, guiding, or teaching qualitative research. Such rigor is the warrant on which validity rests. In addition to this foundation, case studies in music education must attend to additional criteria. They fall short of our expectations when researchers fail to portray the case in its fullness, or when the findings stitch together a patchwork quilt of data that does not sum up to a coherent whole. They also miss the mark when researchers stop short of reintegrating the study's findings into the fabric of what is already known about the topic under study.

5.4. FRAMEWORKS FOR ANALYSIS OF CASE STUDIES

Critical analysis of research efforts is essential for many purposes: to guide the conduct of researchers' efforts toward the submission of publishable reports; to influence peer review and useful professional commentary; and to expand the professional capacity of a field or discipline. Many useful heuristics for the evaluation of qualitative research can be adapted to evaluate case study research. One particularly useful approach involves "big-tent" criteria for determining quality, including worthy topic, rich rigor, sincerity, credibility, resonance, significant contribution, ethical considerations, and meaningful coherence (Tracy 2010). Yin (2009) argues that designating a study as exemplary involves considerations that go far beyond faithful adherence to methodological procedures and criteria. In order to contribute to research efforts in sustainable, lasting, and valid ways, he offers five characteristics tailored specifically to case study, that they "be significant, be complete, consider alternative perspectives, display sufficient evidence, and be composed in an engaging manner" (185–90).

Perhaps one of the most central attributes of a case study is its utility, its descriptive, analytical, or critical power to inform practice, policy, research, civic action, or professional discourse. In order to argue for case study as a valid and worthwhile form of activity, we must be able to articulate what case studies are good for, in addition to being able to identity good examples. Peshkin wrote: "the proof of research conducted by whatever means resides in the pudding of its outcomes" (1993, 23). Thomas puts it plainly: "What the case study is especially good for is getting a rich picture and gaining analytical insights from it" (2011, 23).

After reading methodological literature and numerous critiques of case study research, I launched into the central task of identifying compelling and informative case studies for examination. I sought case studies that went beyond taken-for-granted assumptions, searching for levels of particularity that penetrated beneath and beyond common discourse and common sense. I also searched for case studies that would exemplify complex relationships within theoretical concepts, illustrating intricate and sometimes contradictory tensions in musical experience. To select examples, I examined case studies in prominent English-language journals of music education from the past 10 years, including the *Bulletin of the Council for Research in Music Education*, the *Journal of Research in Music Education*, *Music Education Research*, *Research Studies in Music Education*, and the *Journal of Music Teacher Education*. The studies described in the section that follows are not intended to be representative of a certain typology of case studies, nor are they intended as a review of literature. The findings or topical focus of the studies were of less importance in selection than their utility in illustrating the overall architecture of case studies and the interplay between subject, object, and purpose inherent in the research report. I drew heavily on my reading of methodological literature to select four studies for discussion. Two of the studies (Carlow 2006; Matsunobu 2011) provide particularly complex and intricate "close-up" pictures of participants' experience; two of the studies (Haston and Russell 2012; Langston and M. Barrett 2008) illustrate the usefulness of case studies in expanding theoretical frames toward a "big picture" view. Before discussion of each study, I provide the researcher(s)' abstracts for an encapsulated overview of the purpose, the central phenomenon, identification of the case, methodological processes, and key findings. Following the abstract, I discuss the case study in light of the dimensions outlined in Figure 5.1, concentrating on the subject, object, purpose, and presentation of each project.

5.5. Examining Select Case Studies in Music Education

5.5.1. Diva Irina: An English Language Learner in High School Choir (Carlow 2006)

This article is based on a yearlong collective case study (2003–2004) that examined the perceptions of five English language learner (ELL) high school students enrolled in the same choral class. The article includes a short narrative essay, which highlights the experience of one of the student participants in the larger study. The premise of the research was based on what I perceived as a tension between the socio-cultural institution of traditional American high school choral programs and ELL students' previous and current experiences with singing. The primary research question was "What are the musical experiences of immigrant students who sing in high school choir?" Data included student and teacher surveys, focus groups, in-depth interviews, student journals, classroom and performance observations, and video analysis. Data were analyzed using the NVIVO system, which provided an efficient means for open-coding, analysis, and interpretation. Findings implied that some discourse norms in secondary choral classes can be viewed as culturally incongruent with ELL students' previous musical experiences. (63)

A worn truism in teaching is "get to know your students." In ensemble contexts that constitute the predominant settings for music teaching and learning in US secondary schools, teachers are challenged to live up to this adage in an increasingly diverse, postmodern milieu. Carlow's case study of Irina Choi, a student whose Russian and Korean heritage goes largely unacknowledged within her high school choir, calls the intersections of cultural identity and musical participation into question. Irina is in no way representative of high school choristers; she is likely not representative of immigrant students either. Her typicality is not the point; rather, her "outlierness" (Thomas 2011b, 5) is the provocative bridge to the object of the study—the musical experiences of immigrant students. The explanatory power of this study comes from identifying the tensions of Irina's musical experience in context. Carlow's "casing" stems from her decision to seek out a school setting with a "significant population of immigrant students" (66) and to explore the experiences of the students within the setting of a non-auditioned choir. The case subject was bound by Carlow's interaction with students over a 10-month period, although in many ways the boundaries were drawn larger since a significant source of insight was Irina's description of her previous musical experience in Russia and Kazakhstan. Neither was the study bound to *place* as Carlow observed Irina in settings outside choir—most specifically an International Club talent show at the school where Irina appeared as a diva of Russian popular music. Carlow opens the study with a telling juxtaposition of Irina observed in two contexts—as a vibrant, assured solo performer in the talent show, and as a disgruntled soprano melting into anonymity and indifference in the third row of fourth-period choir.

The evocative presentation of the case hinges on Carlow's skill in presenting Irina in her own voice through a narrative essay, which draws the reader into the uncertain landscape of identity that Irina travels as she contrasts her visceral engagement in Russian music with what she feels are the stultifying rituals, expectations, and repertoires of the high school chorus. As an adolescent English language learner, Irina must "crack the code" of choir to discover what and who is valued; as she does so, she retreats further into disengagement as she waits out the completion of her elective year of choir. From the perspective of case study, the subject of the case is Irina as the central participant, as well as the displaced and mismatched contexts for musical experience in the choral classroom and in her current and remembered Russian realms.

In the introduction of the study and through the thematic discussion, Carlow interweaves data with a theoretical framework that draws from research on musical identity, multicultural perspectives, English language learners, and social justice. The narrative portrayal of Irina is therefore explained in part by relevant literature at the same time that it is problematized and left open. The researcher calls to attention the complex tasks teachers face in discerning students' musical backgrounds and mediating the culture shock of ELL students in particular. In broader fashion, she critiques the tiered hierarchy of ensembles in secondary schools, and the programmatic decisions about repertoire that can distance students as well as draw them closer to the music they perform. This case study, through its particularized account of Irina's experience in her high school choir, informs curriculum and instruction for immigrant students like Irina.

5.5.2. Spirituality as a Universal Experience of Music: A Case Study of North Americans' Approaches to Japanese Music (Matsunobu 2011)

> Ethnomusicologists and music educators are in broad agreement that what makes each cultural expression of music unique are differences, not commonalities, and that these should be understood in culturally sensitive ways. Relevant to the debate was the emphasis on the sociocultural context of music making over the traditional "sound-only" approach. In this study, North American practitioners of shakuhachi music provided a different angle on the view of music as culture-specific. What made these practitioners interested in shakuhachi playing were not so much cultural aspects of Japanese music as universal aspects of human experience identified in Japanese music, such as the feeling of being part of nature and the revitalization of humans' organic sensitivities. For them, the cultural served as a hindrance to accessing the underlying spirituality of Japanese music. From their perspective, the opposite of the sound-only approach was not necessarily posited as a sociocultural approach but as a spiritual or physical approach that transcended cultural boundaries. (273)

The symbiotic nature of musical experience with cultural context is an ongoing source of inquiry for music educators, ethnomusicologists, and other social science researchers. Matsunobu's case study of three North American non-native players who immersed themselves in studying classical (honkyoku) repertoire via the idiosyncratic nature of a particular type of shakuhachi, the ji-nashi, probes the deep realms of musical experience for the performer. In this case study, drawn from a larger ethnographic investigation of 12 practitioners over a two-year period, Matsunobu examines how cultural context influences musical experience, and from fine-grained accounts gleaned from observations and interviews, how cultural context may also hinder understanding. The heart of this study is the phenomenological experience of music as a cultural universal. The subject of the case is compelling in that the three participants selected for the study are examined in context, but this context is unusual. Counter to expectations that context should mean *cultural context*, these non-native players engaged in learning honkyoku in both North American and Japanese settings, including workshops, tours, classes, individual practice, and so on. Thus the boundedness of the case encompasses the experiences of the music for the three individuals regardless of physical setting or specific musical traditions. The overlap of the case's subject with the object is also notable in that the theoretical framework was informed by five dimensions of spiritual awareness the researcher drew from another source, but as the study progressed, the theoretical frame shifted as the analysis oriented toward transcultural meanings of the experience for the players. The fluid alignment of subject and object in this study is illuminated through Matsunobu's description that the players underwent "depth without detour" (279), that is, musical grounding—the rooted experience of sound through sound—without the mediation or interference of cultural knowledge. Matsunobu relates the musical pursuits of the shakuhachi players to the quest for spirituality as a "universal longing and a quest for meaning in life" (284).

The presentation of this case is dependent upon the researcher's fidelity to the phenomenological aspects of musical engagement encountered by the participants. In organizing themes to illustrate the central phenomenon—culture as a hindrance to spirituality—Matsunobu moves fluidly back and forth from discussing honkyoku practices, conveying the universality of simplicity, and articulating the ways that energy moves through the instrument, players' breath, and earth, interwoven with interview excerpts from Liam, Andrew, and Pamela, the three players. Without the benefit of actual sound (which would convey ineffable qualities that text cannot), the researcher expresses the subtleties and textures that carry the significance of this transcultural musical pursuit. The purposeful import of the case comes from Matsunobu's invitation for researchers to investigate how the drive to study this form of music stems from the players' "willingness to explore the shared realm of human music experience, namely spirituality, rather than culture-specific dimensions of music" (284). In light of the industriousness with which music education researchers are investigating culturally specific dimensions of music learning and teaching, Matsunobu's study widens the aperture of inquiry. The implications for teaching and learning are similarly promising as he questions the pedagogical assumptions that attend (and possibly compromise) the impact of the musical experience for students.

5.5.3. Turning into Teachers: Influences of Authentic Context Learning Experiences on Occupational Identity Development of Preservice Music Teachers (Haston and Russell 2012)

The purpose of this study was to examine the occupational identity development of undergraduate music education majors as they participated in a yearlong authentic context learning (ACL) experience situated within a professional development school (PDS). Five undergraduate music education majors enrolled in either a string pedagogy class or an instrumental methods class were required to teach in the band or string projects at the PDS. The authors utilized a multiple case study method and collected data from interviews, observations, and participant written reflections. The transformation of data included transcribing interviews and indexing student reflections. The authors identified four emergent themes: the development of general pedagogical knowledge, knowledge of self, performer/teacher symbiotic outcomes, and professional perspectives. The impact of the perceived positive or negative ACL experiences as well as interactions with peers was mediated by either adaptive or maladaptive participant responses to ACL experiences. Participants' descriptions fit the framework of an extended apprenticeship of what the authors labeled a critical apprenticeship of observation. Based on these findings, they developed a conceptual diagram in order to describe the impact of the ACL experiences on teacher occupational identity development. (369)

Haston and Russell's case study contributes to a growing body of research on music teacher identity development. Their study rests on a conceptual foundation built first upon primary socialization, the development of robust and persistent images of music teaching formed through the "apprenticeship of observation" during primary and secondary school experience, and the catalytic power of preservice teacher education (secondary socialization) to excavate and transform these images into deeper understandings of what teachers actually do, how they think, how teaching feels, and what animates their work. In this instance, the conceptual framework derived from the literature is substantial, which allowed the researchers to situate the study in a particular view of this socialization process related to occupational identity: "the process by which a person learns to adopt, develop, and display the actions and role behaviors typical of and unique to a particular profession" (Merton, as cited in Isbell 2006, 30). The researchers describe the bounded system as the "ACL experiences (band and string projects) that were bound together in place (the same magnet school) and bounded in time (the same academic year)" (373). Within the system, the participation of five undergraduate music education majors in teaching within the professional development school setting was the focus, and perhaps given the nature of the socialization process, one might say further entanglement of person and context occurred as they reflected on the contemporary experiences against the background of the undergraduates' primary socialization as well.

A noteworthy aspect of this case study was the fluidity with which the object of the study was used and transformed. Haston and Russell used the conceptual framework derived from their literature review deductively as they coded interview transcripts. In a subsequent inductive analysis of individual data, the emergent themes (general pedagogical knowledge, knowledge of self, symbiotic outcomes, and professional perspectives) were then incorporated into a conceptual diagram that included findings and insights from the case with a priori findings from the literature, which they titled "conceptualized macro/micro diagram of student occupational identity development loop" (20). The representation of the study's findings in this diagram conveys both complexity and clarity. Identity development is delineated into constituent aspects, arranged to show relationships, and offers concrete pathways for further research or pedagogical development in music teacher education. The components of *case presentation* and *purpose* are more closely linked in this revised, dynamic theoretical framework.

5.5.4. Capitalizing on Community Music: A Case Study of the Manifestation of Social Capital in a Community Choir (Langston and M. Barrett 2008)

There is an extensive literature on social capital and its generation and use in communities, but less is known about the ways in which social capital is manifested in community music settings. The literature suggests that social capital is evidenced through a range of "indicators," including trust, community and civic involvement, and networks. This article reports the findings of a research project that examined the manifestation of social capital in a community choir in regional Tasmania. The study employed multiple data-generation methods including survey, field notes, and artifact-elicited, semi-structured interviews in a qualitative interpretive case study design. An analysis of narrative approach was used to interrogate data generated with the 27 members (the *Tutti*) of the "Milton" Community Choir, and to identify those social capital indicators present. Through analyses of these data, findings suggest that the social capital indicators identified in the literature, specifically those of shared norms and values, trust, civic and community involvement, networks, knowledge resources, and contact with families and friends are present in the community choir. Further a previously unemphasized social capital indicator, that of *fellowship*, is identified as a key component in fostering group cohesion and social capital development in the community choir. (2008, 118)

Langston and M. Barrett (2008) reviewed theories of social capital in their qualitative interpretive case study of the "Milton" Community Choir. The first researcher—Langston—held a 20-year history with the group as its conductor, and thus Thomas might identity the selection of choir members as a *local knowledge case* (2011b, 514), in which the researcher's familiarity with the group opens up avenues of intimate and informed analysis based on long-term relationships and shared history. The researchers provide a strong theoretical framework to outline three forms of social capital (bonding, bridging, and linking, 119) before addressing eight indicators of social capital, constituting the initial conceptual structure (participant, interaction, and civic involvement; networks and connections; families and friends; reciprocity and obligations;

trust; norms and values; learning; and membership in faith-based organizations, 120). Verification strategies included prolonged engagement, triangulation of participant data, and member checking, along with consideration of researcher reflexivity prompted by critical analysis and interactions between the two researchers. The subject of the case is the choir and the 27 singers within, who are bounded by their joint history and membership. The object of the case is the manifestation of these indicators of social capital in the general service of documenting community.

This case study is particularly strong in its articulation of the factors of social capital evidenced in the accounts of the choir members. The data led to the expansion of the theoretical framework with the inclusion of an additional indicator, *fellowship*. Discussion of each indicator balances insights from literature, excerpts from interviews, and interpretive insights. Langston and Barrett's work, with its clear explication of the theoretical frame that guided the study, and the revised frame or object that crystallizes through analysis and interpretation, also leads directly to larger purposes. The researchers imply that the results of the study could be extended to choirs with a similar mission and history, and, as well, could be pointed toward the use of the theoretical framework to guide public policy on the impact of aging on citizens' lives. In addition, the revised structure points to additional research on the impact of musical experience in adult community groups.

5.6. PROMISING AVENUES FOR CASE STUDY IN MUSIC EDUCATION

In the four studies selected as examples, key distinctions emerge, although each treats the subject, object, purpose, and presentation of the case with care. Two of the studies, Carlow and Matsunobu, provide a rich description of individual or musical experience with sufficient vividness that readers can gauge the extendability and correspondence of the case to other situations and instances. These two studies, due to their emphasis on *particularization* of the subject of the case, open up case-to-case transfer. The other two studies, Haston and Russell and Langston and M. Barrett, forward the object of the case in salient ways. Here, the theoretical propositions and their interrelationships—the *complexity* of the object—are more prominent than detailed narrative portrayals. The extended purposes of these studies lend themselves, because of their propositional clarity, to guiding practice, policy, and further research by building on the theoretical structure the researchers have articulated.

For all of the reasons outlined at the beginning of this chapter, case study research has a firm foothold in music education. Yet despite its prevalence, the uneven quality of case study reports calls our attention to the need for more rigor in design and analysis, attention to the analytic path used to draw inferences from the data, and especially the more sophisticated interplay between cases and theoretical frameworks. Additional avenues for development include articulating typologies for categorizing various kinds of case studies and their utility; addressing how lines of inquiry can be developed through a series of case studies; and examining how case studies can be used in complementary ways with other research designs and strategies.

Case studies in music education are well-suited to examine central questions of music teaching and learning. Researchers must know why a case study is a good fit; here, we come back to Thomas's statement: "What the case study is especially good for is getting a rich picture and gaining analytical insights from it" (2011, 23). Case studies allow us to branch out in exploratory ways to map areas of inquiry that are underdeveloped or unexamined. They also allow us to fill in more robust and integrated knowledge about areas of inquiry that need further explication and explanation, such as those aspects of music teaching and learning that are especially complex and intertwined. Paying attention to the dynamic tensions between subject and object, and the ways that these dynamic tensions are brought to light through compelling presentations of the case, will make case study research more powerful and informative within the field.[2]

NOTE

1. Terms used by the German philosopher Wilhelm Windelband, as cited in Thomas (2011a).
2. I wish to thank Julie Bannerman for her invaluable assistance in preparing this chapter.

REFERENCES

Barrett, Janet R. 2007. "The Researcher as Instrument: Learning to Conduct Qualitative Research through Analyzing and Interpreting a Choral Rehearsal." *Music Education Research* 9 (3): 417–33.

Barrett, Margaret S., and Janet Mills. 2009. "The Inter-Reflexive Possibilities of Dual Observations: An Account from and through Experience." *International Journal of Qualitative Studies in Education* 22 (4): 417–29.

Campbell, Donald T. 1975. "'Degrees of Freedom' and the Case Study." *Comparative Political Studies* 8 (2): 178–93.

Carlow, Regina. 2006. "Diva Irina: An English Language Learner in High School Choir." *Bulletin of the Council for Research in Music Education* 170: 63–77.

Creswell, John W. 2007. *Qualitative Inquiry and Research Design: Choosing among Five Traditions*. 2nd ed. Thousand Oaks, CA: Sage Publications.

Flyvbjerg, Bent. 2011. "Case Study." In *The Sage Handbook of Qualitative Research*, edited by Norman K. Denzin and Yvonna S. Lincoln, 301–16. Thousand Oaks, CA: Sage Publications.

Haston, Warren, and Joshua A. Russell. 2012. "Turning into Teachers: Influences of Authentic Context Learning Experiences on Occupational Identity Development of Preservice Music Teachers." *Journal of Research in Music Education* 59: 1–24.

Isbell, Daniel S. 2006. "Socialization and Occupational Identity among Preservice Music Teachers Enrolled in Traditional Baccalaureate Degree Programs." Doctoral diss. Available from ProQuest Dissertations and Theses database (UMI No. 3239420).

Kantorski, Vincent J., and Sandra Frey Stegman. 2006. "A Content Analysis of Qualitative Research Dissertations in Music Education, 1998–2002." *Bulletin of the Council for Research in Music Education* 168: 63–73.

Lane, Jeremy. 2011. "A Descriptive Analysis of Qualitative Research Published in Two Eminent Music Education Research Journals." *Bulletin of the Council for Research in Music Education* 188: 65–76.

Langston, Thomas W., and Margaret S. Barrett. 2008. "Capitalizing on Community Music: A Case Study of the Manifestation of Social Capital in a Community Choir." *Research Studies in Music Education* 30 (2): 118–38.

Matsonobu, Koji. 2011. "Spirituality as a Universal Experience of Music: A Case Study of North Americans' Approaches to Japanese Music." *Journal of Research in Music Education* 59 (3): 273–89.

Merriam, Sharan B. 1998. *Qualitative Research and Case Study Applications in Education*. San Francisco: Jossey-Bass.

Onwuegbuzie, Anthony J., and Nancy L. Leech. 2010. "Generalization Practices in Qualitative Research: A Mixed Methods Case Study." *Quality & Quantity* 44 (5): 881–92.

Peshkin, Alan. 1993. "The Goodness of Qualitative Research." *Educational Researcher* 22 (2): 23–29.

Ragin, Charles C. 1992. "'Casing' and the Process of Social Inquiry." In *What Is a Case? Exploring the Foundations of Social Inquiry*, edited by Charles C. Ragin and Howard S. Becker, 217–26. Cambridge, UK: Cambridge University Press.

Simons, Helen. 2009. *Case Study Research in Practice*. Thousand Oaks, CA: Sage Publications.

Stake, Robert E. 1988. "Case Study Methods in Educational Research: Seeking Sweet Water." In *Complementary Methods for Research in Education*, edited by Richard M. Jaeger, 253–78. Washington, DC: American Educational Research Association.

Stake, Robert E. *The Art of Case Study Research*. 1995. Thousand Oaks, CA: Sage Publications.

Stake, Robert E. "Qualitative Case Studies." 2005. In *The Sage Handbook of Qualitative Research*, edited by Norman K. Denzin and Yvonna S. Lincoln, 443–66. Thousand Oaks, CA: Sage Publications.

Thomas, Gary. 2011a. *How to Do Your Case Study: A Guide for Students and Researchers*. Thousand Oaks, CA: Sage Publications.

Thomas, Gary. 2011b. "A Typology for the Case Study in Social Science Following a Review of Definition, Discourse, and Structure." *Qualitative Inquiry* 17 (6): 511–21.

Tracy, Sarah J. 2010. "Qualitative Quality: Eight 'Big Tent" Criteria for Excellent Qualitative Research." *Qualitative Inquiry* 16 (10): 837–51.

VanWynsberghe, Rob, and Samia Khan. 2007. "Redefining Case Study." *International Journal of Qualitative Methods* 6 (2): 80–94.

Yin, Robert K. 2009. *Case Study Research: Design and Methods*. 4th ed. Thousand Oaks, CA: Sage Publications.

Yin, Robert K. 2012. *Applications of Case Study Research*. Thousand Oaks, CA: Sage Publications.

CHAPTER 6

DOING ETHNOGRAPHY IN MUSIC EDUCATION

PATTI J. KRUEGER

ETHNOGRAPHY is a relatively recent form of inquiry in music education research in the United States (Szego 2002). Though ethnography is now more frequently found in mainstream music education literature, such was not the case before the 1980s. Taylor (1987) writes that at the time, four research methodologies were most widely used in music education: experimental, descriptive, philosophical, and historical. When well-designed, these were often accepted as most valid and reliable for exploring questions relating to music learning and teaching. During the mid-1980s, new research in music, arts, and aesthetic education began to reflect the importance of studying education in relation to its specific and natural context, recognizing the complexities of everyday interaction in schools and the internal dynamics of institutions. Since that time, several researchers have explored how qualitative methodologies such as ethnography are useful when applied to questions in music classrooms and other music education settings (Roulston 2006; Bresler and Stake 2006; Bresler 1995).

The following chapter is an exploration of doing ethnography in schools and in music education research. The chapter defines and describes ethnographic methodologies in education, and discusses the potential for ethnographic methods to contribute information and insights in music education research. The first section is partly drawn from Krueger (1987),[1] an article introducing ethnographic methodology to researchers in music education. The original article provided an early model for crafting ethnographic studies in music education research. Some of the most detailed descriptions of ethnography in education can be found in the literature of the 1970s and early 1980s as this field of study emerged, so I draw generously on this literature and also note some of the most frequently cited resources since that time. Finally, the chapter looks at several examples of how ethnography is used in music education literature from the 1980s to the present, and explores the benefits and contributions of ethnography for music education research.

6.1. Through a Different Lens: Doing Ethnography

Ethnography is a methodological approach that describes, analyzes, and helps one understand a particular culture (Popkewitz 1961). Centered in the qualitative research tradition, ethnography allows the researcher to investigate contextual questions beyond the reach of methodological approaches in which particular variables are isolated. Willis (1977) notes:

> Quantitative studies often consider only the most easily observed and empirically verifiable characteristics of the environment. Qualitative studies usually attempt more fully to consider both observed characteristics and specific qualities perceived as personal forms of meaning. (2)

Willis suggests that the quantitative tradition, in attempting to obtain verifiable data to be quantitatively tabulated, often misses the more interpretive aspects of a social setting, such as qualities and dynamics in the environment or culture of a given school. An ethnographic approach may provide a complementary study, since it allows a view of social interaction occurring within a natural setting.

An experimental approach to educational research often assumes that there are precisely defined variables prior to any evaluation attempt (Fox 1969). The research question then becomes one of choosing which variable to manipulate, examine, or test while controlling all others. In contrast, the problem in ethnography is one of looking into the effects of a particular setting as a whole upon the meanings and interpretations of a particular population and culture, with the intent of disturbing the natural setting as little as possible.

In a thorough resource on this methodology, Spradley (1960) defines ethnography as the process of describing and understanding another culture "from a native's point of view" (3). He outlines three sources of understanding that ethnographers look for: cultural behavior, or what people do; cultural knowledge, or what people know; and cultural artifacts, or what people make and use (5). Spradley distinguishes the ethnographic process as attempting to describe and understand, rather than seeking to find something (26). Through participant observation, Spradley outlines how the researcher is able to explore the dynamics of a particular culture.

Ethnography, then, is useful for looking into questions about educational and classroom practice (Popkewitz and Wehlage 1977). This research approach has long been used by anthropologists and sociologists to help understand schooling, since its focus is on the natural flow of events (Tabachnick 1981). Ethnography is often used as a method for research in the field of ethnomusicology, for exploring music of a particular people, place, or culture. In music education, ethnography often focuses on issues related to teaching and learning music (Bresler 1995). A variety of data collection techniques such as observations, interviews, materials analysis, and occasionally surveys are implemented and compared over an extended period of time. The purpose of data collection in ethnography is to identify and understand patterns of conduct that guide participants' day-to-day practice, as well as to explore structures that shape that practice. Popkewitz and Tabachnick (1981) provide an excellent collected resource on the process of school ethnography.

Educational ethnography evolved from sociology, psychology, and anthropology, and may include single- or multiple-setting case studies developed with a specific process in mind. Spindler (1982) describes this intent:

> Ethnography of schooling refers to educational and enculturative processes that are related to schools and intentional schooling, though this concept leaves room for studies of playgrounds, play groups, peer groups, patterns of violence in schools, and other aspects of school-related life. . . . Native views of reality held by participants make ideas, behavior, and communication sensible to oneself and to others. Therefore a major part of the ethnographic task is to understand what sociocultural knowledge participants bring to and generate in the social setting being studied. (2–7)

Spindler's text (1982) provides a rich collection of insights into the methodology of school ethnography.

An ethnographic methodology has particular advantages for understanding the work of teachers and students. Ethnography permits a closeness to the people, events, and natural practice within the context being studied. Through observation, listening, interviews, and other data collection, the researcher has access not only to what people report about their perceptions, but also to how those understandings actually guide their work. Ethnographic method allows the researcher to take note of unanticipated and unintended consequences of actions, and to observe why events seem to happen in a particular manner. Ethnographic study of naturally occurring situations allows the researcher to consider different types of motivation for actions, such as the goals and beliefs an individual brings to a situation, the needs created by the situation, or pressures originating from outside the school or classroom setting being studied. The investigator can then consider the dynamics of all of these causes (Romberg and Stephens 1983).

6.1.1. Data Collection and Analysis

Many questions posed by educational research require a method of data gathering that allows for the investigation of ideas, attitudes, beliefs, and actions in the context of a school or classroom setting. Observations, conversations, and interviews with participants about school experiences may allow the researcher to understand and link beliefs and attitudes to actions. For instance, the evolving musical orientation of kindergarten students might be most comprehensively studied through ongoing classroom observation, listening, field notes, and interviews of student and teacher participants throughout the year. An ethnographic methodology, involving an in-depth study of a limited number of subjects in their natural setting, may be an appropriate research approach to certain educational problems and questions since it allows for exploration of understandings, meanings, and actions of participants.

Ethnographic methodology includes the use of participant observation and journals, in-depth structured and non-structured interviewing, document analysis, and a variety of other research strategies that allow the investigator to obtain firsthand knowledge about the problem in question. Data collection may involve an extended period of time in the setting by the researchers to understand the culture of the participants being observed. Filstead (1970) notes that these data collection methods allow the researcher to "get close to the data," developing the analytical, conceptual, and categorical components of explanation from the data itself (6). An ethnography evolves from the progression of data collected by the researchers; data becomes the primary source for the evolution and core of an ethnographic study (Emerson, Fretz, and Shaw 1995).

In ethnography, data collection is often closely intertwined with analysis, and issues that shape a study often emerge during data collection and analysis rather than prior to it. Understanding of a particular culture evolves through observation, listening, note-taking, interviews, document analysis, and finding patterns and meaning in all of this emerging data. The lens or framework through which the ethnographer begins the study may evolve and change in the process of data collection, observation, and analysis. Ethnographers are strongly encouraged to describe their initial and evolving theories and assumptions in detail for the reader, since these influence the evolution of analysis and transferability of a study. Documenting methods for data collection, describing relationships with those studied, and sharing data and analysis with participants for their feedback are important for ascertaining accountability and validity (Szeko 2002). Analysis takes on a cyclical pattern of returning to the data to examine and compare with new insights as the study progresses.

6.1.2. Theoretical Framework

Most research methods involve the study of questions and problems, but an ethnographer approaches problems with a unique orientation. Researchers using an ethnographic methodology approach the actions and events to be studied with certain orienting guidelines, and from a particular worldview (Romberg 1981). The theoretical framework and assumptions of ethnography provide an orientation within which the researcher attempts to interpret events and actions. This makes it important for the researcher to clearly outline literature framing the study and assumptions being made for the reader's understanding. Tabachnick (1981) argues that the researcher's chosen orientation, unlike the operational categories of conventional empirical research, is "open to change and development as a result of encountering the action of being studied" (84). This is a direct result of the purposes one brings to a field study. The researcher cannot determine in advance how a theoretical framework will apply to the particular event being studied. Furthermore, the researcher may alter the framework due to events observed during the study. For example, preschoolers being studied may organize sound in creative ways unanticipated by an observing researcher. When recognized, these observed innovations may create new theories to examine. Creswell (1998) summarizes that an ethnographer's framework shapes the initial questions and observations of a study, and the researcher may later alter this lens during data collection and analysis.

Wilcox (1982) also outlines the importance of developing and utilizing orienting categories that arise from a particular theoretical perspective. Wilcox emphasizes the use of theory as a background and framework for study, and she urges the researcher to clearly outline one's general set of assumptions in order to generalize from a particular study. At the same time, she suggests that investigators attempt to set aside other preconceptions and to constantly inquire critically into those assumptions made. In doing so, the ethnographer may understand the beliefs, values, and actions of the people being studied, and abstract the meaning of what is being observed. These findings can then be analyzed with guiding theoretical frameworks in mind. An example in music education might be found in Kennedy's (2004) study on a particular culture of boys with changing voices. The data collected in this study supported previously documented patterns of male voice changes, but also newly revealed the uniqueness of each boy's experience and the impact of mentoring on the voice change process.

Wilcox (1982) further urges researchers to understand the relationship between the particular setting and the larger societal context. For example, school participants typically operate under external constraints. Although there is an important element of creativity in classroom interaction, there are also limits to the extent that definitions of a classroom situation can be negotiated or changed. As relations in schools play out, the participants learn and perpetuate many aspects of their roles. But the social and political environment outside the classroom may be considered critically important for understanding classroom life, such as the values taught by adults to children in a particular community (Willis 1977). By portraying as neutral a particular orientation or specific way of thinking, schools may implicitly define a particular set of cultural values and norms as being acceptable. Accordingly, ethnographic research should be guided by clearly stated orienting and theoretical frameworks generated from related research and experience. The constraints and influences of context cannot be ignored, and these become a part of the basis for new interpretation. The descriptive data generated by a study then becomes the ultimate source of this new interpretation.

Several assumptions involved in the definition of an ethnographic research problem and in the choice of this methodology are important to recognize. The first assumption of ethnography is the belief that a predetermined hypothesis should be avoided in the investigation. Researchers should attempt to remain sensitive and open to the ways in which the subjects, rather than the researchers, make sense of and give meaning to experiences (Spradley 1979). A study may use an orienting framework drawn from related literature, but researchers should remain open to generating new theories that may emerge through data collection and analysis, and to the possibility of discarding the initial theories. A second assumption of ethnography identifies the subjects themselves as important sources of data; both their actions and statements about their beliefs and actions are considered important. Intentions of those being studied are significant, and circumstances alone do not determine their actions. A third assumption considers social and institutional conditions that enhance, shape, or limit actions and events taking place. Describing and noting how these dynamics influence the participants may become an important part of the data collection. Based upon these assumptions, educational ethnography maintains the importance of examining intended and unintended actions and outcomes in an attempt to understand what actually happens in schools, music classrooms, and other settings studied.

6.1.3. Quality in Ethnographic Studies

Clearly defining the role of the investigators becomes significant in ethnography, as the researchers' presence may contribute to the dynamics in many ways. As a non-participant observer, the researcher works to be as unobtrusive as possible and attempts to minimize influence on the participants, trying to understand their world, beliefs, actions, and culture. Nonetheless, defining and acknowledging the observers' presence, views, and the theoretical lens remain significant factors in any ethnographic research. An observer's presence alone may influence the behavior of individuals or a group of students in a particular setting. Researchers become part of the context, and neutrality is not possible.

In some ethnographic studies, investigators may also serve as participant observers in the culture being studied (Spradley 1980). A music teacher in a classroom or setting, for example, may be both a participant and an investigator. As data collectors, participant observers study their subjects' views, and work to remain conscious of the effect that their own presence, biases, values, and assumptions have on the interpretations, dynamics, and other participants that they seek to understand. Recognizing and documenting the effects of one's presence, then, remains important for both participant observers and non-participant observers alike; the researcher must describe roles clearly so that the reader can understand the influences of both non-participant and participant observers.

Detailed descriptions of a study's subjects and setting are equally important for the reader's understanding. Since a sample may include only one or two participants or situations, the detail of the description carries significant weight in one's ability to generalize from the study, as well as in establishing the reliability of the study. Descriptive detail in observations can also bring insights during later stages of analysis and allow for verification and further insights by the reader. Ethnographic research, even of small case studies, can have great power to illuminate the teaching-learning process.

Critics of field research often argue that reliability of qualitative methodology, or its dependability and ability to be replicated, is limited by the uniqueness of each case examined. However, LeCompte and Goetz (1982) identify certain methods that can be used to increase the reliability of a qualitative study. They note five factors to be included in a report of qualitative research that contribute to external reliability: (1) identifying and describing the researcher's role; (2) description and background of the subjects; (3) descriptions of settings in which observations take place; (4) identifying methods for data collection and analysis; and (5) explaining and outlining the theoretical framework guiding the study. All of these factors must be clearly defined in order for an ethnographic study to be reliable, valid, transferable, and generalizable. The reader must be able to clearly interpret descriptions of the researcher's role, the subjects or sample, the setting, methods for data collection, and literature and framework guiding the study in order to draw conclusions specific to another situation or study. LeCompte and Schensul (2010) further assert that a variety of different data sources and several ways of collecting data are necessary for reliability and validity of ethnographic research.

Validity and credibility of research are concerned with the accuracy of the findings drawn from a study. LeCompte and Goetz (1982) claim that validity can be a major strength of qualitative and particularly ethnographic research, since the flexibility of data collection and the power of observations, conversations, and interviews allow the researcher to examine the knowledge and meanings created by the participants. Wehlage (1981) stresses the strength of internal validity in field study, since problems are examined within the context of their natural settings. Bolster (1983) discusses this strength:

> As [qualitative researchers] systematically define the properties of the classroom, observe events in it, and listen to people talk about them, patterns of the events and the interrelationships among them will begin to emerge. . . . The eventual critical description is validated in two ways: referentially—the explanatory generalizations must be consistent with repeated patterns of events recorded in the observational data; and situationally—the explanatory framework must be consistent with the meanings teachers and students draw from and impose upon the classroom situation. (304–05)

Filstead (1970) notes that validity becomes a serious problem in research when previously drawn assumptions and explanations are strictly imposed upon reality through a predefined research design. He supports the notion that when researchers employ a more fluid methodology and process, the problem of validity is considerably lessened. Filstead also suggests that many questions in education are most validly studied in the context of their natural settings.

Other methods that researchers implement to increase validity and credibility in ethnography include comparing and cross-referencing interviews, observations, and materials through triangulation, and having representative participants read and respond to drafts of a study for verification and validation. Creswell (1998) draws on Hammersley and Atkinson (1995) and discusses triangulation of ethnographic data, which he defines as testing and comparing one source of information and data against another. Triangulation, or collecting data from a variety of sources and using ongoing comparisons throughout various stages of data collection and analysis, helps a researcher maintain consistency and accuracy of data. Creswell (1998, 2005) urges ethnographers to interpret data in collaboration with their subjects, and Spindler (1982) encourages investigators to pay attention to participants' points of view through on-going observations and interviews. Berg (2007) outlines similar ethnographic field strategies and methods to enable quality design. Other resources noted in the litera-ture that describe ethnographic methods include LeCompte and Schensul (1999, 2010), Patton (2002), and Bogden and Biklin (2007).

What kind of generalizability should ethnographic research strive for? Field studies are intended to interpret, explain, and produce understanding of the actions being investigated, and in that sense, the researcher is concerned with making generalizable or transferrable conclusions. Again, researchers should take care to clearly describe and ensure that the sample chosen is representative of the population to which one wishes to generalize or transfer conclusions. Romberg (1981) writes that the investigator defines a theoretical framework intending to lead to interpretive generalizations. Once these generalizations are reached, they apply not only to the schools studied, but are likely to apply to other schools as well. Through clear descriptions and theoretical frameworks, an ethnographer can show the reader how to relate the original descriptions and interpretations from a particular context to wider social context.

Wehlage (1981) outlines two levels of generalization made possible through ethno-graphic research. Readers make some generalizations by their own analogies; detailed descriptions are first made by the researcher, leaving the reader to form generalizations. The researcher may also generalize about the structures and frameworks discovered in a particular context. Wehlage notes that research can and should generalize from the expectations, norms, and perceptions that shape and influence the action of people in schools.

Other education and school researchers apply these generalizations in their ap-proach to analysis. For example, through an ethnography of a high school, Cusick (1973) identifies some of the structural characteristics of schools that shape the meanings and experiences of students. Cusick claims that these characteristics are shared by many schools, and that accordingly, conclusions may be generalized or transferred to such schools. Ethnographic research may attempt to uncover what it is about the context and structure of schools that limits, influences, and shapes the actions and beliefs of people in school settings and classrooms. An ethnographic study of schools, then, may provide clear descriptions of the meanings of school and classroom life. When examined in context, researchers may generalize about the relationships between spe-cific features of a setting and the experience of participants by building upon a theoret-ical framework.

All of these factors greatly contribute to the quality of an ethnographic study. Keeping these design factors in mind, how has ethnography been implemented in music education? What can we learn through applying ethnographic research in music education?

6.2. A Sampling of Ethnographic Studies in Music Education

Ethnography first appeared in US music education PhD dissertations in the mid-1980s. In a study of the musical experiences of elementary school children, Zimmerman (1982) provides an ethnographic model for examining the school music culture of elementary students in a particular school. Zimmerman's study explored musical attitudes and behaviors of students and their music teacher within the school setting. Data collection included participant observation of music classes, interviews of students and the music teacher, informal conversations, material analysis of photographs, documents, and classroom tape recordings. Zimmerman's analysis focused on types of activities and literature, teaching methods and style, use of space in the school, and dynamics between students as well as with the music teacher. The study's rich ethnographic descriptions revealed new insights into the musical experiences of children in an elementary school setting. Zimmerman concluded that ethnography is a valuable method for inquiry into music education classrooms since it allows for the discovery of unanticipated questions and the observation of a wide variety of events.

In a study of music student teachers, Krueger (1985) provides another early example of ethnography in music education. This study on the socialization of music student teachers in public school music classrooms sought to understand what influenced music student teacher perspectives amidst clashing cultures of university and public school settings. Inquiry focused on how two student teachers made sense of their world, their students, and their practice. Many influences contributed, including those that were hidden to the music student teachers themselves. Ethnographic inquiry and framework drew on the work of Berlak and Berlak (1981), Lacey (1977), and on other research from outside of music education. The study explored beginning music teachers' actions, beliefs, and perspectives during the process of student teaching, including the effects of expectations, pressures, institutional assumptions, and school rules on student teachers' actions and perceptions. Ethnographic data collection included observational records and tape recordings, document analysis, formal and informal interviews with participants, and personal journals written by the subjects throughout student teaching. Analysis revealed that cooperating teacher practices and institutional traditions, organization, and constraints within the school setting highly influenced evolving student teacher perspectives. Student teachers demonstrated a tendency to perceive classroom situations and pedagogy as given, inflexible, and unalterable. Student teaching experiences significantly modified student teacher perspectives and actions toward increasing acceptance of school organization and practices already in place. Student teachers struggled to navigate the reality of their classrooms, and often sacrificed their ideal curriculum for what they perceived to be expected. Ethnographic methods brought inquiry into the many dynamics of the student teachers' evolving perceptions and practices, and how these affected their emerging commitment to music teaching as a career.

Since the 1980s, ethnography gradually appears more frequently in American music education research (Bresler and Stake 2006), and is used to explore a variety of questions and issues of music teaching and learning. Lane (2011) reports that ethnographic studies appear significantly more often in two eminent research journals, *Bulletin of the Council for Research in Music Education* (CRME) and *Journal of Research in Music Education* (JRME) since the year 2000, possibly indicating an acceptance of qualitative practices in music education and an increase in those doing ethnographic research. Examining dynamics, practices, and meanings in a particular culture or natural setting through ethnography can be beneficial in complementing other types of research methods, as well as in addressing particular research problems and questions. The following examples of ethnographic studies in music education research literature provide insight into a wide range of questions that might be considered through ethnographic inquiry.

The field of ethnomusicology brings examples of ethnography into the realm of music education research (Manes 2009). Music educators with a strong background in ethnomusicology contribute varied examples of how ethnography might be used to explore the music of children and other groups. As an innovative and rich example of ethnography in music education, Campbell (1998) explored how music is significant, valued, and personally meaningful in the lives of children, and what music means to them based on their expressed thoughts and musical behaviors in school and at play. Campbell described children's uses of music at play in a particular American elementary school setting, and engaged in conversation to discover children's understandings, values, and ideas about music. Children in the study sample spanned a variety of economic, ethnic, and cultural backgrounds and engaged in different cultural and social experiences and contexts, all of which contributed to their musical ideas and behaviors.

Other ethnographic studies of music education vary widely. Feay-Shaw (2001) examined a fifth-grade musical production's rehearsal process and performance through ethnographic methodology. The study's framework drew on middle and high school musical research including issues of rehearsal schedules, repertoire, musical development in students, and demands of productions on teachers and students. Data collection included observations, video analysis, conversations, and interviews of student and teacher participants. Significant themes emerged from the data of this study including personal and social growth, musical growth, and theatrical development of students. Analysis also considered value to the music program and school curriculum, and the amount of time devoted to a creating a musical production.

Kennedy (2004) described and interpreted a particular culture of boys with changing voices at the American Boychoir School. Data collection included interviews, observation, participant observation, and exploration of materials such as musical scores, concert programs, and school handbooks. The study's framework drew on voice change research, and analysis focused on references to the voice change process. Evidence from the data supported previously documented patterns of male voice change processes in the literature, but also newly highlighted the uniqueness of each boy's experience and a need for individual mentoring throughout the voice change process.

Lum and Campbell (2007) explored the musical behaviors and culture of children at an American elementary school, with the aim of understanding the nature and context of rhythmic and melodic expressions made and heard by children. The study examined music of both children and adults within the school setting. The time, location, and intent of many spontaneous and planned musical activities all contributed significantly to the children's experiences, including rhythmic and melodic play and the way teachers used music to support learning. This study vividly portrayed and gave focus to music that occurs in the everyday life of children within their school.

In a later ethnographic study, Soto, Lum, and Campbell (2009) documented the process of a year-long public elementary school and university music education student collaboration within a rural community. The project was immersed in a Mexican American migrant community where Spanish was often the primary language for elementary students in their homes. Music education students participated in teaching and training experiences within the context of public elementary school music classrooms. Through an ethnographic framework, observations, structured and unstructured interviews, and materials provided data to explore the benefits and challenges of the collaborative project in a remote community. The research team included participant observers who taught within the partnership program. The study revealed benefits and challenges that might be of interest and significant for similar university/school partnerships.

Several studies use ethnographic techniques to examine music improvisational influences, processes, techniques, and learning. Della Pietra and Campbell (1995) looked at how two music education students developed an understanding of improvisation, with a focus on ways to integrate improvisation into a music teacher education curriculum. Goodrich (2008) examined elements of historic jazz culture in a high school jazz band. Ethnographic observations and interviews explored the role of a director and students in learning jazz through traditional methods. Data collection included observations of sectionals and rehearsals, audio and video recordings, formal interviews, informal conversations, and collection of artifacts. Analysis revealed sharing vocabulary, listening to style, and implementing improvisation during the rehearsal process as significant in sharing jazz culture. In another ethnography, Beegle (2010) examined and described two classes of fifth-graders' music improvisations and interactions within an elementary school music classroom. Data collection included audio and video observations, classroom observations, and interviews of students following a viewing of their own performances on video. Findings included children's planning, strategies, roles, and evaluation of their performances.

In some studies in music education, researchers combined ethnography with other research methodologies and strategies for data collection and analysis. Allsup (2003) combined philosophical and action research data collection methodologies with ethnographic participant observation (exploring the participants' culture and point of view) to look at questions of mutual learning, group compositional process, and democratic practices in a high school instrumental music classroom. Carlow (2006) used ethnographic case studies and narrative inquiry to examine the perceptions, culture, and experiences of English language learners in a high school choral music classroom. Data included student and teacher surveys, focus groups, student journals and narratives, ethnographic interviews and observations, and video analysis. Carlow examined musical experiences and perceptions of the participants as well as customs of the classroom, music department, families, and the school. Sindberg (2007) used a collective case study, employing ethnographic and phenomenological strategies to examine Comprehensive Musicianship through Performance and its effect on student learning in middle school and high school ensemble settings. Data collection in this study included ethnographic observations, interviews, writing prompts, e-mail, teaching plans, and teacher journals. In each of these studies, a combination of strategies explored a particular research question through multiple methodologies.

Ethnographic methods and ethnography appear only sparingly in US music education PhD dissertations since their first appearances in the mid-1980s, though these methods are found more consistently amidst Canadian and other foreign music education dissertations. In one example of ethnography, Bartolome (2010) explored the culture and social structures of the Seattle Girls' Choir, with particular attention to the values and behaviors of the choir members. Data collection focused on the aims, process, and outcomes of rehearsals, performances, and events, and explored the value of musical engagement in the lives of the choir members. The study portrayed the choir's culture as nurturing young women participants musically, personally, and socially. In another example, Snead (2010) investigated the musical lives of adolescents in and out of an American suburban high school through an ethnography. Findings revealed a divide between the musical lives of students in and out of school, and recommended that teachers honor their students' musical knowledge and interests, including students as collaborators in developing music curriculum.

6.3. SUMMARY

As depicted by many of these studies, ethnography offers benefits as a methodological approach for exploring particular questions, problems, or dynamics in music teaching and learning. Flinders and Richardson (2006) propose further ethnographic case studies on the significance to students of music in and out of schools and what this might mean to teachers and music programs. They also suggest that ethnographic study may provide new insights into the impact of various school enrichment programs such as artists-in-residence and school/community partnerships. These and a myriad of other issues and questions in music education may be explored through ethnography, such as the dynamics within music classrooms, the beliefs, values, and understandings of music students and teachers, the influence of societal trends on music classroom culture and curriculum creation, and the effects and process of music teacher education.

Recent resources that guide ethnographic methods include Berg (2007), Bogden and Biklin (2007), and LeCompte and Schensul (2010).

New research designs are currently evolving from ethnography in sociology and other subject areas, and these and other new emerging forms may contribute to and further shape future directions in music education research. Autoethnography, for example, closely related to personal narrative and autobiography, is a researcher's study of one's own experience within a culture or group (Patton 2002). This differs from ethnography, which is a study by researchers of a different culture, group, or context other than one's own. Autoethnographic methods include journaling, poetry, dialogue, performances, and other forms that explore personal experiences within a cultural or group context. Autoethnography has not thus far been readily found in US music education research (Roulston 2006); virtual ethnography (ethnography conducted online and exploring online cultures) and ethnography of place are also new, evolving forms of ethnography that are currently found outside of music education.

In conclusion, ethnography is now an important part of mainstream research literature in music education. I hope that this chapter can assist the music education researcher in constructing ethnographic studies based on clearly defined theoretical frameworks and detailed descriptions of sample, settings, data collection, and analysis that are important to the quality of ethnographic research. Music education ethnographers are contributing significantly to music education research, opening the way for further inquiry into understanding the culture of music classrooms, teachers, and students. Ethnographic inquiry in music education can consider the effects of situational and surrounding influences on practice, and allow for observation within the natural settings of music classrooms and communities. By describing events in detail and examining the relationship of events, music educators and researchers may further interpret and understand the meaning and significance of classroom, cultural, and community dynamics. Ethnographic research may provide new insights into inquiry in the music classroom, community, and music education.

NOTE

1. The material in this chapter draws heavily on previously published material from *Journal of Research in Music* Education 35 (1987): 69, National Association for Music Education (formerly MENC). Adapted and reprinted with permission.

REFERENCES

Allsup, R. E. 2003. "Mutual Learning and Democratic Action in Instrumental Music Education." *Journal of Research in Music Education* 51 (1): 24–37.
Bartolome, S. J. 2010. "Girl Choir Culture: An Ethnography of the Seattle Girls' Choir." PhD diss., University of Washington, Seattle.

Beegle, A. 2010. "A Classroom-Based Study of Small-Group Planned Improvisation with Fifth-Grade Children." *Journal of Research in Music Education* 58 (3): 219–39.

Berg, B. L. 2007. *Qualitative Research Methods for the Social Sciences.* Boston: Allyn and Bacon.

Berlak, A., and H. Berlak. 1981. *Dilemmas of Schooling: Teaching and Social Change.* New York: Methuen.

Bogdan, R. C., and S. K. Biklen. 2007. *Qualitative Research for Education: An Introduction to Theory and Methods.* 5th ed. Boston: Allyn and Bacon.

Bolster, A. S. 1983. "Toward a More Effective Model of Research on Teaching." *Harvard Educational Review* 53 (3): 294–308.

Bresler, L., and R. E. Stake. 2006. "Qualitative Research Methodology in Music Education." In *MENC Handbook of Research Methodologies,* edited by R. Colwell, 270–311. New York: Oxford University Press.

Bresler, L. 1995. "Ethnography, Phenomenology and Action Research in Music Education." *The Quarterly Journal of Music Teaching and Learning* 6 (3): 4–16.

Campbell, P. 1998. *Songs in Their Heads.* New York: Oxford University Press.

Carlow, R. 2006. "Diva Irina: An English Language Learner in High School Choir." *Bulletin of the Council for Research in Music Education* 170: 63–77.

Creswell, J. W. 1998. *Qualitative Inquiry and Research Design: Choosing among Five Traditions.* Thousand Oaks, CA: Sage Publications.

Creswell, J. W. 2005. *Educational Research: Planning, Conducting, and Evaluating Quantitative and Qualitative Research.* Upper Saddle River, NJ: Merrill.

Cusick, P. 1973. *Inside High School.* New York: Holt, Rinehart, and Winston.

Della Pietra, C. J., and P. S. Campbell. 1995. "An Ethnography of Improvisation Training in a Music Methods Course." *Journal of Research in Music Education* 43 (2): 112–26.

Emerson, R. M., R. I. Fretz, and L. L. Shaw. 1995. *Writing Ethnographic Fieldnotes.* Chicago: University of Chicago Press.

Feay-Shaw, S. 2001. "The View through the Lunchroom Window: An Ethnography of a Fifth-Grade Musical." *Bulletin of the Council for Research in Music Education* 150: 37–51.

Filstead W. J., ed. 1970. *Qualitative Methodology.* Chicago: Markham.

Flinders, D. J., and C. P. Richardson. 2006. "Contemporary Issues in Qualitative Research and Music Education." In *MENC Handbook of Research Methodologies,* edited by R. Colwell, 312–42. New York: Oxford University Press.

Fox, D. J. 1969. *The Research Process in Education.* New York: Holt, Rinehart, and Winston.

Goodrich, A. 2008. "Utilizing Elements of the Historic Jazz Culture in a High School Setting." *Bulletin of the Council for Research in Music Education* 175: 11–30.

Hammersley, M., and P. Atkinson. 1995. *Ethnography: Principles in Practice.* 2nd ed. New York: Routledge.

Kennedy, M. C. 2004. "'It's a Metamorphosis': Guiding the Voice Change at the American Boychoir School." *Journal of Research in Music Education* 52 (3): 264–80.

Krueger, P. J. 1985. "Influences of the Hidden Curriculum upon the Perspectives of Music Student Teachers: An Ethnography." PhD diss., University of Wisconsin, Madison.

Krueger, P. J. 1987. "Ethnographic Research Methodology in Music Education." *Journal of Research in Music Education* 35 (2): 69–77.

Lacey, C. 1977. *The Socialization of Teachers.* London: Methuen.

Lane, J. 2011. "A Descriptive Analysis of Qualitative Research Published in Two Eminent Music Education Research Journals." *Bulletin for the Council of Research in Music Education*: 188: 65–76.

LeCompte, M. D., and J. P. Goetz. 1982. "Problems of Reliability and Validity in Ethnographic Research." *Review of Educational Research* 52 (1): 31–60.

LeCompte, M.D., and J. L. Schensul. 1999. *Designing and Conducting Ethnographic Research: Ethnographer's Toolkit.* Vol. 1. Walnut Creek, CA: AltaMira.

LeCompte, M. D., and J. L. Schensul. 2010. *Designing and Conducting Ethnographic Research: An Introduction.* Lanham, MD: AltaMira.

Lum, C. H. and P. S. Campbell. 2007. "The Sonic Surrounds of an Elementary School." *Journal of Research in Music Education* 55 (1): 31–47.

Manes, S. I. 2009. "The Pedagogical Process of a Japanese-American Shamisen Teacher." *Bulletin of the Council for Research in Music Education* 182: 41–50.

Patton, M. Q. 2002. *Qualitative Research and Evaluation Methods.* 3rd ed. Thousand Oaks, CA: Sage Publications.

Popkewitz, T. 1981. "The Study of Schooling: Paradigms and Field-Based Methodologies in Educational Research and Evaluation." In *The Study of Schooling*, edited by T. Popkewitz and R. Tabachnick, 1–26. New York: Praeger.

Popkewitz, T., and R. Tabachnick, eds. 1981. *The Study of Schooling.* New York: Praeger.

Popkewitz, T., and G. Wehlage. 1977. "Schooling as Work: An Approach to Research and Evaluation." *Teachers College Record* 79 (1): 69–86.

Romberg, T. A. 1981. "Field-Based Inquiry and the Development of a Mathematical Methodology for the Study of Schooling." In *The Study of Schooling*, edited by T. S. Popkewitz and B. R. Tabacknick, 183–210. New York: Praeger.

Romberg, T. A., and W. M. Stephens. 1983. "Alternative Research Methodologies for the Study of Mathematics Learning and Teaching." Paper presented at the University of Wisconsin, Madison.

Roulston, K. 2006. "Mapping the Possibilities of Qualitative Research in Music Education: A Primer." *Music Education Research* 4 (2): 153–73.

Sindberg, L. 2007. "Comprehensive Musicianship through Performance (CMP) in Lived Experience of Students." *Bulletin for the Council of Research in Music Education* 174: 25–43.

Snead, T. E. 2010. "Dichotomous Musical Worlds: Interactions between the Musical Lives of Adolescents and School Music-Learning Culture." PhD diss., Georgia State University, Atlanta.

Soto, A. C., C. Lum, and P. S. Campbell. 2009. "A University-School Music Partnership for Music Education Majors in a Culturally Distinctive Community." *Journal of Research in Music Education* 56 (4): 338–56.

Spindler, G, ed. 1982. "Introduction." In *Doing the Ethnography of Schooling*, edited by G. Spindler, 1–13. New York: Holt, Rinehart, and Winston.

Spradley, J. P. 1979. *The Ethnographic Interview.* New York: Holt, Rinehart and Winston.

Spradley, J. P. 1980. *Participant Observer.* New York: Holt, Rinehart, and Winston.

Szeko, C. K. 2002. "Music Transmission and Learning." In *The New Handbook of Research on Music Teaching and Learning*, edited by R. Colwell and C. Richardson, 707–29. New York: Oxford.

Tabachnick, B. R. 1981. "Teacher Education as a Set of Dynamic Social Events." In *Studying Teaching and Learning: Trends in Soviet and American Research*, edited by R. B. Tabachnick, T. S. Popkewitz, and B. B. Szekely, 76–86. New York: Praeger.

Taylor, J. 1987. "Forum." *Journal of Research in Music Education* 35(2): 68.

Wehlage, G. 1981. "The Purpose of Generalization in Field-Study Research." In *The Study of Schooling*, edited by T. S. Popkewitz and B. R. Tabachnick, 211–26. New York: Praeger.

Wilcox, K. 1982. "Ethnography as a Methodology and Its Application to the Study of Schooling: A Review." In *Doing the Ethnography of Schooling*, edited by G. Spindler, 456–88. New York: Holt, Rinehart, and Winston.

Willis, P. 1977. *Learning to Labour*. New York: Columbia University Press.

Zimmerman, J. R. 1982. "The Musical Experiences of Two Groups of Children in one Elementary School: An Ethnographic Study." PhD diss., Ohio State University, Columbus.

CHAPTER 7

....

PHENOMENOLOGICAL RESEARCH IN MUSIC EDUCATION

....

RYAN M. HOURIGAN AND SCOTT N. EDGAR

PHENOMENOLOGY is the essence of qualitative exploration. Understanding the consciousness of the participant as part of a phenomenon can be seen in many theoretical and conceptual constructs making up the body of qualitative research. In education research, phenomenological examinations are crucial to understanding the critical relationships between all stakeholders. Van Manen (1990) states: "It encourages a certain attentive awareness to the details and seemingly trivial dimensions of our everyday educational lives" (8). The purpose of this chapter is to show the potential uses of phenomenology in music education research, to identify models of phenomenological inquiry for future use in music education, and to examine how the phenomenological lens can be used to interpret the lived experience of a person as well as the lived experience of a researcher evaluating a phenomenon. In addition, an examination of the philosophy versus the methodology of phenomenology will be discussed to clarify current and future uses of this framework.

7.1. THE FOUNDATIONS OF PHENOMENOLOGY: EPISTEMOLOGY, METHODOLOGY, AND ANALYSIS

....

Phenomenology is a philosophical discipline that studies the structures of human consciousness from the first-person point of view. This philosophical discipline came to be known in the early twentieth century by the works of Husserl, Merleau-Ponty, and others. The foundations of phenomenological research can be traced to Edmund Husserl's writings in reaction to the positivist argument that thoughts coming from meditations are not rational and should be ignored. Husserl (1977) believed the fundamental flaw of the objective sciences was the inability of positivist thinkers to recognize the subjective world as it is lived and the understandings that may come from examining the human experience. He stated: ". . . the positive sciences, after three centuries of brilliant development, are now feeling themselves greatly hampered by securities in their foundations, in their fundamental concepts and methods" (46). Husserl believed the entire idea of an absolute in science is questionable. He further explained that immersing ourselves into a phenomenon leads us to a fuller understanding beyond that which positive science could provide. Revealing the internal thoughts, conversations, and interactions of all involved in an examination will lead others to a clearer idea of the intent of all parties involved, including the researcher.

Husserl was interested in going beyond exposing the lived experience and intentionality of a person from the first-person point of view. In addition, he believed that revealing researcher intent allowed for others to begin to understand the Ego (realization of our senses) of a scientist and, therefore, for the findings of a researcher to be more credible. The life experience of the researcher or the subjects studied is always changing and subjective. Husserl called this subjectivity *transcendental subjectivity*. The human lived experience is not something that is concrete and stable that can be measured through an objective lens. According to Husserl, phenomenology (or the understandings of the Ego and meditations of the Ego) is the "final sense" of science. This final sense, or understanding of the internal conversation that happens between the objective and subjective world, is defined as transcendental phenomenology.

Recent explorations of phenomenology can be traced through Husserl to Merleau-Ponty, Van Manen, and Moustakas. Unlike Husserl, Merleau-Ponty (1945) did not agree that phenomenology was the final stage of understanding in the scientific world. He believed the human experience was the first step in the understanding of a phenomenon. He stated:

> The whole universe of science is built upon the world as directly experienced, and if we want to subject science itself to scrutiny, and arrive at a precise assessment of its meaning and scope, we must begin by reawakening the basic experience of the world. (Merleau-Ponty, viii)

Both Husserl and Merleau-Ponty agreed that the study of human consciousness, as it exists in the lived experience, is at the heart of credible scientific inquiry. The most important philosophical position of these two philosophers in regard to research is that we can only know what we experience. It is by paying attention to our consciousness (and our senses that are channeled through our consciousness) that we can understand our world.

Phenomenological research is the attempt to study the essence or nature of the lived experience through the eyes of human existence. Van Manen (1990) describes phenomenology as the study of the human being in his or her humanness. He states that the phenomenological point of view is to "always question the way we experience the world, to want to know the world in which we live as human beings" (5). Patton (2002) similarly states that phenomenology is the study of ". . . meaning, structure, and essence of the lived experience of this phenomenon for this person or group of people" (132). It is through phenomenology that researchers attempt to extract meaning by interpreting these experiences (106).

The focus of understanding the human experience is the explication of phenomena as they become apparent to the consciousness of a person or persons. Van Manen (1990) explains that "consciousness is the only access humans have to the world" (9); therefore, phenomenologists are interested in the meaning that can be constructed from the combining of objects of nature and objects of consciousness (Moustakas 1994, 27). Moustakas states: "What appears in consciousness is an absolute reality while what appears in the world is a product of learning" (27). Therefore knowledge can be gained about the world by understanding this relationship through thick self-reflection, as well as description of the events and relationships. Moustakas explains that "the challenge facing the human science researcher is to describe things in themselves, to permit what is before one to enter consciousness and to be understood in its meanings and essences in the light of intuition and self-reflection" (27).

7.1.1. Phenomenological Analysis

As you will see later in this chapter, the word "phenomenological" or "phenomenology" is used in a multitude of studies in qualitative education and music education research. In fact, many scholars consider all qualitative research to be phenomenological in nature. Merriam (2009) explains: "Phenomenology is a school of philosophical thought that underpins all of qualitative research" (15). In music education, Bresler and Stake (1992) explain, "Qualitative researchers tend to be phenomenological in their orientation. Most maintain that knowledge is a human construction" (76). This leads to many inconsistent uses of the term in qualitative research, as some researchers refer to the philosophical essence of phenomenology, while others use phenomenology as a method. A true phenomenological study is concerned with the essence or structure of the experience or phenomenon *and* uses phenomenological analytical processes to determine this structure, all with the understandings that come with exploring the researcher's own perspective and bias in the process.

Van Manen (1990) describes the phenomenological analytical process as a form of phenomenological reflection. He states, "The purpose of phenomenological reflection is to try to grasp the essential meaning of something" (77). However, before a researcher can truly understand a phenomenon, he or she must come to terms with "prejudices, viewpoints or assumptions regarding the phenomenon under investigation" (Patton 2002, 485). This process is called the *epoche*. "Epoche requires that looking precede judgment and that judgment of what is 'real' or 'most real' be suspended until all the evidence is in . . . epoche is an ongoing analytical process rather than a single fixed event" (Patton 2002, 485). This usually takes the form of self-journaling and including these viewpoints within the report to put the researcher's perspective out front for the reader to understand.

With epoche in mind, the researcher conducts theme analysis of data sources. According to Van Manen, theme analysis involves ". . . the process of recovering the theme or themes that are embodied and dramatized in the evolving meanings and imagery of the work" (78). These themes must be grouped and reduced to show a complete picture. "Phenomenological reduction is the process of continually returning to the essence of the experience to derive the inner structure or meaning in and of itself" (Merriam 2009, 26). After the data is coded and bracketed (grouping codes together) the researcher begins to horizontalize the data. This involves organizing the data into what Patton calls *meaningful clusters*. Repetitive and irrelevant themes are eliminated. Horizontalization is the process of laying out all the data for examination and treating the data as having equal weight; that is, all pieces of data have equal value at the initial data analysis stage. These themes are then organized into "clusters" (Merriam 2009, 26) with the end goal of understanding these themes as the "structures of experience" (Van Manen 79).

During the phenomenological reduction and horizontalization of data the researcher must keep in mind the perspective or intention from which the data is realized. There are two terms associated with this process: *noema* and *noesis*. Noema is a phenomenological term used to describe ". . . the perceptual meaning or the perceived as such; in recollection, the remembered as such; in judging, the judged as such" (Husserl 1931, 258). In other words, the noema is the perceived phenomenon through the eyes of the participants (including the researcher). *Noesis* is another phenomenological term used to describe the ". . . mind and spirit, and awaken us to the meaning or sense of whatever is in perception, memory, judgment, thinking, and feeling" (249)—in other words, the 'perfect self-evidence' or the actual experience. Patton explains that in each perceived phenomenon there is a noema and a noesis. Researchers must portray both the perceived experience and the actual experience from the outside perspective of the participants. Patton states: "Phenomenological analysis then involves a 'structural description' that contains the 'bones' of the experience" (486).

In sum, Moustakas (1994) explains the analytical process in the following steps; "a) reduce the numerous significant statements to meaning units or themes; b) analyze the context in which the individuals experienced the meaning units or themes; c) reflect on personal experiences you have had with the phenomenon; and d) write a detailed analysis of the 'essence' of the experience for the participants" (153).

7.2. PHENOMENOLOGICAL INQUIRY IN GENERAL AND MUSIC EDUCATION

Phenomenological inquiry in education has received more research attention internationally than it has in the United States. International journals frequently publish qualitative research articles using phenomenological methodology (e.g., *Asia-Pacific*

Journal of Teacher Education, Hispanic Journal of Behavioral Sciences, Australian Journal of Teacher Education, International Journal of Sustainability in Higher Education, Scandinavian Journal of Educational Research, International Journal of Inclusive Education, and *Teaching and Teacher Education: An International Journal of Research and Studies*). Studies have also appeared in American journals but were conducted internationally (New Zealand, Canada, Australia, Finland, and England). Due to the scope of this *Handbook,* only studies conducted in the United States resulting in articles appearing in American journals during the past five years will be included in this review.

A search for "phenomenology" and "education" on Education Research Information Center (ERIC) resulted in over 1,500 articles. After filtering studies to include American inquiries during the past five years, three themes of inquiry in education using phenomenology emerged: (a) teacher induction/professional development and (b) technology in the classroom. Selected studies were chosen exemplifying these areas of study. Instead of surveying a large number of studies to show a breadth of different uses of phenomenology (of which there are many), the authors have decided to concentrate on a few studies to provide an overview of research, with specific attention to aspects of phenomenology that were made explicit.

7.2.1. Teacher Education

The lived experience of teachers (preservice and in-service) has been a popular area of study (Goodnough 2011; Hart and Swars 2009). For example, Hart and Swars (2009) were concerned by the lack of the preservice teachers' voices when evaluating math education curricula, especially when considering how much upper-level mathematics coursework was necessary in mathematic teacher education programs. Using phenomenological inquiry, the researchers utilized interviews and observations to examine students' perceptions of the math education program. The students described incongruence between the math courses, what they expected to teach in their future classrooms, and perceptions of effective classroom practices. The differences between what was taught in teacher education programs and professional development activities and what was being used in the classroom were of paramount concern; phenomenological inquiry was an appropriate method to explore this issue. Exploring the phenomenon of necessary content knowledge through the lived experience of those teaching could have profound effects on preservice education, teacher induction, and professional development. These researchers focused on both the noema and noesis of this setting. Through extensive observation and interviews, perceptions and reality could be discussed. This study captures both the philosophical and methodological ideals of phenomenology. However, from an analysis perspective, there was little discussion of epoche, phenomenological reduction, and horizontalization of data.

Using Van Manen's (1999) philosophical phenomenological framework, Goodnough (2011) explored the lived experience of ten teachers before, during, and after implementing action research in their classrooms. Using three semi-structured interviews, teachers revealed that action research had a positive effect on their teacher identity, their teaching practices, and perceiving their school in a broader educational context. The teachers were interviewed before conducting their action research study, one year after their study, and an additional two to four years after their study. Each interview lasted 60–90 minutes. The singular use of the interview as a data source did limit this study from fully exploring the phenomenon of action research as professional development: a researcher must be careful of claims that come from only one data source. Furthermore, this form of data collection only captures the noema or perceptions of the participants. Phenomenology was an appropriate philosophical fit in uncovering the issues of the effectiveness of professional development and building meaning from the perspective of the teachers involved in the process. There was little discussion about phenomenological methodology or analysis.

These studies, based in the dynamics of personal learning and growth, are good examples of the kind of topic that could lend itself well to phenomenology both philosophically and methodologically.

7.2.2. Technology

Ever-changing technological advances will always be a part of education. Recently, qualitative researchers utilizing the philosophical and methodological underpinnings of phenomenology have explored technology and social networking (Corwin and Cintron 2011), and teacher's value of technology (Ottenbreit-Leftwich, Glaxewski, Newby, and Ertmer 2010).

Hermeneutical phenomenology "interprets described experience of individuals to understand the phenomenon" (Ottenbreit-Leftwich et al. 2010, 1323). Using hermeneutical phenomenology (van Manen 1999), Ottenbreit-Leftwich et al. (2010) investigated the value beliefs at the basis of teachers' uses of technology. Teachers have varying beliefs as to the value of new technology in the classroom, greatly affecting their implementation of technology. Through the design of a multiple case study (implementing interviews, observations, and electronic portfolios), technology was valued and used for professional and student needs—all focused on benefiting student learning. Technological applications such as attendance taking and grading were less well received. This study provided detailed description of both the philosophical and methodological groundings of hermeneutic phenomenology. The discussion of how phenomenology influenced the multiple case study design was specifically strong.

Building social networks for new college students is an important aspect for their potential success and acclimation to college life. The use of online social networking could help the process of transitioning from high school to college. Corwin and Cintron (2011) used phenomenology as an analytical method to study how social networks are composed among students. The researchers attempted to explain this phenomenon using interviews and observations at multiple campuses, facilitating both noema and noesis. Findings suggested friendship and security were major influential factors in the comfort of college freshmen. Social networks included old friends, new friends, acquaintances, and all students. Online social networking was the strongest manner for staying connected with old friends. The phenomenological analysis included recording biases and categorizing responses as suggested by Strauss and Corbin (1998). A detailed discussion of how the researchers achieved epoche is included.

The use of phenomenology in general education research discussed here represents some of the topics that could be addressed. The use of varied data collection and analysis strategies used within the methodology of phenomenology represents the diverse applications phenomenological research can have.

7.3. PHENOMENOLOGY AS A FRAME OF INQUIRY IN MUSIC EDUCATION

Studies involving phenomenology in music education can be grouped into the following themes: (a) underrepresented populations; (b) professional development; and (c) blended studies. This section of the chapter will explore these studies and their impact on music education. All American studies utilizing a philosophical or methodological phenomenological lens were included regardless of publication data. Randles (2012) offers an additional review of studies using phenomenology as a research lens. He suggests, "the majority of phenomenological studies focus on meaning as it relates to identity—perceptions of individuals about themselves, others, acts, society, culture, and of course the business of music teaching and learning" (18).

7.3.1. Underrepresented Populations

Students from underrepresented populations have been examined using phenomenology within the following populations: (a) students with special needs (Hourigan 2009; Jellison and Flowers 1991); (b) students from multicultural settings (Drake 2010; Southcott and Joseph 2010); and (c) adult learners (Reed 2008; Thornton 2010). These studies are presented historically.

One of the earliest phenomenological studies conducted in music education addressed students with disabilities (Jellison and Flowers 1991). The researchers do not use the term "phenomenology"; however, this investigation of the lived experiences of students with disabilities represents the earliest study in music education suggesting a phenomenological philosophical orientation, which the researchers describe as "naturalistic inquiry." One key finding was the similarities in responses from the two groups (students with and without disabilities) regarding how they respond to music. This early study laid the groundwork for research to be conducted in music education looking at the lived experiences of participants.

Adult learners have different needs than children and adolescents. Understanding the lived experiences of adult music-makers and learners is especially important for music education, and phenomenology is conducive to exploring this topic. Using narrative inquiry, closely informed by phenomenology, Reed (2008) looked to determine the role music plays in meaning-making. Nine adult music-makers in a community band, aged 72 to 93, participated in both personal and focus group interviews. Findings suggest that performing may lead to good health, foster community, and facilitate knowledge of self. The data collection was the most salient part of this study informed by phenomenology. There was little discussion of phenomenological data analysis or philosophy.

Hourigan (2009) continued this vein of research, exploring preservice music teachers' perceptions of working with students with special needs. This phenomenological investigation utilized a qualitative particularistic case study design to explore preservice music teachers' experiences working with music students with special needs and he labeled phenomenology as his theoretical framework (Husserl 1970). Preparation for teaching diverse populations, including students with special needs, is a problematic area for both teacher educators and preservice teachers. Journals, participant interviews, and observations were used as data. This triangulation of data collection helped strengthen this study to provide both noema and noesis. Hourigan's experience as a researcher participant allowed him to account for the lived experience of all participants. His discussion of epoche and his role in analysis strengthened his use of phenomenology. Findings suggest that orientation to working with students with special needs was beneficial for the preservice teachers, and the act of participating in the study (observation, journaling, and discussion) was beneficial.

Students from multicultural settings have also received attention in phenomenological research. One area of music receiving little music education research attention is hip-hop. Due to this underrepresentation, Drake (2010) explored, through a phenomenological philosophical lens, the lived experience of youth in a hip-hop culture (Moustakas 1994). The guiding research question was: "What is the meaning of hip-hop as described by the lived experience of adolescents?" Interviews of eight high school participants were the singular source of data. Findings suggest that hip-hop is not only music, but also a lifestyle, and understanding of this culture is important to teaching and building relationships with students who identify with this culture. The limited data set prevented discussion on the reality of what was happening in the hip-hop lives of the students. Further, there was little discussion on how phenomenology informed data analysis. The philosophical discussion of how phenomenology was used as a lens was strong.

Thornton (2010) explored a similar phenomenon: adult music engagement of those not currently participating in music-making that is an extension of traditional music curricular offerings. The three participants were an avid listener, a church praise team member, and a bluegrass musician. Using individual interviews, participants discussed their musical life histories, the importance of their current musical lives, what meaning they attach to their music-making, and how their musical engagement changed over the course of their lives. Phenomenological analysis was achieved by joining participant and researcher interpretation to construct accurate perspectives. Themes that emerged were that music connected participants to humanity, it gave them a sense of fulfillment, and it was profound that participants could choose to be involved. Phenomenology philosophy informed data collection and analysis.

7.3.2. Professional Development

Just as in general education, phenomenology has been used to explore music education professional development (Bower 2008; Conway 2000, 2003, 2008; Conway, Eros, Hourigan, and Stanley 2007; Conway and Hodgman 2008; Conway and Holcomb 2008; Pellegrino 2010; Lippitt Kazee 2010; Nichols 2005).

Conway (2000) represents the earliest example of phenomenology in this category. Due to the potential in-depth data collection of the teachers' experience, coupled with observation, phenomenology can be used to explore music teacher practice and the realities of music education in schools. Conway (2000) utilized a phenomenological interview design informed by Seidman to explore instrumental music students' perspectives of instrument gender stereotypes. The use of in-depth interviews provided perspectives that instrument stereotypes do exist and student instrument choice is influenced by gender stereotypes. Phenomenology solely informed data collection.

Conway (2003) did not explicitly call her investigation of district mentoring programs phenomenology; however, the findings represent the phenomenon and lived experience of beginning teachers, mentors, and administrators in the mentor/mentee relationship. Conway utilized interviews, focus groups, and an investigator's log to develop a holistic perspective of this phenomenon. Findings suggest there was little consistency in mentoring programs across contexts, and the content of mentoring practices included administrative duties, classroom management, parent interaction, policy, and building issues. Her use of diverse data collection, researcher journaling, and varied perspectives represents phenomenological methodology.

Homeschooling and music education are an area that has received little research attention. Nichols (2005) explored the music education curriculum choices of three homeschooled families. Using interviews and observations, findings suggest the lived experiences of these families are very different in terms of what they teach their children about music. The parents' fundamental philosophy of education, their belief in the value of music education, and their own prior experiences in music learning and performance affected their curriculum. Data collection and the theoretical framework were both influenced by a phenomenological philosophy.

Conway, Eros, Hourigan, and Stanley (2007) explored the perceptions of beginning teachers regarding their brass and woodwind technique classes in undergraduate teacher preparation. Observations, interviews, focus groups, and self-study researcher logs comprised the data set. The diversity of data sets aided in providing a holistic perspective of the beginning teacher, allowing for both noema and noesis to be discussed. Findings suggest that there is a great deal of diversity in how these courses are taught across contexts, instrument proficiency is difficult, priority should be given to broad teaching strategies, and a realization that different ages of P–12 students require different types of instrument instruction. Notebooks, handouts, and resources are some of the most valuable elements of instrument technique courses. Utilizing a phenomenological framework, this study represents an example of how data collection can be phenomenology.

Using case study methodology informed by heuristic phenomenology, Conway and Holcomb (2008) explored preparation and experiences of 11 music mentors. Data sources included interviews with mentors, research logs, and notecards from participant interactions. Findings suggest that mentors themselves need mentors, time constraints are challenging, communication with mentees is difficult, technology can be a positive variable, and it is difficult to provide support to mentees in a non-evaluative role. The importance of the heuristic approach is that the researcher, as a professional development facilitator for mentors, could be involved from the inside so that she could reflect as both participant and researcher. This study was closely informed philosophically by phenomenology. A heuristic phenomenological framework also informed data collection and analysis.

Continuing to draw from heuristic phenomenology, Conway and Hodgman (2008) explored the experiences of college and community choir members performing collaboratively. Hodgman conducted a concert combining two of his ensembles: one college and one community. Using focus group interviews, journals, individual interviews, and a teacher-research log, findings included that this concert fostered a heightened performance experience, improved understanding of each other, and no signs of age barriers. It was stressed that preparation for collaboration was critical. Due to the heuristic inquiry drawing on the personal experience and insight of the researcher, Hodgman was a participant-researcher, as well as facilitator for the experience. Beyond the choice to include the conductor as researcher, the use of phenomenology was philosophical and had little influence on data analysis.

Conway (2008) explored the professional development perceptions of experienced music teachers over the course of their career. The lived experiences of the participants are especially relevant, as the study explored how their perceptions and experiences had changed. Within a phenomenological interview design, data sets included interviews with 13 mid-career teachers, interviews with six veteran teachers, a focus group with four of the veteran teachers, and an investigator's log. The sole use of interview limited discussion to noema. Findings suggest that informal interactions with other music teachers are some of the most valuable forms of professional development, and that professional development needs for music teachers change over the course of their career. Phenomenology also informed data collection, as Conway used phenomenological interviews (Seidman 2006). Phenomenological interviewing combines life history with in-depth interviewing (Seidman 2006):

The first interview establishes the context of the participants' experience. The second interview allows participants to reconstruct the details of their experience within the context in which it occurs. And the third encourages the participants to reflect on the meanings their experiences holds for them. . . . In the first interview, the interviewer's task is to put the participant's experience in context by asking him or her to tell as much as possible about him or herself in light of the topic up to the present time. . . . The purpose of the second interview is to concentrate on the concrete details of the participants' present lived experience in the topic area of study. . . . In the third interview, we ask participants to reflect on the meaning of their experience. (Seidman 2006, 17–18)

Bower (2008) utilized an action research methodology within a phenomenological perspective to explore the researcher's transformation in using technology to compose in a fourth- and fifth-grade choral classroom. The use of self-reflection, journaling, and student interview allowed the researcher/teacher to adopt a constructivist approach to his classroom. The self-study/action research approach was a unique interpretation of phenomenology, but was able to describe the lived experiences of both the teacher and students. The findings suggest teachers are able to transform their classroom by using technology to compose. The use of researcher reflection and the role of the researcher in the data analysis were greatly influenced by phenomenological methodology.

Southcott and Joseph (2010) utilized interpretive phenomenological analysis to explore undergraduate preservice teacher education students' perspectives of multicultural music and how this affects their understanding of cultural diversity in school music. Interpretive phenomenological analysis "employs a phenomenological, idiographic approach that attempts to explore personal experience in a participant's personal and social life-world" (14). Within this analysis technique, the interpretive role of the researcher is stressed. Using primarily semi-structured interviews, participants' perspectives—though not necessarily the reality of practice—were explored. Findings suggest that students were aware of the importance of multicultural music in schools, preservice teachers should be exposed to multicultural musical settings in field experiences, and artist-in-school programs are one way to expose students to multicultural music. Phenomenology most closely informed data analysis.

Lippitt Kazee (2010) explored teachers' perspectives of teaching musicianship. Three music teachers were interviewed and observed to see how they implemented musicianship in an assessment-driven academic climate. This allowed for both noema and noesis. The rich description of the settings, teachers, and teaching practices suggest that phenomenology was conducive to exploring music teacher practices. Participants believed that expressive qualities in music are important, and this was evident through their teaching practices. This study utilized phenomenology primarily as a philosophical lens through which to view the data.

7.3.3. Blended Studies

Phenomenology is often combined with other theoretical frameworks or research methodologies. Examples in music education include heuristic phenomenology

(Conway and Holcomb 2008; Conway and Hodgman 2008), phenomenological case study (Amoriello 2010; Mirabal 2008; Pellegrino 2010; Sindberg 2007), narrative phenomenology (Reed 2008), hermeneutic phenomenology (Ruthmann 2006), and as part of a mixed method study (Nolan 2008). As discussed earlier, heuristic phenomenology is beneficial in that the researcher is able to analyze the phenomenon from the inside (an emic perspective), as Hodgman did as conductor (Conway and Hodgman 2008), and Conway did as professional development facilitator (Conway and Holcomb 2008).

Case study has also been an approach blended with phenomenology. Sindberg (2007) explored teachers' and students' lived experience of music education based on comprehensive musicianship. Designed as a collective case study, observations, interviews, writing prompts, e-mail correspondence, teaching plans, and teacher journals revealed both teachers and students found this model beneficial, and found it went beyond the technical elements of the music. She also drew upon some ethnographic research techniques, as she was a participant observer.

Using a phenomenological case study methodology, Pellegrino (2010) examined the meanings and values of music-making and how they intersect with teaching. Using background surveys, individual interviews, classroom observations, focus group interviews, researcher self-interview, and researcher's journals, music-making was connected to the formation of teacher identity and well-being. Music-making further reminded participants why they valued playing, helped make them better teachers, helped them be more compassionate to their students, helped inspire both them and their students, helped to address classroom management, helped gain credibility with students, and modeled performance. The use of case study and phenomenology allowed Pellegrino to explore both detailed profiles of the participants and the broad scope of music-making in the lives of string teachers. Phenomenology provided a philosophical lens and method for data collection and analysis. Aspects of phenomenology that impacted the study were: (a) data collection design of conversational interviews, videotaping teachers while music-making in the classroom with their students, music-making in the focus group interview, and researcher's self-interviews; (b) analysis process (Moustakas 1994); and (c) the focus of describing the phenomenon of the lived experience of four string teachers' music-making (past, present inside and outside of the classroom, as well as in their imagined futures). Aspects of case study, such as the unit of analysis, were also defined and cited.

Amoriello (2010) also conducted a phenomenological case study utilizing interviews, research journals, focus group interviews, and observations to explore the phenomenon and lived experience of undergraduate music majors and piano proficiency. Mirabal (2008) similarly utilized a phenomenological case study to explore primary public school students' perspectives on performing sacred songs. The underrepresented student perspective was observed through a discourse curriculum where the researcher observed discussions based on the research topic. Findings suggest children are interested in performing sacred songs as long as religion is not indoctrinated. Because of the importance for phenomenology to account for varied perspectives, noema and noesis, and researcher perspective, case study is especially conducive to blend with phenomenology.

Reed (2008) was able to explore a phenomenon through telling the stories of older performing musicians using narrative phenomenology. Using hermeneutic phenomenology (van Manen 1999), Ruthmann (2006) explored the lived experiences of sixth-graders in a music technology lab. The use of hermeneutics allowed Ruthmann to explore the students' knowledge and to adequately interpret the phenomenon being observed. This view allowed for the study to be completely "other-oriented" and focused on the students (etic perspective).

Mixing qualitative and quantitative data is increasing in frequency in music education literature (see Fitzpatrick in this *Handbook*). Nolan (2008) used phenomenology (Moustakas 1994) to inform the qualitative portion of her mixed method study exploring the role of parents in instrumental music education. She utilized thick description to describe the parents' role. Findings suggest that parents are influential in children's participation and retention in instrumental music education programs. Data analysis and collection were influenced by phenomenology and were described in detail in this study.

Phenomenology, when combined with other frameworks and methodologies, can provide different ways of exploring a phenomenon. The examples used in the preceding represent the potential uses of phenomenology within music education. It is important for researchers in music to understand that meaning cannot always be found from the perspective of an outsider. In order to understand a situation, relations, scenario, or phenomenon, a researcher must include as many perspectives as possible. Phenomenology is one means to accomplish this goal.

7.3.4. Suggestions for Future Use of Phenomenology in Music Education

At the heart of the phenomenological lens is the attempt to observe a phenomenon through the eyes of the person(s) who are truly living within the structure of the experience. Within music education, this framework lends itself to being a useful tool of inquiry into phenomena where these experiences are unique and useful to our understanding within the field. Beginning in-service teachers, experienced music teachers, and underrepresented students are all groups for which a qualitative perspective of the participants is vital to the overall understanding; therefore, it is important for our field to continue with these strands of research.

The use of the analytical processes involved with phenomenology can be used in other forms of qualitative research. For example, case study, grounded theory, and hermeneutics all have a need to examine the data from the noema/noesis perspective. In addition, as qualitative researchers, we should all come to terms with our own biases (as Husserl suggests) in order to clarify data and offer a clear picture to the reader.

Phenomenological research in both general and music education have provided insight into the lived experiences of the participants. Because the focus of qualitative inquiry is on the particular and is rarely meant for generalizability, further use of phenomenology in diverse settings is recommended. The stories of the participants outlined in this review offer the thick description that phenomenological researchers strive for. Thoughtful research design that raises the question, "what are your experiences in terms of the phenomenon and what contexts or situations have typically influenced or affected your experiences with the phenomenon?" (Creswell 2007, 61) could continue to provide rich, thick description of the lives of stakeholders in all aspects of music education.

REFERENCES

Amoriello, L. 2010. "Teaching Undergraduate Class Piano: A Study of Perspectives from Self, Students, and Colleagues." EdD diss., Teachers College, Columbia University.

Bower, D. N. 2008. "Constructivism in Music Education Technology: Creating an Environment for Choral Composition in the Fourth and Fifth Grades." PhD diss., New York University.

Bresler, L., and R. E. Stake. 1992. "Qualitative Research Methodology in Music Education." In *The Handbook of Research on Music Teaching and Learning*, edited by R. Colwell, 75–90. New York: Schirmer.

Conway, C. M. 2000. "Gender and Musical Instrument Choice." *Bulletin of the Council for Research in Music Education* 146: 1–17.

Conway, C. M. 2003. "An Examination of District-Sponsored Beginning Music Teacher Mentor Practices." *Journal of Research in Music Education* 51: 6–23.

Conway, C. M. 2008. "Experienced Music Teacher Perceptions of Professional Development throughout Their Careers." *Bulletin of the Council for Research in Music Education* 176: 7–18.

Conway, C. M., J. Eros, R. Hourigan, and A. M. Stanley. 2007. "Perceptions of Beginning Teachers Regarding Brass and Woodwind Technique Classes in Preservice Education." *Bulletin of the Council for Research in Music Education* 173: 39–51.

Conway, C. M., and T. M. Hodgman. 2008. "College and Community Choir Member Experiences in a Collaborative Intergenerational Performance Project." *Journal of Research in Music Education* 56 (3): 220–37.

Conway, C. M., and A. Holcomb. 2008. "Perceptions of Experienced Music Teachers Regarding Their Work as Music Mentors." *Journal of Research in Music Education* 56 (1): 55–67.

Corwin, J. R., and R. Cintron. 2011. "Social Networking Phenomena in the First-Year Experience." *Journal of College Teaching and Learning* 18: 25–37.

Creswell, J. W. 2007. *Qualitative Inquiry and Research Design: Choosing among Five Approaches.* Thousand Oaks, CA: Sage Publications.

Drake, C. Y. 2010. "Phenomenological Study into the Lived Experiences of Youth in the Hip Hop Culture." PhD diss., Capella University.

Goodnaugh, K. 2011. "Examining the Long-Term Impact of Collaborative Action Research on Teacher Identity and Practice: The Perceptions of K–12 Teachers." *Educational Action Research* 19: 73–86.

Hart, L. C., and S. L. Swars. 2009. "The Lived Experiences of Elementary Prospective Teachers in Mathematics Content Coursework." *Teacher Development* 13: 159–72.

Hourigan, R. M. 2009. "Preservice Music Teachers' Perceptions of a Fieldwork Experience in a Special Needs Classroom." *Journal of Research in Music Education* 57 (2): 152–68.

Husserl, E. 1970. *Cartesian Meditations.* Translated by D. Cairns. The Hague: Martinus Nijhoff (Original work published 1933).

Husserl, E. 1931. *Ideas*. Translated by W. R. Boyce Gibson. London: George Allen and Unwin.

Jellison, J. A., and P. J. Flowers 1991. "Talking about Music: Interviews with Disabled and Nondisabled Children." *Journal of Research in Music Education* 39: 322–33.

Lippitt Kazee, S. 2010. "The Extent to Which Expressive Qualities Are Valued by K-12 Public School Music Teachers, and the Impact of Those Values on Educational Leadership Practices and Policy Initiatives." PhD diss., University of South Carolina.

Merleau-Ponty, M. 1945. *Phenomenology of Perception*. Delhi, India: Gallimard Press.

Merriam, S. B. 2009. *Qualitative Research*. San Francisco: Jossey-Bass.

Mirabal, L. B. 2008. "Singing Sacred Songs in Public Schools: Perspectives of Primary School Students." EdD diss., Teachers College, Columbia University.

Moustakas, C. E. 1994. *Phenomenological Research Methods*. Thousand Oaks, CA: Sage Publications.

Nichols, J. 2005. "Music Education and Homeschooling: A Preliminary Inquiry." *A Bulletin of Council for Research in Music Education* 166: 27–42.

Nolan, M. R. 2008. "Parent Involvement in Instrumental Music: A Parent's Perspective." PhD diss., University of Phoenix.

Ottenbreit-Leftwich, A. T., K. D. Glazewski, T. J. Newby, and P. A. Ertmer. 2010. "Teacher Values and Beliefs Associated with Using Technology: Addressing Professional and Student Needs." *Computers and Education* 55: 1321–35.

Patton, M. Q. 2002. *Qualitative Research and Evaluation Methods*. 2nd ed. Thousand Oaks, CA: Sage Publications.

Pellegrino, K. 2010. "The Meanings and Values of Music-Making in the Lives of String Teachers: Exploring the Intersections of Music-Making and Teaching." PhD diss. University of Michigan.

Randles, C. 2012. "Phenomenology: A Review of Literature." *Update: Applications of Research in Music Education* 30: 11–21.

Reed, S. M. 2008. "Sentimental Journey: The Role of Music in the Meaning-Making Processes of Older Performing Musicians." PhD diss., Pennsylvania State University.

Ruthmann, S. A. 2006. "Negotiating Learning and Teaching in a Music Technology Lab: Curricular, Pedagogical, and Ecological Issues." PhD diss., Oakland University, Rochester, MI.

Seidman, I. 2006. *Interviewing as Qualitative Research: A Guide for Researchers in Education*. New York: Teachers College, Columbia University.

Sindberg, L. 2007. "Comprehensive Musicianship through Performance (CMP) in the Lived Experiences of Students." *Bulletin of the Council for Research in Music Education* 174: 25–43.

Southcott, J., and D. Joseph. 2010. "Engaging, Exploring, and Experiencing Multicultural Music in Australian Music Teacher Education: The Changing Landscape of Multicultural Music Education." *Journal of Music Teacher Education* 20 (1): 8–26.

Strauss, A., and J. Corbin. 1998. *Basics of Qualitative Research: Techniques and Procedures for Developing Grounded Theory*. 2nd ed. Thousand Oaks, CA: Sage Publications.

Thornton, D. H. 2010. "Adult Music Engagement: Perspectives from Three Musically Engaged Cases." PhD diss., Pennsylvania State University.

Van Manen, M. 1999. *Researching Lived Experience*. New York: State University of New York Press.

....

CHAPTER 8

NARRATIVE INQUIRY AND THE USES OF NARRATIVE IN MUSIC EDUCATION RESEARCH

....

SANDRA L. STAUFFER

DURING the 1980s, eminent psychologist Jerome Bruner described two distinct yet complementary modes of cognition that humans use to order experience and construct reality—the paradigmatic or logico-scientific mode, and the narrative mode.[1] "A good story and a well-formed argument are different natural kinds," Bruner argued, and each "way of knowing" functions differently, is structured differently, and aims at fundamentally different ways of "convincing" (1986, 11). The paradigmatic or logico-scientific mode of thinking employs categorization, relies on formal description, and makes use of observation and hypothesis testing to generate arguments that aim to "convince one of their truth" (1986, 11–13). The narrative mode of thinking has to do with "how we come to endow experience with meaning," with "epiphanies of the ordinary," and with "human or human-like intention and action and the vicissitudes and consequences that mark their course" (1986, 12–13). Narratives aim at meaning rather than truth and convince through lifelikeness or *verisimilitude*. Drawing upon his own study of "how people tell the stories of their lives," Bruner described narrative as a way to make sense of lived time and a means self-making (1987/2004, 700). "A life as led is inseparable from a life as told" (1987/2004, 708), Bruner claimed, and the study of narratives provides an opportunity to understand the human condition.

Bruner stands as a key figure in the community of narrative scholarship. Yet at the time of his 1980 writings, narrative work was already well underway in disciplines as diverse as psychology, anthropology, sociology, literary theory, and historiography. Since then, scholars in these disciplines and others have continued to take what has been called "the narrative turn"—a move toward narrative *as* scholarship and narrative *in* scholarship (Pinnegar and Daynes 2007). The result has been a proliferation of ways of using narrative in research, as well as rather healthy debates about what narrative inquiry is and even what constitutes a narrative.

Consider an example from the one-man play "Second Chair," by Johnny Saldaña, published in *Research Studies in Music Education.*

> (setting: two metal folding chairs with metal music stands in front of each one; the music stands hold all necessary props for the production; first chair appears shiny and pristine; second chair appears worn, rusty, and beaten)
>
> *(pre-show music: various selections composed by W. Francis McBeth [The Feast of Trumpets, Praises, Caccia, Flourishes]; lights rise; JOHNNY enters at the beginning of Flourishes, looks longingly at first chair, then sits in second chair and looks occasionally toward the empty first chair; music fades out; he speaks to the audience)*
>
> JOHNNY: In high school band, Tammi Jo thought she was so special. She played an ebony wood Selmer clarinet with a glass mouthpiece, while all I had was this cheap-ass plastic Bundy. Her family was typically middle-class and she was the only child, thus receiving all of the attention and all of the spoils. My family was transitioning from lower class to middle, but that was kind of hard with so many children to take care of.
>
> In our junior year, I was second chair; and Tammy Jo was first chair
>
> (brief pause)
>
> And I think you know where this story is going.
>
> (Saldaña 2008, 179, italics in the original)

Do you? Do you know where this story is going? What it is that you "know," and how do you know it? Are you curious enough to want to read more of Johnny's story? Why? Saldaña, the author, describes this piece as an "autoethnodrama." But is it narrative?

Although storytelling is an ancient and even venerated human practice, narrative is a relatively recent addition to the panoply of approaches within the larger domain of qualitative scholarship. The disciplinary roots of narrative stretch into phenomenology, psychology, sociology, anthropology, literature, and the arts, and are intertwined in diverse ways, making narrative scholarship a complex, multidisciplinary, polyvocal, and evolving mode of inquiry (Barrett and Stauffer 2009, 2012; Clandinin and Rosiek 2007; Holstein and Gubrim 2012; Reissman 2008; Squire, Andrews, and Tomboukou 2008). One purpose of this chapter is to summarize current definitions of narrative and narrative inquiry, and to describe narrative scholarship from perspectives that may be useful to music education researchers.

Another purpose of this chapter is to point to markers or characteristics of narrative inquiry and to provide examples that illustrate those markers. Wherever possible, these examples are drawn from the music education literature. Reading the music education literature only, however, affords insufficient grounding for engaging in narrative scholarship, not because extant music studies are flawed (though quality does vary), but because there is much to be learned from our colleagues in other disciplines who have been about the practice of narrative inquiry longer and who have taken different positions, drawn on different sources, asked different questions, and made use of different processes. Thinking through various disciplinary approaches may open multiple possibilities for music education researchers and can help to clarify thinking about what constitutes narrative inquiry.

As suggested earlier, variants of narrative inquiry within the larger domain of qualitative research are quite easily found, to the extent that "it is easier to identify complexities and multiplicities in the field of narrative inquiry than it is to identify commonalities" (Chase 2011, 429). Yet, both commonalities and distinctions do exist in this rather messy state of affairs, and these commonalities and distinctions raise two sets of questions. One set of questions has to do with the fundamental assumptions of narrative inquiry. Every research tradition—every means or method—is fraught with problems of definitions, process, bias, truth claims, quality criteria, ethics, and more, whether researchers choose to articulate them or not. Narrative inquiry is no different. Given the variants of narrative research one might encounter, questions range from philosophical matters having to do with reality, knowledge, and self, to practical problems of procedure, interpretation, and representation. All the more reason, then, to heed the counsel of those who advise considering one's own ontological and epistemological commitments before beginning narrative work and throughout the inquiry process (Clandinin and Murphy 2009).

The second set of questions has to do with the potential uses of narrative and narrative inquiry in music education. For what reasons would a researcher choose narrative inquiry? What purposes can narrative inquiry serve in music education scholarship? When and how might narrative modes of research be used or useful? And why should narrative matter? In other words, "Why narrative? Why now?" (Bowman 2006, 5).

8.1. Pathways to Narrative

What is narrative? What is narrative inquiry? The answers to these questions may seem simple: A narrative is a story one tells of one's lived experience—of sitting (or not) in "second chair" in band, for example. Narrative inquiry, then, might appear to be simply a matter of finding and recording someone's story, writing it up, and putting some explanatory text around it. Done. But not so fast. What counts as a narrative? The story you told to a friend about what happened during yesterday's class? The story you might tell about reading this chapter? A novel? A text message exchange? Does music, a dance, or an artwork count as narrative? As *part* of a narrative? Why was a particular story told in the first place? Would the teller change the story depending upon when or to whom the story was told? Does that matter? Is it ethical to "get" stories and write them up? Why would one do that?

And what, exactly, is under investigation in narrative inquiry? The story itself? The person who told the story? The act of telling? The incident to which the story refers? The purpose of the teller and the telling? The teller's psychological state? The culture in which the story is situated? The social practices or oral conventions of narrating that both enable and constrain the story, the telling, and the teller? What makes a particular narrative of interest to a researcher? Are the researcher's interests the only interests that matter?

These questions (and more) matter to narrative researchers, and all of them may be answered somewhat differently, depending on one's approach to narrative and purposes for choosing narrative as a research mode. In music education those who have engaged in narrative scholarship have generally taken one of three pathways into their studies. The first pathway originates in the writing and thinking of Jerome Bruner and dates to his work in the 1980s. In *Actual Minds, Possible Worlds* (1986) and articles written at about the same time, Bruner described narrative as a way of knowing and a distinctly human achievement. This view became important in psychology and in other social science disciplines. A second pathway derives from the work of D. Jean Clandinin and F. Michael Connelly. Their book, *Narrative Inquiry: Experience and Story in Qualitative Research* (2000), followed their previous writings about personal experience methods. This early work and their subsequent writings mark a distinct path in narrative inquiry that has been influential in teacher education research and curriculum studies. A third pathway to narrative in music education research has followed the writing and thinking of Tom Barone. Barone's *Touching Eternity: The Enduring Outcomes of Teaching* (2001) and other works pointed to the power of what he has called critical storytelling in educational research. A brief examination of these three pathways follows.

8.1.1. Jerome Bruner and Narrative Knowing

As noted earlier, Bruner outlined narrative as a distinct way of human knowing, a "form of thought" or "mode of cognitive functioning" (1987/2004, 691; 1986, 11). Narrative, Bruner posits, is a means by which "we go about constructing and representing the rich and messy domain of human interaction(s)," a way in which we organize "our memory of human happenings" (1991, 4). Bruner's distinction between paradigmatic and narrative modes of thinking and knowing underpin these claims. Rather than position the paradigmatic and narrative modes as dichotomous, Bruner suggests that they are two "distinct ways of ordering experience" that are "complementary" and "irreducible to each other." Each way of knowing represents the world differently, is constructed in different ways, and has different aims (1986, 11), and both are useful.

Bruner describes the paradigmatic or logico-scientific mode as logical thought using formal systems of description and explanation aimed at certainty or truth through "good theory, tight analysis, logical proof, sound argument, and empirical discovery guided by reasoned hypothesis" (13). In the logico-scientific mode, the mind is an instrument of reason. In contrast, narrative forms of thought have to do with ways in which we make sense of lived time, deal with the ambiguities of daily life, and construct our conceptions of selves. These two ideas—narrative as a means of making sense of experience and narrative as a means of constructing our selves—are fundamental in the Brunerian perspective. A central concern for narrative scholars on the Brunerian pathway is how narrative "operates as an instrument of the mind in the construction of reality" (1991, 6), or "how we come to endow experience with meaning" (1986, 12).

Throughout more than three decades of writing about narrative, Bruner puzzles over two complex and intertwined matters crucial to his perspective: narrative as a means of self-making, and narrative in and as culture. "A self is probably the most impressive work of art we ever produce, surely the most intricate," he writes, "For we create not just one self-making story but many of them . . . it is not just who and what we are that what we want to get straight (in our story making) but who and what we might have been" as well as who and what we wish to be (2002, 14). Bruner suggests that self-making through storying is "our principal means for establishing our uniqueness, . . . we distinguish ourselves from others by comparing our accounts of ourselves with the accounts that others give us of themselves" (2002, 66). He describes this human capacity for narrative as a cognitive achievement, an "interpretive feat" that we acquire in the course of living (1987, 693). "Has anybody ever found it necessary to teach a young child what a story *is*," Bruner asks, "or how to understand it?" (2010, 45, italics in the original). No, rather, to story is to be human.

Stories are not context free, however, but rather are situated in and continuous with cultural worlds. If "self-making is a narrative art," as Bruner suggests, then it is often "guided by unspoken, implicit cultural models of what selfhood should be, might be— and, of course, shouldn't be" (2002, 65). Like selves, cultures are made and remade through, in and with narrative. Drawing on anthropologist Clifford Geertz and others, Bruner posits that culture comes about in part through "a local capacity for accruing stories of happenings of the past into some sort of diachronic structure that permits continuity into the present" (1991, 19–20). Cultures as large as societies and as small as families "rely upon narrative conventions to maintain their coherence" and to "pass on their norms to successive generations," often through canonical forms and figures, linguistic conventions, and implicit rules of telling that, while arbitrary (and typically value-laden), allow speakers and listeners to (at least begin to) grasp what one is saying and the other hearing (2010, 45).

Yet the small stories—the local, particular, and individual narratives of who we are or what is, was, or might be—are "forever in dialectical tension" with larger cultural and canonical narratives (2002, 13–14). "Life in culture is perpetually open to improvisation," Bruner suggests, for it is full of "ambiguities and multiple demands," and while "our narrative capacity . . . may make culturally mediated life possible," the stories we tell are rarely neutral (2010, 45–46). Rather, "in their very nature, [stories] inevitably throw their weight in support of or against what is culturally taken for granted, however subtly" (46). Cultures provide models, presuppositions, and perspectives about self-hood; telling others about one's self often "depends on what *we* think *they* think we ought to be like" (2002, 66, italics in original), and that means trouble.

Narrative comes about because of trouble or plight, Bruner suggests, and plight may involve a mismatch of agent, act, purpose, scene, and/or means—a pentad derived from philosopher and rhetorician Kenneth Burke (Bruner 1986, 2000, 2002; see also Rutten and Soetaert 2013). Consider the inferences of plight in Johnny's narrative at the beginning of this chapter: female and male, middle class and not yet middle class, only child and large family, ebony and plastic clarinets, first chair and second chair—all wrapped up in one paragraph, two characters, and an enormously complex context. Trouble is most certainly brewing, and even more tensions unfold as Johnny's narrative continues. For Bruner, the purpose of narrative scholarship is to understand how these particular characters, and how people in general, see and tell about themselves and their lives and to understand how they have made sense of their experiences, including their plights—"to see not what they are *about* but how the narrators construct themselves" (1987/2000, 702).

While Bruner is a principal character in this particular story of narrative scholarship, he is not a solitary figure on the pathway. In 1988, Donald Polkinghorne described the value of narrative scholarship in clinical psychology practice. By 1991, the first issue of the *Journal of Narrative and Life History* (later *Narrative Inquiry*) appeared, edited by psychologists Allyssa McCabe and Michael Bamberg, and in 1993, psychologists Amia Lieblich and Ruthellen Josselson began a series of edited books entitled *The Narrative Study of Lives*. At the same time, other social scientists also took the narrative turn. During the 1980s Ivor Goodson began a series of life history studies, including studies of teachers and schools (e.g., 1980/1981), and Elliot Mishler began to question the talk that occurred between doctors and patients during medical interviews (1984). The biennial *Narrative Matters* conference began in 1990. Just a few years later, sociologist Catherine Kohler Reismann published one of the early texts on narrative analysis (1993).

Since then, narrative research has proliferated in the social sciences, where scholars have used narrative techniques or narrative data in a wide variety of ways and within multiple kinds of research designs. Yet the Brunerian emphases on self-making and culture often remain. For example, Dan McAdams, who joined Lieblich and Josselson in co-editing the books aligned with the *Narrative Study of Lives* series, developed a life story interview protocol (McAdams 1993) that he and others have used to examine questions related to identity and self-making in life history narratives. In one study, McAdams and Bowman (2001) interrogate both how highly generative and relatively low non-generative adults narrate important turns in their lives, and how the ways in which they narrate their turning points speak more broadly to the quality of their lives. More specifically, McAdams and Bowman identify redemption and contamination sequences, or stories, in the narratives of the participants, and the authors describe how participants use these narrative strategies to make sense of their life transitions. In another study, McAdams and Logan (2006) examine "the stories academics tell about the questions, the ideas, the projects, the collaborations, the insights, and the scholarly pursuits that have animated their intellectual lives" in order to look at the intersections of their creative work and identities (89). In both studies, the life stories of participants are a primary component of the presentation of the research; the details of how the researchers conduct the study, as well as literature and theories, appear throughout rather than in separately labeled sections, except for a final discussion.

Life histories can be extensive, and yet the small stories that occur in face-to-face conversation, as well as in text messages, e-mails, and social media posts are also potential narrative data, and narrative researchers suggest that these everyday storying practices are sites of engagement for identity work (Bamberg 2006; Bamberg and Georgakopoulou 2008; Georgakopoulou 2006). For example, Georgakopoulou (2013) investigated the identities that students in a London comprehensive school constructed for themselves in their daily lives, and in particular "how the students' engagement with new media shaped their identities at school" (60). Data for the study included text message conversations, which appear in the article. Paugh (2012) examined work narratives that occurred during dinnertime conversations of dual-earner middle-class families, particularly the ways in which the dinnertime discourses socialized the children into family life and future work orientations. In both articles, the authors present small-story narratives in the form of conversations drawn from the data, then surround those conversation with an analysis of matters such as the lexical choices of the speakers, what the discourses communicate, the positioning and relationships of the story tellers, and the tensions among and between their small stories and larger canonical cultural tales.

Researchers in music education have also followed the Brunerian pathway, using narrative data and techniques to investigate questions of self-making and culture in music, often embedding narrative in research designs that appear similar to multiple case studies, single case studies, and ethnographies. Ferguson (2009), for example, examined the self-views of two preservice music educators, gathering data through conversations with them and observations of their teaching over an academic year. More specifically, Ferguson sought to understand the individuals' self-views—both those of which they were fully aware and those that appeared ambiguous or even invisible to participants—as well as how their self-views were reflected in their narratives and actions. Ferguson structures the presentation of the study similarly to many published case studies: a review of literature section and a methods section; two case presentations of the participants in narrative form; an interpretation section peppered with quotes from the participants that functions as a cross-case analysis; and a final section in which Ferguson challenges music teacher educators to consider the multiple and evolving (or not) nature of preservice teachers' self-views and the ways in which self-views, evident in their stories are connected to experiences, relationships, and meanings (101).

Margaret Barrett makes use of narrative in recent articles from her series of studies of young children's musicing (2009, 2011, 2012). Although Barrett's approach is a hybrid of all three narrative pathways described in this chapter, her focus is Brunerian in its aim at revealing children's self-making in and through music (2009), including the ways in which children construct "an emergent identity as a musical and sociocultured being" (2011, 403) and the "beginnings of an individual and personal style" in their music making (2012, 66). Barrett provides narrative descriptions of the children's spontaneous singing and musical play in all three articles, and drawing on Brunerian lines of thinking, she shows how these musical engagements occur within the small cultures of the children's families. Barrett suggests that "invented song and music-making provide narrative forms and structures through which children *perform* and *enact* ways of being in their developing identity work" (2011, 420)—a perspective clearly aligned with the Brunerian pathway in narrative scholarship.

8.1.2. Jean Clandinin and Michael Connelly and Narrative Inquiry

Clandinin and Connelly's *Narrative Inquiry: Experience and Story in Qualitative Inquiry* (2000) marks a different and well-worn pathway to narrative. Clandinin, a student of Connelly at the University of Toronto, later edited the *Handbook of Narrative Inquiry* (2007) and authored the more recent *Engaging in Narrative Inquiry* (2013), which updates her approach to narrative scholarship. Clandinin and Connelly's "Personal Experience Methods" chapter in the first Sage *Handbook of Qualitative Research* (Denzin and Lincoln 1994) points to their theoretical grounding, which, while related, is different from that of Bruner.

In their 1994 chapter, Clandinin and Connelly define narrative as both phenomenon and method:

> Narrative names the structured quality of experience to be studied, and it names the patterns of inquiry for its study. To preserve this distinction, we used the reasonably well-established device of calling the phenomenon *story* and the inquiry *narrative*. Thus we say that people by nature lead storied lives and tell stories of those lives, whereas narrative researchers describe such lives, collect and tell stories of them, and write narratives of experience. (416)

The connection between experience, story, and meaning is crucial in their approach. More than a decade later, Clandinin and Connelly clarified their definitions in this oft-quoted passage:

> Arguments for the development and use of narrative inquiry come out of a view of human experience in which humans, individually and socially, lead storied lives. People shape their daily lives by stories of who they and others are and they interpret their past in terms of these stories. Story, in the current idiom is a portal through which a person enters the world and by which his or her experience of the world is interpreted and made personally meaningful. . . . Narrative inquiry, the study of experience as story, then, is first and foremost a way of thinking about experi-ence. . . . To use narrative inquiry methodology is to adopt a particular view of expe-rience as phenomena under study. (2006, 477)

The purposes of narrative inquiry, according to Clandinin and Connelly, have to do with understanding how knowledge is narratively composed, embodied, and lived (2000, 124), in other words, to understand how people use story as a means of interpreting ex-perience, how they construct knowledge and meaning from their experiences, and how people live and relive, and tell and retell, their stories.

Clandinin and Connelly's disciplinary roots are in teacher education, teacher knowl-edge, and curriculum-making. Their approach to narrative is firmly grounded in the writings of John Dewey and a Deweyan ontology and epistemology. "Narrative in-quiry is the study of experience," they write, "and experience, as John Dewey taught, is a matter of people in relation contextually and personally" (2000, 189). The insep-arability of experience and relationship is fundamental in Clandinin and Connelly's perspective on narrative. Story is a means by which "we come in touch with our expe-rience, come to know what we know of our experience" (418–19). Experience is contin-uous, and relationship is the "middle ground" where conversation about experiences occurs, often in the form of stories (1994, 425). This Dewey-inspired conception of ex-perience and story are fundamental in Clandinin and Connelly's perspective on narra-tive; it distinguishes their position from other narrative pathways and from other kinds of qualitative approaches that, while similar, have different ontological and epistemo-logical underpinnings (see Clandinin and Rosiek 2007; Pinnegar and Hamilton 2011). Their Dewey-inspired conceptions of experience and story also have implications for how researchers conceive of and engage in narrative inquiry. If humans live storied lives, then any story one might tell or hear is not a discrete unit that can be extracted and analyzed, but rather part of a complex, continuous experiential and relational whole that must be considered throughout the research process.

Based on Dewey's theory of experience and his conceptions of situation, interaction, and continuity, Connelly and Clandinin imagine "a metaphorical three-dimensional narrative inquiry space, with temporality along one dimension, the personal and the social along a second dimension, and place along a third dimension" (50); they de-scribe these dimensions as the "three commonplaces" of narrative inquiry (2006, 479). Temporality has to do with the continuity of past, present, and future, and with how any single story exists within temporal history. The sociality commonplace includes both the personal and social conditions. Narrative inquiry focuses neither exclusively on a person's thoughts and feelings nor on studies of social conditions in which an indi-vidual may be treated as "a hegemonic expression of social structure and social process" (2006, 480); rather, narrative inquiry attends to "the personal and social and existen-tial conditions involved for various actors in the situation," including the researcher, throughout the inquiry process (480). Place, the third commonplace, has to do with "the specific concrete, physical, and topological boundaries of place," or location, where the inquiry, events, and story (including the telling and hearing) occur (480–81).

While Clandinin and Connelly assert the importance of attending to all three commonplaces in any study, they also suggest that researchers attend to four narrative directions: inward, outward, forward, and backward. Inward has to do with "feelings, hopes, aesthetic reactions, and moral disposition," outward with existential, social, and environmental conditions, and forward and backward with past, present, and fu-ture (2000, 50). They posit these directions as avenues of questioning to be pursued throughout the inquiry, commenting that "to *experience an experience*—that is, to do research into an experience—is to experience simultaneously in these four ways and to ask questions pointing each way" (50, italics in original).

While Clandinin, Connelly, and others following this pathway eschew defining a nar-rative method, they do outline certain practices or ways of being in the research (see, for example, Clandinin 2006, 2013; Clandinin and Connelly 2000; Clandinin, Pushor, and Orr 2007). Studies begin with a "research puzzle" that is framed and reframed as the study progresses. The researcher begins to think narratively about the phenomenon or experience before entering the field and upon leaving the field. Thinking narratively may include telling one's own story to oneself, not simply as a matter of being reflective, but as a matter of understanding how the story unfolds and what one's own experiences of similar phenomena or events mean in one's own life. Once in the field, researchers spend considerable time with participants, described variously as "living alongside" or "being in the midst." The participants, the researcher, and the participants and researcher together may generate data in various forms as they story and restory, tell and retell, live and relive experiences. Writing progresses gradually and moves between field texts, interim texts, and research texts, all of which are considered "composed" in that all texts are interpretations of experience. Research texts include the voices of both participants and researcher, as the inquiry and the process are part of the experience of both. The entire process is not linear, but rather involves tacking back and forth between the field, writing, field texts, research texts, participant stories, the researcher story, literature, and theory. The final published account, and the process of doing the inquiry, raises questions that invite consideration of matters of social significance and allow for growth and change (see Clandinin and Connelly 2000; Clandinin 2013).

The narrative inquiry pathway defined by Clandinin and Connelly has been highly influential in education. Narrative researchers have conducted studies of early school leavers (Clandinin, Steeves, and Caine 2013), teacher and student identities (e.g., Clandinin, J. Huber, M. Huber, Murphy, Orr, Pearce, and Steeves 2006), curriculum-making (e.g., Huber, Murphy, and Clandinin 2011), and the tensions inherent in stories of (and inquiry into) achievement testing practices and policies (e.g., Clandinin, Murphy, Huber, and Orr 2009). In an extensive series of articles spanning more than a decade, Cheryl Craig has used narrative inquiry to examine the impact of education reform on teachers, students, families, and communities (e.g., 2012a, 2012b, 2010a, 2010b), including the ways in which classrooms have become increasingly contested spaces (2009).

In music education, several researchers have followed the narrative pathway outlined by Clandinin and Connelly to inquire about experiences of teaching and learning. For example, in a series of articles from a study of second- and third-grade children, Shelly Griffin interrogates how children experience music in school and outside of school, as well as the intersections (or lack thereof) of children's in-school and out-of-school music experiences (2009, 2011b) and the social justice implications behind attending (or not attending) to children's lived musical realities (2011a). While Griffin's articles appear in different forms, the children's perspectives, as illustrated in their commentary to and conversations with Griffin, provide rather stunning (and not very flattering) views of what children think about their school musical experiences and the meanings they associate with them.

Deborah Blair's (2009) narrative inquiry in a secondary school classroom for students with special needs begins with her own story of becoming a guest music teacher in that context. While Blair includes descriptions of her interactions with the students and their responses to and participation in various musical engagements, the focus of the study turns to the ways in which the adults, particularly the classroom teacher, create an environment that fosters a sense of belonging and family in the classroom. Blair characterizes the teacher's practice as a pedagogy of thoughtfulness that provides students who struggle to make and express emotional connections with classroom a place in which risking to learn, to express, to be valued, and to be loved becomes possible (33). While Blair references Clandinin and Connelly in her description of her methods and narrative intentions, she also describes her approach as informed by arts-based educational research and the writings of Tom Barone, to whom we turn next.

8.1.3. Tom Barone, Literary Nonfiction, and Critical Storytelling

The third pathway to narrative within the music education research community follows the work of Tom Barone. Barone's work is informed by his background in literature and literary theory, and by his long association with Elliot Eisner and arts-based educational research (Barone and Eisner 2006, 2012). In *Touching Eternity: The Enduring Outcomes of Teaching* (2001) and in various essays and articles, Barone describes his work and that of others as literary or creative nonfiction (Barone 2008) and critical storytelling (Barone 2000a, 2000b). Barone holds up these narrative modes as powerful means of engaging in social science research, including educational inquiry.

Following a literary path based on the theoretical work of Mikhail Bakhtin (1975/1981), Roland Barthes (1975, 1977), Wolfgang Iser (1974, 1980, 1993), and others, Barone makes no apologies for the intentions and aims of literary nonfiction and critical storytelling. The purpose of narrativists and the aim of "researcher-storytellers," he writes, "is not to seek certainty about correct perspectives on educational phenomena but to raise significant questions about prevailing policy and practice that enrich an ongoing conversation" about education (Barone 2007, 466). Pointing to the capacity of novelists such as Charles Dickens (1839/1950; 1854/1955), Sinclair Lewis (1920), and John Updike (1959) to bring social issues to public consciousness, Barone challenges critical storytellers to be similarly rigorous in their investigations and to write in artful, honest, and powerful ways. The purpose of inquiry and of narrative writing from this perspective, Barone suggests, is "to rhetorically persuade [readers] to ask questions about important educational issues" and "to entice the reader into wondering about what has been previously taken for granted" (2001, 162, 179). The persuasive story is "one with the capacity for promoting a kind of critical reflection that results in a reconstruction of the reader's value system" (2000c, 214), or, for writers in education, to challenge and change the educational imaginary (Barone 2003).

While persuasion and the reconstruction of values may raise the metaphorical eyebrow, Barone (2000a) associates "persuasive" with *useful* in that reading persuasive texts may reorganize the reader's experiences of what seems familiar, thereby challenging habitual ways of thinking (145). In other words, the reader's interaction with the text (and author and characters) becomes "an occasion for conspiracy" in which the reader, though wary and skeptical, may come to see "a social reality that may have gone previously unnoticed," may engage in questioning and sharing of ideas, and may "plot against inadequate present conditions in favor of an emancipatory social arrangement in the future" (146). The reader, in this literary perspective, is not subservient to the author or the text, but is, rather, a thoughtful and engaged individual who can grapple with dilemmas and ambiguities in the text (and in life) and who can write and speak on her own. For Barone, whose eye is clearly toward education, the aim of narrative is to "prick the consciences of readers by inviting a re-examination of the values and interests undergirding certain discourses, practices, and institutional arrangements in today's schools" (a passage that although written in 1992 certainly continues to resonate), to make the lives of school people within that system evident to each other, and to empower them and embolden transformation.

The opening of Barone's early piece, "Ways of Being at Risk: The Case of Billy Charles Barnett" (1989), points to some of the qualities of narrative and critical storytelling that follow the literary pathway. He writes:

> We are the representatives of two subcultures, meeting at a McDonald's along an interstate highway in northeastern Tennessee. Sitting across from me is Billy Charles Barnett, a tall lanky boy with dark hair, green eyes, a pug nose, and an infectious grin. He is a member of the rural "disadvantaged," a fifteen-year-old nominated by the vice-principal as the student least likely to remain in Dusty Hollow Middle School. I am a middle-aged urban academic who, secure in a tenured university position, will never leave school.
>
> I am inclined to believe the warnings of others like me—teachers and administrators at Billy Charles' school—that this teenager from the hills will be "slow" and "hard to talk to." I am, therefore, surprised to discover almost immediately a keen intelligence and an eagerness to share his knowledge about his world. Even more jolting is a sudden realization of my vast ignorance about the ways of people who live within a two-hour drive of my home and about the fundamentals of a world no longer honored in the dominant culture.

Between slurps on a straw, Billy Charles speaks:

> You don't know what jugging is? When you go jugging, first you take a jug that bleach comes in. You rinse it out and tighten the lid and get some soft but strong nylon string. Then you need to get a two-inch turtle hook, real strong . . . and a three-or-four-foot line. The best bait is a bluegill, cut in half. You know, you really should use the head part. It's better than the tail, because turtles always go for the head of the fish first. But you can [also] catch catfish, bass, like this. I caught me a seven-and-a-half pound bass once, jugging. The jug just hangs in the water and nothing can get off the line unless they break it. I can catch a mess of turtles [this way], and then I make turtle soup. Do you know how to make turtle soup?
>
> I find myself squirming in my seat. But why should I be the one feeling inadequate and defensive? No, I didn't know—until Billy Charles told me—that the market was bearish on coonskins this year, and that I could expect no more than $40 for a flawless one of average size. The topic had simply never come up in any graduate course

on curriculum theory. Moreover, E. D. Hirsch and his co-authors had included no such items in their *Dictionary of Cultural Literacy: What Every American Needs to Know*. (Barone 1989, 147)

This passage includes several qualities of narrative consistent with critical storytelling. First, the power of the story rests, in part, in artful writing. Barone (2000b) describes the structure of the piece as a story-within-a-story-within-an-essay, wherein the central story is that of Billy Charles, the surrounding story provides a glimpse of the author, and the essay questions the meanings of the story for educators and for society, including consideration of the ways in which educators and society are implicated in the heartbreak of Billy Charles's life. Second, the piece is published without headings and references in the text, and yet, the work of rigorous scholarship is clearly evident, another quality of a well-crafted critical story. We know from the preceding passage, for example, details about the singular participant (Billy Charles), about the writer (Barone), about the research context (rural northeastern Tennessee), and, in part, about how the inquiry was conducted (through face-to-face conversation in at least one setting). Barone hints at the tensions about to be explored in the essay that follows, including the meeting of "two subcultures," the paradox of education as experienced and education as studied, and questions about epistemology and whose knowing counts, adding references as part of the story. Third, consistent with the literary theory in which Barone bases his work, we (the readers) are drawn into these tensions (note the words "surprised," "jolting," "squirming") and into the ambiguities of the text, and, even more, are invited to consider, question, and make our own interpretations. A symbiotic relationship exists between the qualities of artful writing, depth of inquiry, and faith in the reader. By the end of the essay, one wonders just who or what is at risk.

In music, Jeananne Nichols (2013) uses critical storytelling in a piece that challenges readers to consider the places and experiences of transgender students in music education. Although Nichols draws on both the Brunerian and the Clandinin and Connelly pathways, her narrative account and the approach throughout are consistent with critical storytelling—a purpose Nichols claims in the text. Her writing is literary and richly descriptive, with the participant's story as the centerpiece. She writes:

Ryan has always known two things about himself—he is musical and he is unapologetically "Rie." Friends and family struggle to describe this artistic, free spirit who dresses in short skirts and tight halter tops that reveal both an ornate chest tattoo and an Adam's apple. Faltering in their explanations, they typically fall back to, "He's just Ryan." Ryan loathes the all-too-human practice of categorizing and labeling, but suffers my "how do you identify yourself" question patiently and answers:

I consider myself transgender, but I call myself a cross-dresser because I have never taken hormones. I have never considered SRS (sexual reassignment surgery). It took me a long time to be comfortable in my skin, and now I am. I have always loved the saying, "If it ain't broke don't fix it," and that is kind of how I feel.

I met Rie in the course of my professional life as a conductor. Rie played the flute in a band I directed, but she was not my student. She projected a funny, fearless persona and I noted her acceptance and popularity with the other band members. I wondered how difficult the gender transition process had been for her, how she navigated the rural, Midwestern school system in her hometown, and if she had been supported by family, friends, and teachers. I was particularly interested in her experiences with school music, so I asked her if she would be willing to tell me her story. (Nichols 2013, 266)

Like Barone, Nichols interweaves artful writing with details of a rigorous research process. We know a great deal about the participant, a bit about the writer, something about the research context, and part of the research process in these three paragraphs. Note, too, the tensions of the transgender experience embodied in the pronoun shift between paragraphs—an intentional device that, Nichols explains later, was determined *with* Rie, who participated in every phase of the research process, right up to publication. Consistent with the aims of critical storytelling described by Barone, Nichols, along with Rie, positions the narrative not as a singular or essentialized story, but rather as an account that "offers readers the opportunity to test their own convictions, to seek their positionality within the text, to explore their identification with Rie, and to refine their insight into the responses of her peers, her parents, and her teachers" (276). Nichols' (2016) subsequent article on the ethics of writing this account are a must read for narrative scholars on any pathway.

8.2. Markers, Critiques, Possibilities

The three pathways to narrative described in this chapter are not the only story of narrative scholarship that can be told. Others have told it differently and will do so in the future. Healthy debates continue within and between those committed to each pathway about everything from definitions of narrative, to purposes of narrative scholarship, to techniques for data generation, to how to write narrative accounts. The blending and hybridization of perspectives within narrative scholarship add even more complexity. Those seeking the certainty of a straight-and-narrow research pathway or who are attracted to narrative simply by the romance of telling a story should look elsewhere.

While narrative scholarship is, as Chase (2011) suggests, "still a field in the making" (421), Barone (2009) argues that the presence of both commonalities and variegations is "a sign of the maturation of a field of study, one that refuses a tight set of methodological and definitional prescriptions, but that is still being tilled by members of a community of discourse who sense a certain degree of professional affinity" (152). The variegations may be obvious, but what are the commonalities? I posit five. First, those engaged in narrative are socially situated researchers working within a larger interpretivist community of qualitative scholars. They share with other qualitative researchers and have inherited from them fundamental (though often contested) ontological and epistemo-logical assumptions that are discussed in depth in other chapters in this *Handbook* (see Allsup, chapter 4) and elsewhere. For many, reality is a social construction that is indi-vidually understood and therefore never completely knowable; the politics of meaning, the interplay of local concerns and global conditions, and the tensions arising from them are always in play. A child's musical self evolves not only in her own backyard but also within larger social frames and cultural conditions; the lives of teachers continue to be complicated by politics and policies made by others for them and about them, but not with them; Rie continues to live her story as a transgender person within a changing social and political discourse about who others think she is or should be. Whatever nar-rative scholarship is, it falls within this basic interpretive, humanistic framework: the stories that are part of any narrative inquiry are stories of human experiences, stories of when, where, and how people are in the world, stories of self and sense, stories that are contested and contextualized. Those stories and the "sense" made from them are always provisional, always evolving.

Second, narrative work occurs with living people, over time, face to face, and usually *in the places where narrators or participants are*. While this marker may sound typical of qualitative research in general, narrative emphasizes relationship and relationality. While relationality is "not the sole prerogative of narrative inquiry, [it is] a central tenet" (Barrett and Stauffer 2009, 12) that figures into narrative work in two ways. First, stories are relational phenomena—unique to the individual, constructed from her experiences, shared between teller and listener, and told in different ways depending on time and context as well as the relationship between speaker and listener. How you tell the story of your reading of this chapter (if you do) will change depending on who you tell the story to (a confidant, a colleague, an acquaintance, a family member), when you tell it (today, tomorrow, in a month, in a year, after your next study), and where you tell it (in a cab, over dinner, at a conference, in a class). In other words, storying occurs within a speaker-listener relationship located in time and place contexts. Further, once told, the story becomes part of the relationship, a reference point, part of the experiences and the story that the speaker and listener have together. If you tell the story of reading this chapter to the same person a second time, you will not tell it in the same way or for the same reasons.

In narrative studies, researchers attend not only to the relationality of participants' stories, but also to the qualities of their relationships with participants. One-time encounters are flimsy grounds for narrative work, for they afford insufficient time for understanding plight in the Brunerian pathway, insufficient time for developing a collaborative trusting relationship in the Clandinin and Connelly pathway, and in-sufficient time to grapple with nuances and paradoxes in the Barone pathway. In nar-rative studies, the researcher is personally engaged in an ongoing relationship of trust with the participants that affords them a space in which stories—including disturbing ones—can be told. In a description of his and a colleague's research with the Goodhertz family, Bruner describes a moment when an uncomfortable conversation between two family members occurred and notes, "Like anybody invested in keeping an atmosphere congenial I took advantage of the pause that ensued to announce that a new pot of coffee had arrived. I realized only later that I was 'behaving family' " (1990, 126). Later, he notes, "When [my colleague] and I were vaguely invited by Mrs. Goodhertz to have an Italian dinner with them at home, we took it for the semiotic act that it was: *we* had become real people too, resident selves of the world that is 'home' " (135). Narrative inquiry is inquiry *with* participants.

Relationality has to do with a third marker of narrative research: that is, the data are narrative, and may include not only spoken stories and tales told in conversation, but also written stories, letters, journals, photographs, artwork, and music, as well as the researcher's story. These narrative data, these texts, are not generated through questionnaires, open-ended responses, or even sets of interview questions. Bruner comments that the "recognition that people narrativize their experience of the world and of their own role in it has . . . forced social scientists to reconsider how they use their principle instrument of research—the interview" (115). He notes that while he and his colleague planned questions for the Goodhertz family members, their visits sometimes extended for hours and unfolded in a conversational manner without occasion or need to use the prompts (125). Similarly, Chase (1995) cautions against interviews that become interrogations. Such an approach is likely to elicit dry and hollow responses aimed at pleasing the researcher rather than narratives of experience. Instead, Chase challenges researchers to create relational and conversational conditions that invite the participants' stories. Conversation rather than interrogation serves the narrative researcher well.

A fourth marker of narrative studies—analysis or, better, interpretation—is a highly contested one within the narrative community. Polkinghorne's (1995) distinction between narrative analysis and analysis of narratives provides an interesting starting point. In narrative analysis, the researcher re-stories narrative data into a plot, story, or stories consistent with narrative reasoning, whereas analysis of narratives is more consistent with paradigmatic reasoning and results in "descriptions of themes that hold across the stories or in taxonomies of types of stories, characters, or settings" (12). "In other words," Polkinghorne writes, "analysis of narratives moves from stories to common elements, and narrative analysis from elements to stories" (12). The heart of the debate begins there.

Scholars who use narrative within case studies or ethnographies may indeed code data and organize the report in various themes that emerge from the process. In Polkinghorne's terms, they are conducting "analysis of narratives," although that term is infrequently used, even in titles of articles and books explaining various procedures. Detractors of analysis of narratives argue that the parsing and coding of stories is a reductionist treatment of narrative data that serves only the researcher's interests and may render the participants' meanings and even their stories invisible. Such practices are the antithesis of narrative knowing, they argue, and are contrary to the relational ethic that underpins narrative inquiry.

Rather than parsing and coding, other narrative scholars engage in analysis via reading the generated data and writing and rewriting narrative texts in a process that deepens and refines understanding with each pass—Polkinghorne's "narrative analysis."

Matters of voice, plot, and other literary qualities become central in the writing-as-analysis process, which sometimes occurs *with* the participants instead of apart from them. Detractors of this approach argue that, narrative sensibilities aside, such processes are too intuitive. But, St. Pierre counters, "writing *is* thinking, writing *is* analysis, writing *is* indeed a seductive and tangled *method* of discovery" (in Richardson and St. Pierre 2005, 967, italics hers).

Still other narrative researchers use a combination of these approaches and more, including techniques derived from discourse analysis. Numerous authors provide descriptions of interpretive processes from different positions in the debate, usually using the term *narrative analysis* (even when outlining what Polkinghorne would describe as analysis of narratives) or sometimes avoiding the word "analysis" altogether (e.g., Clandinin 2013; Daiute and Lightfoot 2004; Gubrium and Holstein 2012; Reissman 1993, 2008; Squire, Andrews, and Tamboukou 2008). Regardless of approach, interpretive processes are neither ready-formed nor linear, but rather invented within the context of each study and composed of multiple recursive moves between data, work in the field, literature and theory, and writing.

These recursive moves are interpretive ones, raising questions of whose interpretations or which interpretations matter. Most stories have multiple meanings, therefore multiple possible interpretations. While one interpretation may be different from another, one interpretation is not necessarily better than another. Cape and Nichols (2012) illustrate this quality of openness to multiple interpretations in an account of the stories of two women who served in military bands in the United States and Canada from World War II through 1961. They present an interpretation in which the women "carve out a place for themselves in a domain not accustomed to women," thereby "[easing] the way for subsequent generations of female musicians" (29). However, during their recursive moves between participants, fieldwork, data, and writing, the women in their study suggest to Cape and Nichols that while this interpretation is indeed credible, their experience at the time was more of a "grand adventure" that continues to play out in their lives and which they recount with pride (33–34). Cape and Nichols present both interpretations in the published account, refusing to position one over the other. They challenge narrative scholars and their readers to "imagine the possibilities" and to remain "open to ambiguities" of multiple interpretive moves (35).

The fifth marker of narrative inquiry has to do with writing, including qualities of writing and the ways in which narrative appears in published accounts. As illustrated by the examples in this chapter, the forms and formats for publishing narrative studies vary extensively. To be clear, there is no standard narrative article, chapter, or dissertation structure. At their most conservative, authors use formats similar to well-worn positivist articles, complete with headings and sections that begin with literature review and end with discussion. However, other structures are also common in the narrative literature, including forms in which storied passages are supported by essay or essay-like writing designed to engaged the reader in questioning. Such accounts include the voices of participants and researcher, as well as connections to the literature and theorizing moves, though not necessarily in any anticipated ordering or imposed structure.

The writing in such accounts is literary, metaphoric, artful, but not at the expense of the detail required of scholars. Consider the passages of narrative included in this chapter, which are thick with detail communicated in artful ways. Honing writing ability is crucial. Narrative requires writing design choices—symbolism, plot, foreshadowing, juxtaposition, motif, turning point, dénouement. Narrative accounts include the voice of the author, but not at the expense of the participants' voices, stories, and meanings. A researcher fully invested in the assumptions of narrative inquiry simply cannot write "my study," "my data," or "my participants." Narrative researchers do not own the people, the data, or the research. Rather, narrative scholars live and study *with* those who choose to allow researchers to talk with them, listen to them, and hold up their stories for others to hear. Finally, narrative writing places faith in the reader, leaving open spaces for the reader to engage with the text and the story, to wonder and to question. There are no "conclusions" and often no recommendations. In narrative scholarship, the reader is the author of what comes next.

The five markers suggested here are full of internal tensions. Like good stories open to multiple interpretations, the pathways in narrative scholarship are not clearly hewn trails. So, how might narrative inquiry be assessed? Elsewhere, Margaret Barrett and I have written about narrative inquiry as resonant work composed of four intertwined and inseparable qualities: respect, responsibility, rigor, and resiliency (Stauffer and Barrett 2009; Barrett and Stauffer 2012). Respect has to do with the relational qualities of the narrative work. Beyond acts of deference and civility, narrative inquirers respect the integrity of narrator-participants as persons with stories and meanings of their own, told in their own languages and gestures that are deeply embedded in their lives and lifeways. Responsibility has to do not only with the procedural concerns and the obligation to demonstrate trustworthiness, but also with conscious and continuous attention to the well-being of the participants, one's self, and the public good as well as one's professional community, and to the potential impacts of inquiry throughout the immediate research process and beyond.

Rigor in narrative research inheres not only in the attention to details throughout, but in the recursive shifting from fieldwork to literature to writing, and in the researcher's ability to act reflexively, examining her own values, motivations, and assumptions at every turn. Rigor also has to do with purpose. Narrative inquiry in music education is not mere storytelling; rather, narrative inquiry in music education is scholarly engagement with stories of experience as a means of interrogating critical matters in education, in music, in the world. Finally, resiliency has to do with the researcher's ability to grapple with persistent questions and to be open to new means and meanings in thinking and practice while remaining grounded in the epistemological underpinnings of narrative. Rather than a way of doing, resonant work is as a way of *being* in narrative research—a conscious ethic enacted and embodied by narrative researchers. I suggest here that narrative accounts might be assessed with a view to the qualities of resonant work as well, and that the power of narrative inquiry lies, in part, in the ability of the researcher to do resonant work.

Attending to the qualities of resonant work may help narrative inquirers avoid and address some of the criticisms leveled at narrative scholarship. One criticism is that narrative research and writing is a self-indulgent navel-gazing exercise. This occurs when narrative inquirers lose sight of the participants and become enamored with their own role in the study. Another criticism is that narrative research is an excuse for telling "nice" stories. This occurs when the researcher becomes more entranced by a story than attentive to the experiences and meanings that the story represents. Another criticism is that narratives are valorizing tales. This occurs when narrative scholars essentialize participants or their stories through some poorly conceived notion of giving them voice without thinking about social and political contexts. Another reservation is that the stories people tell are things of the past, prone to misrememberings and fictionalizations, and therefore inappropriate grounds for scholarship in the first place. Narrative scholarship is not about measuring the accuracy of detail, but rather about the constructing of selves and meanings and lives in a world where ambiguity is the normal state of affairs. Still another criticism is that narrative research suffers from the tyranny of the local—a charge leveled at qualitative research in general. Yet what we know of the larger world we know through the particular instances of our own experiences. What readers gain from the particular stories of Johnny or Billy Charles or Rie or anyone is insight into larger questions and problems of the human condition.

Why narrative, why now? Well-wrought critical stories raise questions that provoke readers to dig deep and think again, from a different perspective. Narrative scholarship can empower researchers, readers, and the participant storytellers to question, to think, to act, and to question yet again. The power of narrative inquiry lies in the possibility of troubling certainty and, once troubled, in the possibility of change.

NOTE

1. Thank you to Jeananne Nichols, University of Illinois, for critical commentary on drafts of this chapter.

REFERENCES

Andrews, M., C. Squire, and M. Tamboukou. 2008. *Doing Narrative Research.* Thousand Oaks, CA: Sage Publications.
Bakhtin, M. 1975/1981. *The Dialogic Imagination: Four Essays.* Austin: University of Texas Press.
Bamberg, M. 2006. "Stories: Big or Small? Why Do We Care?" *Narrative Inquiry* 16: 147–55.
Bamberg, M., and A. Georgakopoulou. 2008. "Small Stories as a New Perspective in Narrative and Identity Analysis." *Text and Talk* 28: 377–96.
Barone, T. 1989. "Ways of Being at Risk: The Case of Billy Charles Barnett." *Phi Delta Kappan* 71 (2): 147–51.
Barone, T. 2000a. "Using the Narrative Text as an Occasion for Conspiracy." In *Aesthetics, Politics, and Educational Inquiry: Essays and Examples,* edited by T. Barone, 137–60. New York: Peter Lang.
Barone, T. 2000b. "Beyond Theory and Method: A Case of Critical Storytelling." In *Aesthetics, Politics, and Educational Inquiry: Essays and Examples,* edited by T. Barone, 191–200. New York: Peter Lang.

Barone, T. 2000c. "A Narrative of Enhanced Professionalism: Educational Researchers and Popular Storybooks about Schoolpeople." In *Aesthetics, Politics, and Educational Inquiry: Essays and Examples*, edited by T. Barone, 201–28. New York: Peter Lang.

Barone, T. 2001. *Touching Eternity: The Enduring Outcomes of Teaching*. New York: Teachers College Press.

Barone, T. 2003. "Challenging the Educational Imaginary: Issues of Form, Substance, and Quality in Film-Based Research." *Qualitative Inquiry* 9: 202–17.

Barone, T. 2007. "A Return to the Gold Standard? Questioning the Future of Narrative Construction as Educational Research." *Qualitative Inquiry* 13: 454–70.

Barone, T. 2008. "Creative Nonfiction and Social Research." In *Handbook of the Arts in Qualitative Research*, edited by J. G. Knowles and A. L. Cole, 105–16. Thousand Oaks, CA: Sage Publications.

Barone, T. 2009. "Commonalities and Variegations: Notes on the Maturation of the Field of Narrative Research." *The Journal of Educational Research* 103: 149–53. DOI: 10.1080/00220670903333189.

Barone, T., and E. Eisner. 2006. "Arts-Based Educational Research." In *Handbook of Complementary Methods in Education Research*, edited by J. L. Green, G. Camilli, and P. B. Elmore, 95–109. Mahwah, NJ: Lawrence Erlbaum Associates.

Barone, T., and E. W. Eisner. 2012. *Arts-Based Research*. Thousand Oaks, CA: Sage Publications.

Barrett, M. S. 2009. "Sounding Lives in and through Music: A Narrative Inquiry of the 'Everyday' Musical Engagement of a Young Child." *Journal of Early Childhood Research* 7: 115–34.

Barrett, M. S. 2011. "Musical Narratives: A Study of a Young Child's Identity Work in and through Music-Making." *Psychology of Music* 39: 402–23.

Barrett, M. S. 2012. "Preparing the Mind for Musical Creativity: Early Music Learning and Engagement." In *Musical Creativity: Insights from Music Education Research*, edited by O. Odena, 51–71. Surrey, UK: Ashgate.

Barrett, M. S., and S. L. Stauffer. 2009. "Narrative Inquiry: From Story to Method." In *Narrative Inquiry in Music Education: Troubling Certainty*, edited by M. S. Barrett and S. L. Stauffer, 7–17. Dordrecht, The Netherlands: Springer.

Barrett, M. S., and S. L. Stauffer. 2012. "Resonant Work: Toward an Ethic of Narrative Research." In *Narrative Soundings: An Anthology of Narrative Inquiry in Music Education*, edited by M. S. Barrett and S. L. Stauffer, 1–17. Dordrecht, The Netherlands: Springer.

Barthes, R. 1975. *The Pleasure of the Text*. Translated by R. Miller. New York: Hill and Wang.

Barthes, R. 1977. "The Death of the Author." In *Images, Music, Text*, edited by R. Barthes, 142–48. New York: Hill and Wang.

Blair, D. 2009. "Nurturing Music Learners in Mrs. Miller's 'Family Room': A Secondary Classroom for Students with Special Needs." *Research Studies in Music Education* 31: 20–36.

Bowman, W. 2006. "Why Narrative? Why Now?". *Research Studies in Music Education* 27: 5–20.

Bruner, J. 1986. *Actual Minds, Possible Worlds*. Cambridge, MA: Harvard University Press.

Bruner, J. 1987/2004. "Life a Narrative." *Social Research* 71: 691–710. First published in *Social Research* 54 (Spring 1987).

Bruner, J. 1990. *Acts of Meaning*. Cambridge, MA: Harvard University Press.

Bruner, J. 1991. "The Narrative Construction of Reality." *Critical Inquiry* 18 (1): 1–21.

Bruner, J. 2002. *Making Stories: Law, Literature, Life*. Cambridge, MA: Harvard University Press.

Bruner, J. 2010. "Narrative, Culture, and Mind." In *Telling Stories: Language, Narrative, and Social Life*, edited by D. Schiffrin, A. De Fina, and A. Nylund, 45–50. Washington, DC: Georgetown University Press.

Cape, J., and Nichols, J. 2012. "Engaging Stories: Constructing Narratives of Women's Military Band Members." In *Narrative Soundings: An Anthology of Narrative Inquiry in Music Education*, edited by M. S. Barrett and S. L. Stauffer, 21–35. Dordrecht, The Netherlands: Springer.

Chase, S. 1995. "Taking Narrative Seriously: Consequences for Method and Theory in Interview Studies." In *Interpreting Experience: The Narrative Study of Lives,*" vol. 3, edited by R. Josselson and A. Lieblich, 1–26. Thousand Oaks, CA: Sage Publications.

Chase, S. 2011. "Narrative Inquiry: Still a Field in the Making." In *The SAGE Handbook of Qualitative Research*, edited by N. K. Denzin and Y. S. Lincoln, 421–34. Thousand Oaks, CA: Sage Publications.

Clandinin, D. J. 2006. "Narrative Inquiry: A Methodology for Studying Lived Experience." *Research Studies in Music Education* 27: 44–53.

Clandinin, D. J., ed. 2007. *Handbook of Narrative Inquiry: Mapping a Methodology*. Thousand Oaks, CA: Sage Publications.

Clandinin, D. J. 2013. *Engaging in Narrative Inquiry*. Walnut Creek, CA: Left Coast Press.

Clandinin, D. J., and F. M. Connelly. 1994. "Personal Experience Methods." In *Handbook of Qualitative Research*, edited by N. K. Denzin and Y. S. Lincoln, 413–27). Thousand Oaks, CA: Sage.

Clandinin, D. J., and F. M. Connelly. 2000. *Narrative Inquiry: Experience and Story in Qualitative Research*. San Francisco: Jossey-Bass.

Clandinin, D. J., J. Huber, M. Huber, M.S. Murphy, A. M. Orr, M. Pearce, and P. Steeves. 2006. *Composing Diverse Identities: Narrative Inquires into the Interwoven Lives of Children and Teachers*. New York: Routledge.

Clandinin, D. J., and M. S. Murphy. 2009. "Comments on Coulter and Smith: Relational Ontological Commitments in Narrative Research." *Educational Researcher* 38: 596–602.

Clandinin, D. J., M. S. Murphy, J. Huber, and A. M. Orr. 2009. "Negotiating Narrative Inquires: Living in a Tension-Filled Midst." *The Journal of Educational Research* 103 (2): 81–90.

Clandinin, D. J., D. Pushor, and A. M. Orr. 2007. "Navigating Sites for Narrative Inquiry." *Journal of Teacher Education* 58: 21–35.

Clandinin, D. J., and J. Rosiek. 2007. "Mapping a Landscape of Narrative Inquiry: Borderland Spaces and Territories." In *Handbook of Narrative Inquiry: Mapping a Methodology*, edited by J. D. Clandinin, 35–75. Thousand Oaks, CA: Sage Publications.

Clandinin, D. J., P. Steeves, and V. Caine. 2013. *Composing Lives in Transition: A Narrative Inquiry into the Experiences of Early School Leavers*. Bingley, UK: Emerald Group.

Connelly, F. M., and D. J. Clandinin. 2006. "Narrative Inquiry." In *Handbook of Complementary Methods in Education Research*, edited by J. L. Green, G. Camilli, and P. B. Elmore, 477–502. Washington, DC: American Educational Research Association.

Craig, C. J. 2009. "The Contested Classroom Space: A Decade of Lived Educational Policy in Texas Schools." *American Educational Research Journal* 46: 1034–59.

Craig, C. J. 2010a. "Evaluation Gone Awry: The Teacher Experience of the Summative Evaluation of a School Reform Initiative." *Teaching and Teacher Education* 26: 1290–99.

Craig, C. J. 2010b. "Research on the Boundaries: Narrative Inquiry in the Midst of Organized School Reform." *The Journal of Educational Research* 103: 123–36.

Craig, C. J. 2012a. "Butterfly under a Pin: An Emergent Teacher Image amid Mandated Curricular Reform." *The Journal of Educational Research* 105: 90–101.

Craig, C. J. 2012b. "Tensions in Teacher Development and Community: Variations on a Recurring School Reform Theme." *Teachers College Record* 114 (2). Online http://www.tcrecord.org.

Daiute, C., and C. Lightfoot, eds. 2004. *Studying the Development of Individuals in Society.* Thousand Oaks, CA: Sage Publications.

Denzin, N. K., and Y. S. Lincoln. 1994. *Handbook of Qualitative Research.* Thousand Oaks, CA: Sage Publications.

Dickens, C. 1839/1950. *The Life and Adventures of Nicholas Nickleby.* Oxford: Oxford University Press.

Dickens, C. 1854/1955. *Hard Times for These times.* Oxford: Oxford University Press.

Ferguson, K. 2009. "Filtered through the Lens of Self: Experiences of Two Preservice Music Teachers." In *Narrative Inquiry in Music Education: Troubling Certainty,* edited by M. S. Barrett and S. L. Stauffer, 87–106. Dordrecht, The Netherlands: Springer.

Georgakopoulou, A. 2006. "Thinking Big with Small Stories in Narrative and Identity Analysis." *Narrative Inquiry* 16: 122–30.

Georgakopoulou, A. 2013. "Small Stories and Identities Analysis as a Framework for the Study of Im/politeness-in-Interaction." *Journal of Politeness Research: Language, Behaviour, Culture* 9: 55–74.

Goodson, I. 1980/1981. "Life Histories and the Study of Schooling." *Interchange* 4 (11): 62–76.

Griffin, S. M. 2009. "Listening to Children's Music Perspectives: In- and out-of-School Thoughts." *Research Studies in Music Education* 31: 161–77.

Griffin, S. M. 2011a. "The Social Justice behind Children's Tales of in- and out-of-School Music Experiences." *Bulletin of the Council for Research in Music Education* 188: 72–92.

Griffin, S. M. 2011b. "Through the Eyes of children: Telling Insights into Music Experiences." *Visions of Research in Music Education* 19. Retrieved from http://www-usr.rider.edu/vrme~/

Holstein, J. A., and J. F. Gubrium, eds. 2012. *Varieties of Narrative Analysis.* Thousand Oaks, CA: Sage Publications.

Huber, J., M. S. Murphy, and D. J. Clandinin. 2011. *Places of Curriculum Making: Narrative Inquiries into Children's Lives in Motion.* Bingley, UK: Emerald Group.

Iser, W. 1974. *The Implied Reader.* Baltimore, MD: Johns Hopkins University Press.

Iser, W. 1980. "The Reading Process: A Phenomenological Approach." In *Reader-Response Criticism: From Formalism to Post-Structuralism,* edited by J. P. Thompkins, 50–69. Baltimore, MD: Johns Hopkins University Press.

Iser, W. 1993. *The Fictive and the Imaginary: Charting Literary Anthropology.* Baltimore, MD: Johns Hopkins University Press.

Lewis, S. 1920. *Main Street.* New York: Harcourt, Brace, and World.

McAdams, D. P. 1993. *The Stories We Live by: Personal Myths and the Making of the Self.* New York: William Morrow.

McAdams, D. P., and P. J. Bowman. 2001. "Narrating Life's Turning Points: Redemption and Contamination." In *Turns in the Road: Narrative Studies of Lives in Transition,* edited by D. P. McAdams, R. Josselson, and A. Lieblich, 3–34. Washington, DC: American Psychological Association.

McAdams, D. P., and R. L. Logan. 2006. "Creative Work, Love, and the Dialectic in Selected Life Stories of Academics." In *Identity and Story: Creating Self in Narrative,* 89–108. Washington, DC: American Psychological Association.

Mishler, E. G. 1984. *The Discourse of Medicine: Dialectics of Medical Interviews.* Norwood, NJ: Ablex.

Nichols, J. 2013. "Rie's Story, Ryan's Journey: Music in the Life of a Transgender Student." *Journal of Research in Music Education* 61: 262–79.

Nichols, J. 2016. "Sharing the Stage: Ethical Dimensions of Narrative Inquiry in Music Education." *Journal of Research in Music Education* 63: 439–54.

Paugh, A. 2012. "Speculating about Work: Dinnertime Narratives among Dual-Earner American Families." *Text and Talk* 32: 615–36.

Pinnegar, S., and J. D. Daynes. 2007. "Situating Narrative Inquiry." In *Handbook of Narrative Inquiry: Mapping a Methodology*, edited by J. D. Clandinin, 3–34. Thousand Oaks, CA: Sage Publications.

Pinnegar, S., and M. L. Hamilton. 2011, "Narrating the Tensions of Teacher Educator Researcher in Moving Story to Research." In *Narrative Inquiries into Curriculum Making in Teacher Education, Advances in Research on Teaching*, vol. 13, edited by J. Kitchen, D. C. Parker, and D. Pushor 43–68. Bingley, UK: Emerald Group.

Polkinghorne, D. E. 1988. *Narrative Knowing and the Human Sciences*. Albany: State University of New York Press.

Polkinghorne, D. E. 1995. "Narrative Configuration in Qualitative Analysis." *International Journal of Qualitative Studies* 8: 5–23.

Reissman, C. K. 1993. *Narrative Analysis*. Qualitative Research Methods Series, Vol. 30. Newbury Park, CA: Sage Publications.

Reissman, C. K. 2008. *Narrative Methods for the Human Sciences*. Thousand Oaks, CA: Sage Publications.

Richardson, L., and E. A. St. Pierre. 2005. "Writing: A Method of Inquiry." In *The Sage Handbook of Qualitative Research*, 3rd ed., edited by N. K. Denzin and Y. S. Lincoln, 959–78. Thousand Oaks, CA: Sage Publications.

Rutten, K., and R. Soetaert. 2013. "Narrative and Rhetorical Approaches to Problems of Education. Jerome Bruner and Kenneth Burke Revisited." *Studies in Philosophy and Education* 32, 327–43.

Saldaña, J. 2008. "Second Chair: An Autoethnodrama." *Research Studies in Music Education* 30 (2): 177–91.

Squire, C., M. Andrews, and M. Tomboukou. 2008. "Introduction: What Is Narrative Research?" In *Doing Narrative Research*, edited by M. Andrews, C. Squire, and M. Tamboukou, 1–21. London: Sage Publications.

Stauffer, S. L., and M. S. Barrett. 2009. "Narrative Inquiry in Music Education: Toward Resonant Work." In *Narrative Inquiry in Music Education: Troubling Certainty*, edited by M. S. Barrett and S. L. Stauffer, 19–29. Dordrecht, The Netherlands: Springer.

Updike, J. 1959. *Pigeon Feathers and Other Stories*. New York: Fawcett Books.

CHAPTER 9

PRACTITIONER INQUIRY

JANET ROBBINS

9.1. Defining Qualities
of Practitioner Inquiry

> As more teachers become researchers in their schools and classrooms,
> they explore innovative forms and formats for documenting class-
> room activities, interrogating conventional assumptions about the re-
> search itself, and questioning relationships between researchers and the
> researched.
>
> (Cochran-Smith and Lytle 1993, 40)

TEACHERS who are researching their own practice are part of a "wonderful new breed of artists-in-residence" who are using their classrooms as settings for studying teaching and learning (Hubbard and Power 2003, xiii). They are practicing a form of educational research known as *practitioner inquiry* that involves systematic and intentional inquiry of their own practice and their students' learning. Given the many genres of practitioner inquiry, it is not surprising that the answer to the question, "What is practitioner inquiry?" is complicated. *Teacher research* and *action research* are two of the more widely known approaches of practitioner inquiry, but the current landscape includes many versions and variants, such as participatory action research, self-study, and the scholarship of teaching (Cochran-Smith and Donnell 2006; Zeichner and Noffke 2001). This chapter will take an expanded view of practitioner inquiry in music education to include multiple traditions being conducted by P–12 teachers, graduate students, teacher candidates, and teacher educators.

Despite differences in various genres of practitioner inquiry, there are several defining qualities that connect and cut across multiple traditions. At the heart of all intellectual traditions of practitioner inquiry is an assumption that teachers' intimate knowledge of teaching provides an important "insider" perspective on teaching and learning. Researching teachers recognize the value of looking at daily routines and examining (as anthropologists have always done) the "humdrum elements of experience (Jackson 1968, 4). When teachers' classrooms become inquiry sites for intentional and systematic inquiry of their own teaching and students' learning, they become knowers and producers of knowledge, rather than consumers of knowledge being worked out somewhere else by someone else. In one sense they are "students of teaching" (Bullough and Gitlin 1995), open to new approaches, curious about students' learning, and intent on understanding "both the impact and the limitation of what they are doing" (Perl and Wilson 1988, 252).

The symbiotic relationship between inquiry and practice is another defining quality of practitioner inquiry. Researching teachers assume dual roles as researcher and teacher, negotiating the borders between research and practice in ways that raise questions about "what can be known about teaching, who can know it, how it can be known, and how that knowledge can be used" (Cochran-Smith and Lytle 1993, 40). Questions driving practitioner inquiry derive from teachers' observations and reflections on real-world dilemmas, a curiosity about students' perspectives, and tensions related to daily practices or larger professional issues. Ann Berthoff's (1987) idea of RE-searching practice involves looking and looking again at what happens in the classroom. "We do not need new information; we need to think about the information we have . . . to interpret what goes on . . . and interpret our interpretations" (1987, 30).

Although some practitioner research looks "remarkably similar to traditional forms of empirical or interpretative research," many researching teachers design innovative data collection techniques that function naturally and organically within teaching schedules and daily routines. (Noffke 2009, 7). Teacher and student journals, observational notes, anecdotal records, interviews, surveys, audio and video recordings, photographs, students' work, and classroom artifacts are all of part of the "artist's toolbox" that Hubbard and Power discuss in their chapter on strategies for data collection (2003). They argue that "research is both art and craft" and recommend using multiple data-collection tools in some combination. Their chapter, "The Artist's Toolbox: Strategies for Data Collection," is an excellent resource for teachers embarking on classroom research for the first time.

A successful research design is flexible, innovative, and deliberate rather than spontaneous, occurring within phases of problem-posing, application, and recasting practice. Data collection and analysis may vary according to theoretical frameworks but are closely tied to specific needs of students and core theories of teaching. "Teacher research doesn't have to involve hundreds of students, establish control groups and perform complex statistical analyses; nor does it start with a hypothesis to test; instead teacher researchers begin with wonderings to pursue" (Bissex 1987, 3).

Practitioner inquiry is often a collaborative enterprise aimed at social change. Knowledge about teaching and learning is constructed by school-based teachers, administrators, university researchers, or parents and community activists (Cochran-Smith and Donnell 2006) working in the same school, across sites, in learning communities, and through networks. Reciprocity and shared decision-making enable teachers to move back and forth equitably within each other's worlds, listening and learning from each other.

Finally, practitioner inquiry can be a "path to empowerment" (Kinchloe 1991) when participants are mindful of the personal, professional, and political dimensions and purposes of practitioner inquiry (Noffke 2009). Such purposes reach beyond a "close-up" view of teaching in ways that challenge the status quo and taken-for-granted assumptions about forms of knowledge (Zeichner and Noffe 2001). Practitioner inquiry is aimed at "breaking the silence" and raising the voices of teachers and students at all levels in ways that are emancipatory and transformative (McDonald 1986).

9.2. CONNECTING TO THE ROOTS OF PRACTITIONER INQUIRY

A paradigm shift in the 1980s supported a different view of teacher—as knower, thinker, and *re*-searcher (Berthoff 1987) who did not necessarily need more findings about best practice produced by university-based researchers, but instead found greater relevance in dialogue with other teachers who would generate theories about teaching grounded in practice (Cochran-Smith and Lytle 1999). A number of intellectual traditions and educational projects sparked renewed interest in action research and the emergence of the North American teacher research movement (Zeichner and Noffke 2001; Cochran-Smith and Lytle 1999).

Eleanor Duckworth's (1987) notion of teaching *as* research opened the door for teachers to document their students' work through observation and inquiry, which positioned them as expert knowers of their own students and classrooms (Cochran-Smith and Lytle 1992, 16). Shulman's work with the Carnegie Foundation was another initiative that supported teachers-as-knowers and as "authorities in their own right" (Leglar and Collay 2002, 856). To engage in excellent teaching, Shulman argued, was indeed a scholarly act (Shulman 2011, 3). Schön was another who changed the conversation in teacher education by extending Dewey's notion of teachers as *reflective practitioners* (Leglar and Collay 2002, 859–60). The increased inclusion of inquiry-centered approaches in university methods courses, as well as a growing acceptance of graduate-level research that used teacher research and action research methodologies, provided momentum for the practitioner inquiry movement.

All of these efforts to professionalize the teaching force emphasized teachers' critical role in school change and educational reform. At the center of the reform are the varied traditions of practitioner inquiry. Despite the different histories and purposes of these traditions, it is useful to note that action research, teacher research, self-study, and communities of practice all remain "grounded in a respect for the intellectual work of teaching, and all are concerned about the way professional and cultural discourses can distort teachers' thinking and practice" (Rosiek and Atkinson 2005, 422).

9.2.1. Action Research

Action research is an international movement with a long history and a host of predecessors (Noffke 1994). Many attribute the term "action research" to Kurt Lewin, a social psychologist who viewed action research as a means to "counteract racial prejudice, to reform agricultural practices, and to promote more democratic forms of leadership in the workplace" (Zeichner and Noffke 2001, 301). Lewin was interested in improving the work of "ordinary people," and his work at the Research Center for Group Dynamics at MIT in the 1940s represented a "radical new direction for research in psychology" (Somekh and Zeichner 2009, 8). Adelman's (1993) discussion of the origin of action research is useful in linking Lewinian traditions of "action science" grounded in social psychology with concepts of educational action research (13).

Corey was one of the first to use action research in education. He and colleagues at the Horace-Mann-Lincoln Institute of School Experimentation at Columbia University worked cooperatively with teachers and administrators in school districts across the United States in the late 1940s and 1950s (Zeichner and Noffke 2001, 301), advocating for teachers to conduct research on their own practices as one way to address the gap that existed between research and practice.

A resurgence of action research in the 1970s and 1980s is evident in the "teacher-as-research" movement spearheaded by Lawrence Stenhouse and John Elliott in the United Kingdom. The transformative intentions and a commitment to curriculum innovation and reform characterized the movement, and Stenhouse's vision for "democratizing research as a way to emancipate practitioners and genuinely improve practice" became a widely accepted premise of action research (Cochran-Smith and Lytle 1999, 16). Like Stenhouse, Elliott (2006) recognized the democratic nature of action research, promoting research *in* education shaped by practitioners' practical theory and knowledge, as opposed to research *on* education influenced by a "spectator theory" of knowledge (179).

Participatory action research was another variant emerging in Australia as part of a "broad ranging movement toward collaborative curriculum planning" (Noffke 1994). The critical theory framework of participatory action research (Carr and Kemmis 1986) was reflective of Lewin's emancipatory vision to improve students' education and resist oppressive conditions in schools (Somekh and Zeichner 2009, 8).

Research methods are characterized most notably by a cyclical and reflexive design. Lewin's early model of action research consisted of "moments of action" that proceeded in a spiral of steps: planning, action, observation, and reflection or evaluation of the result of the action (Kemmis and McTaggart 1988, 8). Elliott argued that action research was not a "unique research paradigm in terms of data collection methods" (Zeichner and Noffke 2001, 302) but rather a process of phases or cycles. Teachers would first identify a pedagogical aim or ideal; following that, they would gather and interpret evidence to examine the ways their practice was or was not consistent with realizing that aim; finally they would reflect on, develop, and test possible strategies and solutions (Elliott

2006). The overlapping of action and reflection were necessary for a flexible and responsive design aimed at studying change and the "intended and unintended consequences" of innovations and interventions teachers plan and carry out (Cain 2008, 284).

9.2.2. Teacher Research

Tracing the roots of the teacher research movement, one finds a discourse dominated by "dissatisfaction with business as usual" and tensions related to the way university-generated research was assumed to encompass everything one needed to know about teaching (Cochran-Smith and Lytle 2010). *Reclaiming the Classroom* (1987) by Goswami and Stillman and *Seeing for Ourselves* (1987) by Bissex and Bullock are two early publications that provide exemplars of classroom-based studies and illuminate the work of researching teachers who are challenging the status quo.

Many factors led to the emergence of the North American Teacher Research Movement in the 1980s (Zeichner and Noffke 2001, 303). Among those were the pioneering work of writing teacher Nancie Atwell (1989), who developed case studies on the teaching of writing with the Breadloaf Project and Patricia Carini's "Descriptive Review of a Child," a collaborative inquiry process used at the Prospect School to examine children's growth and learning (Carini 2001).

Cochran-Smith and Lytle's 1993 landmark book, *Inside-Outside: Teacher Research and Knowledge*, provides a comprehensive view of the history and scope of teacher research traditions. Of particular interest is their working typology that groups teachers' research in two broad categories: classroom studies (empirical research) and teachers' essays on school life (conceptual research) that are more theoretical and philosophical in nature. Vivian Paley's *The Girl with the Brown Crayon* (1997) and Sylvia Ashton-Warner's *Teacher* (1963) are examples of well-known, firsthand accounts of teachers' struggles and solutions written *by* teachers.

Teacher research is most often associated with classroom studies characterized by *systematic and intentional inquiry*. Intentionality "signals teachers' deliberate and planned (rather than spontaneous) inquiry" (Cochran-Smith and Lytle 1993, 23–24) that embodies a recursive process. Although not as cyclical in design as action research, Cochran-Smith and Lytle suggest that teacher research emerged from Lewin's action research principles as well as Dewey's vision of teachers as students of learning (9). Like its qualitative ancestor ethnography, data in teacher research come from multiple sources, including teacher journals, student logs, videotaped lessons, simple surveys, and interviews.

Studies are often conducted by school-based teachers in collaboration with university-based colleagues and are shaped by teachers in ways that give the work a "distinctly grassroots character" (Cochran-Smith and Lytle 1999, 16). The University of Pennsylvania and Philadelphia-area schools have a long-standing tradition of collaboration. Many of the teachers present their research at the Teacher Research Day that was established in 1986 as part of the University of Pennsylvania's Annual Ethnography and Education Forum.

9.2.3. Self-Study

Self-study is a form of practitioner inquiry conducted almost exclusively by teacher educators who are interested in interrogating self, their practice, and reinventing teacher education. Many self-study researchers "moved into the area of self-study through [their] involvement in action research" (Samaras and Freese 2009, 5) and began *doing* research rather than simply teaching students how to engage in research. Two developments that influenced the emergence of self-study were the acceptance of qualitative research methods in education and new notions about the relationship between research and practice prompted by the action research movement (Bullough and Pinnegar 2001, 13). The reflective practitioner movement was another influence that draws upon Dewey's concept of reflection; it should be purposeful, seek to solve a problem, and lead to a deeper understanding of students and practices, resulting in a view of new possibilities (Dinkleman 2003, 7).

Self-study emerged in the 1990s and gained momentum through a special interest group that formed within the American Educational Research Association in 1993. "The establishment of S-STEP [Self-Study of Teacher Education Practices] proved to be a significant turning point in creating a community of self-study researchers (Samaras and Freese 2009, 6). In 1996, the first Castle Conference in Castle, England, drew researchers together from around the world; it continues to be a valuable forum for exploring philosophy, methodologies, and self-study practices.

Self-study "operates from the post-modern assumption that it is never possible to divorce the self from either the research process or from educational practice" (Cochran-Smith and Donnell 2006, 506). Knowledge production begins with thoughtful reflection on one's own practice and questions that "arise from concerns about and interest in the self-as-teacher educator with others in context, over time. . . ." The "focus is not on the self per se, but on the space between self and the practice engaged in" (Bullough and Pinnegar 2001, 15).

Research tipping too far toward self and confessional reporting has little chance of generating conversations about broader issues or affecting change. Samaras and Freese (2009) posit that what distinguishes self-study from action research is a focus on who the researcher *is* more than what the researcher *does*, with a focus on "reframing and reconceptualizing the role of the teacher" (5).

Self-study uses multiple qualitative research approaches such as biography, personal history, memory work, reflective portfolios, and narrative inquiry (Samaras and Freese 2009). Narrative accounts resembling essays found in the North American Teacher Research movement, as well as story and metaphor, are sometimes used to "bring the discipline of teaching to life" (Loughran and Russell 2007, 225). The multiple methodologies and emphases within self-study research make it difficult to pin down a definition, although some argue that it is not possible or even desirable, since self-study's inclusive nature is an important characteristic (Samaras and Freese 2009, 11; Bullough and Pinnegar 2001).

9.2.4. Communities of Practice

Although working collaboratively is a common practice across all genres of practitioner inquiry, research taking place within "communities of practice" is gaining momentum as a version of practitioner inquiry. Wenger, McDermott, and Snyder (2002) define communities of practice as "groups of people who share a concern, a set of problems, or a passion for a topic, and who deepen their knowledge and expertise in this area by interacting on an ongoing basis" (Gruenhagen 2009, 145).

Often tied to professional development, teacher inquiry groups are sometimes organized and led by P–12 teachers; in other instances they are initiated by administrators, university professors, or external facilitators. When professional development promotes inquiry and collaborative study of teaching and learning, it has the potential to foster "local teaching movements" that position teachers as leaders in their schools and communities, as well as change agents in the profession.

Oral inquiry becomes a way for teachers to study their practice as they engage in conversations about teaching strategies, students' work, or curriculum materials. Collaborative work goes beyond simply sharing stories when teachers shift from congenial but superficial conversations to dialogue that entails risk-taking and trust (Nelson et al. 2010). Whether the conversations spring up naturally within groups of teachers who share similar backgrounds and experiences or are guided by an external facilitator, all teachers must function as "fellow learners rather than experts" (Cochran-Smith and Lytle 1999a, 278). Over time, teachers begin to analyze commonalities and differences across contexts and co-construct knowledge in communities.

9.3. A View of Practitioner Inquiry in Music Education

Looking back at the literature in music education, one finds several "early soundings" that signaled an interest in practitioner inquiry in music education. Pernecky's article in a 1963 publication of the *Bulletin for the Council of Research in Music Education* may have been one of the first in a music education journal to raise consciousness about action research. His instructional piece describes how to conduct action research and outlines issues drawn from the work of action research pioneers Steven Corey and Abraham Schumsky. Another early voice was Paul Haack's (1968). More than 30 years ago, he warned of the wide gulf between research and practice and argued that teaching and research have a significant relationship; both involve problem-posing, formulation of a hypothesis, and a search for solutions. His ideas about the reciprocal nature of research and practice reflect a vision of practitioner inquiry that had yet to emerge in music education.

Fast-forward to the first Qualitative Research Methodologies Conference held at the University of Illinois in 1994 for a glimpse of conversations and presentations about action research and teacher research that were taking place. A subsequent issue of the Bulletin of the Council for Research in Music Education (*BCRME*) featuring roundtable papers (Hookey, Miller, Robbins, Wiggins 1994/1995) and keynote addresses by Liora Bresler and Fred Erickson provide further evidence that the qualitative umbrella was opening up to include teacher research and action research alongside phenomenology and ethnography (Bresler 1994/1995). The time had come to create "new structures" that would bridge the gap between research and practice (Reimer 1992).

9.3.1. Action Research and Teacher Research

"Terms like action research and teacher research have been widely appropriated and have come to mean many things as they are attached to various teacher learning initiatives and various educational purposes" (Cochran-Smith and Lytle 1999a, 282). Some studies are reminiscent of Britton's "quiet form of research" (1987) with teaching and inquiry aimed at renewing personal practice; others are more complex and larger in scope. Rather than trying to categorize studies as *either* action research *or* teacher research, it may be more productive to examine the focusing questions of music teachers' inquiry—questions about schedules and the organization of time, about why students choose music and what they understand; questions about students' responses to new approaches, flare points in lessons, and who is floundering and flourishing. The following studies were selected to provide a sense of "where the action is" (Erikson 1994/1995) and to illustrate the ways music teachers' inquiry is situated at the intersection of theory and practice.

Learning from students' points of view. When a teacher asks, "What will happen if I use journals in my middle school instrumental class?" she might also be asking, "What will writing about music reveal about students' musical knowledge and development?" Several studies used writing to look at student learning in the general music class, tapping into the legacy of so many writing teachers who recognize that writing is a way for students to express ideas and feelings and to generate meaning (Berthoff 1987). An investigation by Eichenlaub (1996) involved integrating dialogue journals at the end of music classes with her fourth-grade students over a six-month period. Her analysis of students' writing revealed what students were learning and struggling with and gave her an up-close view of how children articulate multiple ways of knowing in music. The journals were not only a tool for assessment but also a window on students' interests that allowed her to see them as individuals. After 30 years of teaching, she found herself assuming a new role as learner in her classroom.

Itinerant teacher Heidi Dunkle designed a similar study of fourth-grade students' writing (Robbins, Burbank, and Dunkle 2006). The primary purpose was to investigate what students were learning and what was important to them; Dunkle was curious about what she would learn from one-on-one communication with students through journal exchanges. Borrowing from Thompson's "Letters to a Math Teacher" (1990), she invited students to write letters about each music class over a six-week period. Her researcher journal and videotaped lessons provided additional data. The recursive nature of the inquiry was evident as she adjusted writing prompts in response to students' questions and moved conversations about music and music-making to the center of her teaching. "I learned not only about how my students learn, but also about how I teach and how I influence them in ways I had never imagined" (2006, 65).

Reflective writing was the focus of "teacher inquiry" with middle school instrumental students (Reynolds and Beitler 2007). Beitler's interests in reflective practice became the basis for her professional development plan and partnership grant that supported writing across the curriculum. Beitler initiated a two-phase project: the first phase involved integrating reflective writing into her middle school instrumental classes following weekly group lessons. The second phase was dedicated to data analysis and reflecting on the research process through journal writing and conversations with her university-based collaborator. Although it was time-consuming for Beitler to read and reflect on so many students' reflective responses, she found journaling to be a "fair trade" for what she was learning about students' needs. Students' reflections "spurred decisions to review or re-teach" portions of her lessons and re-examine her assumptions about students (62). Unexpected benefits of her study included the collaborative exchange of ideas, which in turn led to reinterpreting and reframing practice.

What do students value about participation in music class? Because music is often an elective course, recruiting and retaining students in classes and ensembles is part of the music teacher's job. It is not surprising that research questions grow out of a curiosity about why students participate and what students might say "in their own words" about their "lived" experience in music. A study that looked at participation in choir (Conway and Borst 2001) was sparked by the teacher's (Borst) puzzlement about attrition when choristers from his middle school did not return for choir in 10th grade. This tension led to an investigation of the factors and influences motivating students' decisions to enroll. Six students and their parents elected to participate in a series of face-to-face and/or phone interviews in this collaborative action research study. Seven categories related to students' perspectives on and reasons for participation in choir emerged, the most prominent being "social aspects," "personal gain," and "entertainment." Borst's discussion of future plans to implement more opportunities for students to socialize in music class reflects a cyclical action research process of planning, action, and recasting practice.

Understanding the phenomenon of social belonging was the focus of Parker's study with her high school choirs (2010). She wanted to learn more about the factors comprising students' approach to ensemble music-making and membership and to reflect on her role in supporting students' sense of belonging at school. Parker used purposive sampling to select 26 students in her high school choral program for the study, encouraging participation from students who had already manifested a strong sense of belonging during informal conversations. Data included her researcher journal and seven small-group interviews that took place during student lunch periods in the chorus room. Her systematic and intentional design included triangulation and member checking. Excerpts from interviews with students were used to illuminate five themes of social belonging that emerged.

"What if" questions of practice. Several studies emerged from "what if" questions that prompted teachers to study student engagement and response to specific instructional strategies and curriculum innovation. Hookey's research is an extension of Bresler's (1993) ethnographic study of non-specialists' use of music in the elementary school. The central question of Hookey's research (1994/1995) was: "What would it mean to have a music specialist work in a consultative manner with classroom teachers?" (39). She describes her shift in role from music teacher to consultant who worked with two generalist teachers to plan and implement music in their classrooms. Together they met for pre-observation planning sessions and follow-up conferencing to reflect upon and analyze videotaped teaching episodes. What stands out in her report are the collaborative process and the storied approach to curriculum planning that unfolded when she (as music specialist) was "linked" to classroom teachers to bring music into the general classroom.

Several studies by Miller (2003, 1996, 1994/1995) explored what a collaborative curriculum might look like when music is integrated into whole language classrooms. Miller was curious about the possibilities for "authentic intersections" between music and core curriculum, student learning in music and across disciplines, student enthusiasm and engagement, and the influence of integrated pedagogies on classroom teachers' perceptions of music. Her willingness to press herself beyond what she already knew and to engage in systematic inquiry about what she did not know is reflective of an inquiry stance (Ashburn 1995, 84). All of Miller's studies used qualitative methods of observations, journaling by collaborating teachers, and videotaping to collect data. Her use of a "critical friend" (Costa and Kallick 1993) points to the important role of collaboration when teachers plan, implement, and research curriculum together.

Another focus of several studies by Wiggins involved children's compositional thinking and the teacher's role in facilitating composing in the classroom (1999/2000; 1995; 1994/1995; 1994; 1993). Wiggins's dissertation research was one of the first, if not the first, teacher-research dissertations in the United States. Wiggins studied the processes her fifth-grade students used when working together to solve compositional problems. Data were drawn from videotapes of class sessions, as well as audio data from two targeted children who wore lapel microphones and small tape recorders. Additional data included interviews with target children and their parents, researcher field notes, and artifacts from lessons. Wiggins's close-up view of her students' compositional decision-making transformed her teaching and thinking about the important role of shared musical understanding in empowering students' independent musical thinking.

Strand (2003, 2005) was interested in studying how children transfer conceptual learning in music to composing tasks. Her action research involved designing and field-testing a curriculum with eight students, ages 9–12, during a four-week summer enrichment program. Data included written lesson plans, video recordings of lessons, researcher field notes, audio recordings, and students' composition artifacts. Her discussion of the reflective spiral design that involved generating, modeling, and mediating ideas in her teaching illuminates the recursive nature of action research. Strand (2009) also published a narrative analysis and critique of a wide range of action research studies on teaching composition taking place internationally.

On becoming reflective practitioners. The idea that "reflection is central to the concept of teacher as inquirer" (Leglar and Collay 2002, 860) has prompted a variety of reflective practices in music teacher education. Journals and autobiographical essays are being implemented to jog students' memories about beliefs about "good" teaching that were formed during their "apprenticeship of observation" (Lortie 1975). Students work collaboratively to plan, teach, and reflect on practice in ways that promote the construction of knowledge about teaching. With inquiry approaches moving to the center of methods courses and teaching internships, one finds studies of the ways preservice music teachers are beginning to act and think like researching teachers.

Preparing preservice teachers to conduct research was the focus of two studies. Conway (2000) was one of the first to document the application of action research in preservice music teacher preparation. Her recognition of the usefulness of action research in general classrooms prompted her to introduce several action research "lessons" in a three-credit methods course that was required for music education students. Four examples of students' mock action research studies are discussed. Strand (2006) introduced students to action research methods in a two-semester sequence that involved introduction to action research during a general methods course, followed by implementation of projects with cooperating teachers in a subsequent semester. Most of the novice teacher-researchers focused their inquiry on cooperating teachers' strategies; only one examined the efficacy of an instructional strategy she wanted to try. Strand's discussion of students' "fledging attempts" provides insight into the rewards and challenges.

Walls and Samuels (2011) used a collaborative action research design to study an innovation strategy aimed at engaging students in more meaningful conversation about observing and assessing teaching. Data included analysis of students' course assignments, instructor journals, and interviews with students. Through individual and collaborative reflection, both researchers found that students took ownership of and had greater interest in observation and recognized important connections between student-designed observation instruments and improved practice. Students were empowered "to think as innovators and leaders" as they shifted from "student-type thinking to teacher-type thinking" (33).

9.3.2. Self-Study in Music Teacher Education

Although the term "self-study" is rarely used in music education, it is worth noting that some research in music teacher education is moving in the direction of self-study. In the past two decades, scholarship undertaken by music teacher educators has been fueled by the revitalization of the Society for Music Teacher Education and its biennial symposia and accompanying "action groups" or ASPA's (Areas of Strategic Planning and Action). The Instrumental Music Teacher Educators (IMTE) Colloquium and the

Mountain Lake Colloquium are two other forums that have prompted conversations and scholarship on music teaching and learning. Five volumes of *The Mountain Lake Reader* (1997–2010) feature music teacher education scholarship in the form of essays that embody some of the qualities of self-study.

A general methods course was the setting for an examination of general music methods students' "in-flight" decision-making (Robbins 1999). Robbins's essay opens with her deliberating over course content and requirements in search of ways to help students become more responsive in their weekly teaching practicum.

> The recognition that I had, to a great degree, ignored the thousands of interactive decisions that my preservice teachers were making and missing led to a minor yet significant adjustment in my own plan. (26)

A small change of plan to encourage "in-flight" decision-making led to new insights about students' fear of "letting go" of their plans and losing control of the lesson. Analysis of students' reflective writing led to a discovery of students' tensions between planning and teaching and Robbins's own growing awareness of the ways prescriptive planning models limit rather than liberate her students as artist-teachers.

Mills's (2001) study of a music course for elementary education majors begins with an autobiographical voice that often characterizes self-study. A past experience led her to wonder how she might help her elementary education students begin to see themselves as musicians. Students' reflective writing led to the realization that "something was missing in their backgrounds" (18).

> I focused my concern on the following question: How could I teach the basic musical skills and concepts necessary for an elementary educator when students rejected themselves as musicians? (19)

Her semester-long journey with elementary preservice teachers as she plotted a new course brings to life the ways she adjusted course outcomes and source materials to include world music repertoire (19), collaborating with students in ways that "forever changed [her] perspective" (20).

Another project that moves in the direction of self-study is a collaborative investigation by Cooper and Berger (2004). Theirs is a story of two graduate students studying themselves as researchers and writers. They formed a learning community of two in order to systematically and intentionally connect through a process they describe as "negotiated thought." Their collaboration included shared texts and time for "critical conversations" that led to growth as researchers and writers. Their interest in "making their own thinking public" (75) looked not only at their present practice but beyond to the kind of graduate classes they aspire to teach in the future.

Barrett's (2007) study makes explicit her "pedagogical moves" to include more active engagement with the research process in a qualitative research in music education (QRME) course.

After teaching QRME only once before, I resolved to tip the balance from my previous emphasis on learning about qualitative research to active engagement in qualitative research. (420)

Data for this "pedagogical action research" were drawn from in-class discussions,
students' written assignments, final projects, and end-of-semester reflections. A dual
focus on her teaching and her students' "resultant insights to analyze and interpret qualitative data" (420) is instructional on multiple levels. The narrative account takes the
reader inside a sequence of assignments—what Barrett calls "five-movements"—to
view graduate students working collaboratively as Barrett witnesses the complexities of
teaching qualitative research.

9.3.3. Communities of Practice

Teacher learning communities involve the work of teachers who typically meet outside of school time to reflect on practice and share concerns about students' learning.
Informal talk shifts to more formal inquiry as they puzzle out problems and co-construct
knowledge over time. Within music education, several studies are illustrative of practitioner inquiry taking place in learning communities. A study by Montgomery, deFrece,
and Robinson (2010) involved an on-campus collaborative inquiry group made up of
five mentor teachers "in partnership with three elementary music education professor-
researchers" (231). A primary purpose was to examine the student teaching practicum
experience through the eyes of the mentor teacher; university researchers also wanted
to find an auxiliary model for connecting to and honoring the work of mentor teachers.
The collaborative inquiry group became the context for examining the experiences of
music mentor teachers as well as the role of collaborative inquiry. Analysis of group
conversations, interviews with mentor teachers, and e-mail exchanges revealed the
benefits, goals, and tensions experienced by mentor teachers and also the potential for
collaborative inquiry groups to level the playing field for university and mentor teachers
engaged in the student teaching process.

As the director of an early childhood program in a community music school,
Gruenhagen (2008, 2009) studied teachers' "collaborative conversations" during
monthly meetings that took place over one academic year. The primary purpose was
to understand the extent to which teachers' conversations might function as a form of
"collaborative professional development." Gruenhagen's research presents a "case" of
11 teachers who participated in teacher-centered, collaborative professional development that led to "understanding, articulating, and ultimately altering practice and social
relationships" (2008, 281). What distinguishes this research as practitioner inquiry is its
reliance on oral inquiry within a "community of practice" that involved all members (including the facilitator) as learners.

Stanley (2009) facilitated a *collaborative teacher study group* (CTSG) for the purpose
of creating a "different kind of professional development for teachers" (3). This social

constructivist inquiry looked at collaboration on two levels: in the teacher study group and also in the elementary music classroom. Three teachers joined Stanley for weekly meetings that involved looking in on and analyzing video of each other's lessons in a "non-hierarchical community." Teachers took turns leading discussion using an analysis protocol to support conversations about challenges related to applying student-initiated cooperative learning approaches. Stanley analyzed interviews, video records, and artifacts from the CTSG meetings and her teacher log to "tease out" the ways teachers were affected by the CTSG. Her research supports the democratic values associated with practitioner inquiry and supports teachers' honest talk about teaching tensions.

Several studies of teacher inquiry groups involved supporting in-service teachers' efforts to conduct research in their classrooms. Orff SPIEL (Schulwerk Project: Implementing Eastman's Levels) involved six teachers who volunteered to participate in a three-year project designed to support the implementation of what they were learning in Eastman's two-week summer Orff Schulwerk course. Teachers met throughout the school year and during the summer course to share ideas from their classrooms and talk about challenges they faced as they explored new approaches with their students. Teachers also read several texts related to conducting teacher research and subsequently identified questions they wanted to pursue for systematic and intentional inquiry in their own classrooms in year three. Eichenlaub's research with her fourth-grade students (previously discussed) is one published example.

A study by Roulston et al. (2005) involved the development of a collaborative teacher-research group made up of university educators and early-career elementary music teachers. A question for the university-based researchers was "how, and in what ways might a teacher-research community contribute to the professional development of early-career elementary music teachers" (4). A unique aspect of this study involved coaching early-career elementary music teachers in the use of action research over the course of one year. Excerpts from interviews with teachers and transcriptions of the collaborative meetings bring early-career teachers' voices into view as they reflect on the benefits and challenges of conducting action research. The addition of university-based researchers' reflections on their interactions and roles as members of the teacher-research group creates a polyvocal texture to the descriptions of learning taking place.

9.4. CRITIQUES AND CONSIDERATIONS

Although there are many values that unite the various genres of practitioner inquiry, there are a number of issues that lead to misunderstandings and continue to create a divide with traditional forms of research. More than 10 years ago, Cochran-Smith and Donnell (2006) identified several common critiques of practitioner inquiry that raised questions about the value of practitioner inquiry, what counts as research, and whose knowledge matters.

First is the "knowledge critique" that questions the extent to which teachers' idiosyncratic and situated knowledge can contribute to the professional knowledge base. Critics describe teachers' practical knowledge "pejoratively as lore, anecdote, fad or intuitive" as compared to formal knowledge generated by university research (Cochran-Smith and Lytle 2009, 129). The knowledge critique underestimates the potential for teachers' local knowledge to invoke complex and provocative questions and fails to recognize that the kind of knowledge generated by teachers "comes through closeness as well as distance, through intuition as well as logic" (Bissex 1987, 3). Not only do teachers conduct research on their own practice, they also consider the knowledge and theory produced by others as generative material for interrogation and interpretation (Cochran-Smith and Lytle 131).

A second critique calls into question whether teachers have the necessary skills, distance, and analytic capabilities to conduct research on their own practice. The "science critique" argues that the small, single-site samples of practitioner inquiry are incapable of producing generalizable results and identifying factors that increase teaching effectiveness (Cochran-Smith and Donnell 2006). Practitioner inquiry findings are not intended to be generalizable; instead they provide an important lens on issues taking place at the ground level with a "potential to move outside to influence schools, communities, and new policies of practice" (Schmidt and Robbins 2011, 100). The science critique is most problematic for practitioner research when it "operates invisibly by excluding the work of practitioner research from consideration of what is known about a particular topic" (Cochran-Smith and Donnell 2006, 513). To some extent the science critique is a silencing factor that prevents practitioner inquiry from being widely published or publicly presented. Much of the work of P–12 researching teachers is rarely accessible beyond district-wide networks, local conferences, and graduate capstone projects and remains part of the "fugitive literature" (Zeichner and Noffke 2001, 304).

Another criticism claims that practitioner inquiry is either too personal or too political. Research that looks like professional development and is aimed at personal renewal is considered too narrow. Alternatively, practitioner research that proposes to reform traditional school structures or critically examine social dimensions of school and society is considered too political and "not research at all, but advocacy, activism, or political maneuvering by disenfranchised groups" (Cochran-Smith and Donnell 2006 513). Ideally, practitioner inquiry involves a balance of the personal and political—of technical and theoretical pursuits—that promotes inquiry and collaborative study of critical dimensions in their classrooms while simultaneously enacting change on a larger scale.

Democratic validity involves the extent to which the research is done in collaboration with all parties who have a stake in the problem under investigation. Erikson (1994/1995) addresses the complexity of power relationships when doing collaborative action research. In some instances, action research is directed and carried out by a school-based teacher; in other cases, the university researcher is primarily in charge of posing the questions and conducting the research. Like Erikson, Cochran-Smith and Lytle (2009) point out that not all instances of collaboration serve the same purposes or are "connected to the same larger social and political agendas" (59). Awareness of power relationships between P–12 and university teachers will be important to the work of music teacher educators interested in forging new partnerships with school-based teacher researchers.

Too often, practitioner inquiry falls under the same scrutiny as traditional research and is held up to the same standards rather than being recognized as a new, different genre of research. Practitioner inquiry is not less than, but different from, traditional research, with the potential to provide "insight into the particulars of how and why something works and for whom it works within the context of particular classrooms" (Cochran-Smith and Lytle 1993, 15). Alternative criteria are needed when assessing the quality of practitioner inquiry. Foremost in any consideration of the worthwhileness of practitioner inquiry in music education is the extent to which it involves a commitment to change at both micro and macro levels—change in personal practice, institutional culture, or in social structures. Practitioner inquiry can and should be much more than self-discovery. Even if practitioner research does not change unjust social structures, it can make important differences in students' lives. "Every classroom issue has a critical dimension; the critical and political are right in front of us" (Zeichner 1993, 201)

In addition to conceptual critiques of the value of practitioner research, several facets of school culture can create paths of resistance for the work of researching teachers. Among these are lack of time, teacher isolation, and an occupational culture that equates good teaching with answers rather than questions.

One way to deepen and sustain the work of researching teachers is to create school structures that provide time for inquiry and collaboration. Researching teachers need time to observe students, conduct interviews, gather supporting artifacts, and meet with colleagues. "Finding the requisite time for such work is particularly relevant for music teachers who invariably work with large numbers of students, often in back-to-back lessons, and commonly coordinate regular performances" (Roulston et al. 2005, 15). Unfortunately, many school schedules typically do not allow adequate time for music teachers to meet, talk, and reflect with other teachers.

Teacher isolation can be another obstacle for music teachers who travel between schools or teach in spaces located apart from the rest of the school. Separation from colleagues discourages conversations about critical issues that define teacher inquiry. Teacher communities have the potential to break down barriers that discourage rather than encourage open, honest discussion. The literature suggests that ". . . teachers who planned and worked together over time built commitment not only to each other but to further learning. Even the act of 'struggling' together at the same time in the same ways helped teachers to master new practice" (Lieberman and Mace 2010, 78).

Occupational culture is another deep-seated problem that works against the grain of practitioner inquiry. "Going public with questions" is often viewed as inappropriate behavior for teachers (Cochran-Smith and Lytle 1992, 303). The work of researching teachers is challenged within a culture that views uncertainty as a sign of weakness or worse, failing. A supportive culture recognizes that researching teachers are noted for their questions, not because they are failing but because they are curious and want to learn. Researching teachers embrace uncertainty and welcome change, rather than waiting for it to happen. Teachers' intimate knowledge of the uncertainties about teaching are the very thing that is missing from both our theories and our research (McDonald 1986). Imagine the shift in conversation if teachers were to raise questions rather than grow silent when they recognize uncertainty. "Knowledge about teaching might begin to ripple out in ever-widening circles, moving from inside to outside, and create a very different dynamic between teaching and research" (Robbins, Burbank, and Dunkle 2006, 68).

9.5. A Way Forward

If knowledge about teaching is "fluid and socially constructed" (Cochran-Smith and Lytle 1993), then we have a great deal to learn from teachers' lived experiences. "New ways to communicate about research are still very much needed—ones that recognize and value multiple ways of knowing and forms of theorizing and that assume all educational work, whether in P–12 classrooms or university research centers, is a form of practice with political implications" (Zeichner and Noffke 2001, 310).

In music education, we can create new venues and networks that will make public the work of researching teachers. Regional and national conferences might include a teacher research day similar to the one established by Marilyn Cochran-Smith and Susan Lytle more than 30 years ago as part of the Ethnography and Education Forum at the University of Pennsylvania. Published accounts of practitioner inquiry are another way to increase the visibility of work taking place. The *Practitioner Inquiry Series* is one model that includes "rich insider accounts of the complex, day-to-day work of educational practice as well as how practitioners theorize and understand their work from the inside" (Cochran-Smith and Lytle 2009, x).

Another way to move forward is for university- and school-based teachers to continue working collaboratively toward change. Current initiatives in preservice music teacher education point to new partnerships between P–12 and university teachers that are creating and sustaining greater ownership and equity among all stakeholders. When teacher educators model reflective practices for and with their students, they make visible the very uncertainties and complexities of teaching that preservice teachers need to understand that teaching is complex, at times messy, fluid, and socially constructed. Teacher educators who study their own practice "create and recreate teacher education as a living educational theory" (Hamilton and Pinnegar 2000, 239).

There are many opportunities to involve undergraduate students in thinking about research issues and techniques, but also in learning how to conduct research. Preservice music teachers can become researching teachers, too, when they are engaged in work that highlights the intimate relationship between research and practice. Possibilities include making teaching labs inquiry sites where preservice teachers work in cohorts to document and study students' learning, collaborate on designing lessons, and join host teachers for discussion about observations of music teaching and learning. Establishing early habits of collaborative inquiry can prepare preservice teachers to take an inquiry stance across the professional life span.

9.5.1. Taking an Inquiry Stance

More than 20 years ago (in their 1993 book *Inside/Outside*), Cochran-Smith and Lytle proposed the concept of "inquiry as stance" as distinct from the more common notion of inquiry as a time-bound project. They use the metaphor of stance to suggest perspectival and positional ideas—the positions teachers take toward knowledge and its relationship to practice (Cochran-Smith and Lytle 1999a, 289). Inquiry as stance makes visible and problematic the various perspectives through which researching teachers frame their questions, observations, and interpretations of data. It reflects a way to "capture the ways we stand, the ways we see, and the lenses we see through" (Cochran-Smith and Lytle 1999a, 288–89). Questions become lenses for seeing and making sense of practice: Who am I as a music teacher? In what ways are my students making meaning from the musical experiences in my classes? In what ways are my choices of materials and teaching strategies making a difference in student engagement and learning? How are my efforts to connect to the school community influencing the music program and larger school agenda?

Across the life span, inquiry has the potential to invoke larger questions grounded within the changing culture of school—questions about assessment, standardization, promotion, school schedules, and research methods (Cochran-Smith 1999a). In this sense, inquiry as stance becomes a frame for imagining and enacting change over time. Drawing upon Freire's notion of "praxis," Cochran-Smith and Lytle suggest that an inquiry stance is grounded by a dialectical relationship with theory and action. When teachers "work the dialect" they simultaneously practice and theorize about practice. More like a dance than a linear process, taking an inquiry stance recognizes that pedagogies are constantly invented, reinvented, and negotiated with learners, colleagues, and in different contexts (Cochran-Smith and Lytle 2009a). From a music teaching perspective, framing and reframing practice is essential to understanding students, materials, and school culture. Lessons are adjusted each time a different second-grade class comes through the door; repertoire is regularly adapted for varied ability levels of students' within each context; and music curriculum is reinvented in response to collaborative school-wide themes and program demands. "What if" questions about music teaching and learning are compounded by multiple classes and hundreds of students.

Practitioners take on an expanded view of practice when they assume an inquiry stance and see themselves as learners and leaders. "Behind the framework of inquiry as stance is a new idea of professionalism . . . when practitioners work from an inquiry stance they are working both within and against the system—the ultimate purpose is enhancing students' learning and life chances for participation in and contribution to a diverse and democratic society" (Cochran-Smith and Lytle 2009, 146). When teachers reconstruct practice as inquiry across the professional life span, they challenge the notion that practitioners are technicians, consumers, receivers, and transmitters of other people's knowledge. A move in this direction has greater potential to reposition music teachers as learners and leaders in the profession. When we view teaching *as* research, we recognize the thoughtful and important work of researching teachers who are naturally curious about students' learning, collect information to inform their practice, interrogate the research of others, and experiment with new approaches and repertoire. They are the change agents, working both within and against the system for change. Cochran-Smith and Lytle call for a "renegotiation of the boundaries of research and practice and reconfiguration of relationships inside and outside schools and universities, all in the interest of school and social change" (2009, vii).

Practitioner inquiry not only challenges traditional views about the relationship of knowledge and practice and the roles of teachers in educational change, it also promises to bridge the divide that has too long existed between teachers and researchers and to address the problem that knowledge about teaching resides "elsewhere" (Boomer 1987, 8). Practitioner inquiry has the potential to link teaching and curriculum to wider political and social issues. "When this happens teacher research creates a dissonance, often calling attention to the constraints of the hierarchical arrangements in schools and universities . . ." (Cochran-Smith and Lytle 1999, 22). Such a dissonance can be energizing and necessary for change. In music education we can listen for and look forward to more dissonance created by researching teachers, and regard this as a signal of music educators who are on the move and more mindful of the gap between research and practice.

REFERENCES

Adelman, Clem. 1993. "Kurt Lewin and the Origins of Action Research." *Educational Action Research* 1 (1): 7–24.

Ashburn, Elizabeth. 1995. "Teacher-Led Inquiry: A Compelling Direction for the Education of Teachers." *Action in Teacher Education* 17 (3): 79–86. Portsmouth, NH: Heinemann.

Atwell, Nancie, ed. 1989. *Coming to Know: Writing to Learn in the Intermediate Grades.* Portsmouth, NH: Heinemann.

Barrett, Janet. 2007. "The Researcher as Instrument: Learning to Conduct Qualitative Research through Analyzing and Interpreting a Choral Rehearsal." *Music Education Research* 9 (3): 417–33.

Berthoff, Ann. 1987. "The Teacher as Researcher." In *Reclaiming the Classroom: Teacher Research as an Agency for Change,* edited by Dixie Goswami and Peter Stillman, 28–39. Upper Montclair, NJ: Boynton/Cook.

Bissex, Glenda. 1987. "What Is a Teacher-Researcher?" In *Seeing for Ourselves: Case-Study Research by Teachers of Writing,* edited by Glenda Bissex and Robert Bullock, 3–5. Portsmouth, NH: Heinemann.

Bissex, Glenda, and Robert Bullock, eds. 1987. *Seeing for Ourselves: Case-Study Research by Teachers of Writing.* Portsmouth, NH: Heinemann.

Boomer, Garth. 1987. "Addressing the Problem of Elsewhereness: A Case for Action Research in Schools." In *Reclaiming the Classroom: Teacher Research as an Agency for Change*, edited by Dixie Goswami and Peter Stillman. Upper Montclair, NJ: Boynton/Cook.

Bresler, Liora. 1994/1995. "Teacher Knowledge: A Framework and Discussion." *Bulletin of the Council for Research in Music Education* 123: 26–30.

Bresler, Liora. 1995. "Ethnography, Phenomenology and Action Research in Music Education." *Quarterly Journal of Music Teaching and Learning* 6 (3): 4–16.

Britton, James. 1987. "A Quiet Form of Research." In *Reclaiming the Classroom: Teacher Research as an Agency for Change*, edited by Dixie Goswami and Peter Stillman, 13–19. Upper Montclair, NJ: Boynton/Cook.

Bullough, Robert, and Andrew Gitlin. 1995. *Becoming a Student of Teaching: Methodologies for Exploring Self and School Context*. New York: Garland.

Bullough, Robert, and Stefinee Pinnegar. 2001. "Guidelines for Quality in Autobiographical Forms of Self-Study Research." *Educational Researcher* 30 (3): 13–21.

Cain, Tim. 2008. "The Characteristics of Action Research in Music Education." *British Journal of Music Education* 25 (3): 283–313.

Carini, Patricia. 2001. *Starting Strong: A Different Look at Children, Schools and Standards*. New York: Teachers College Press.

Carr, Wilfred, and Stephen Kemmis.1986. *Becoming Critical: Education, Knowledge and Action Research*. Geelong, Victoria: Deakin University Press.

Cochran-Smith, Marilyn, and Kelly Donnell. 2006. "Practitioner Inquiry: Blurring the Boundaries of Research and Practice." In *Handbook of Complementary Methods in Education Research*, edited by Judith Green, Gregory Camilli, and Patricia Elmore, 503–18. Washington, DC: American Educational Research Association.

Cochran-Smith, Marilyn, and Susan Lytle. 1993. *Inside Outside: Teacher Research and Knowledge*. New York: Teachers College Press.

Cochran-Smith, Marilyn, and Susan Lytle. 1999. "The Teacher Research Movement: A Decade Later." *Educational Researcher* 28 (7): 15–25.

Cochran-Smith, Marilyn, and Susan Lytle. 1999a. "Relationships of Knowledge and Practice: Teacher Learning in Communities." *Review of Research in Education* 24: 249–305.

Cochran-Smith, Marilyn, and Susan Lytle. 2009. *Inquiry as Stance: Practitioner Research for the Next Generation*. New York: Teachers College Press.

Cochran-Smith, Marilyn, and Susan Lytle. 2009a. Teacher Research as Stance." In *Sage Handbook of Educational Action Research*, edited by Susan Noffke and Bridget Somekh, 39-49. London: Sage Publications.

Cochran-Smith, Marilyn, and Susan Lytle. 2010. "Inquiry as Stance: Practitioner Research for the Next Generation." Keynote Address for the 31st Ethnography and Education Forum. University of Pennsylvania. Accessed via *iTunes U Collections*.

Conway, Colleen. 2000. "The Preparation of Teacher-Researchers in Pre-Service Teacher Education." *Journal of Music Teacher Education* 9 (2): 22–30.

Conway, Colleen, and James Borst. 2001. "Action Research in Music Education." *Update: Application of Research in Music Education* 19 (3): 3–8.

Cooper, Shelly, and Audrey Berger. 2004. "Negotiated Thought: Joining Individual Voices in Co-Authorship." *Mountain Lake Reader* (3): 72–75.

Costa, Arthur, and Bena Kallick. 1993. "Through the Lens of a Critical Friend." *Educational Leadership* 51 (2): 49–51.

Dinkelman, Todd. 2003. "Self-Study in Teacher Education: A Means and Ends Tool for Promoting Reflective Teaching." *Journal of Teacher Education* 54 (6): 6–18.

Eichenlaub, Rosemary. 1996. "Journaling in Music: A Different Kind of Assessment." *The Orff Echo* 28 (20): 36–41.

Elliott, John. 2006. "Educational Research as a Form of Democratic Rationality." *Journal of Philosophy of Education* 40 (2): 169–85.

Erikson, Frederick. 1994/1995. "Where the Action Is: Collaborative Action Research in Education." *Bulletin of the Council for Research in Music Education* 123: 10–25.

Goswami, Dixie, and Peter Stillman, eds. 1987. *Reclaiming the Classroom: Teacher Research as an Agency for Change.* Portsmouth, NJ: Heinemann.

Gruenhagen, Lisa Marie. 2008. "Investigating Professional Development: Early Childhood Music Teacher Learning in a Community of Practice." Order No. 3295323, University of Rochester, Eastman School of Music. http://search.proquest.com/docview/304314947?accountid=2837.

Gruenhagen, Lisa. 2009. "Developing Professional Knowledge about Music Teaching and Learning through Collaborative Conversations." In *Research Perspectives: Thought and Practice in Music Education*, edited by L. Thompson and M. Campbell, 125–51. Charlotte, NC: Information Age.

Haack, Paul. 1968. "Teachers Can Be Researchers Can Be Teachers." *Music Educators Journal* 54 (7): 81–83.

Hamilton, Mary Lynn, and Stefinee Pinnegar. 2000. "On the Threshold of a New Century: Trustworthiness, Integrity and Self-Study in Teacher Education." *Journal of Teacher Education* 5 (3): 234–40.

Hookey, Mary. 1994/1995. "Music Education as a Collaborative Project: Insights from Teacher Research." *Bulletin of the Council for Research in Music Education* 123: 39–46.

Hubbard, Ruth, and Brenda Power. 2003. *The Art of Classroom Inquiry.* Portsmouth, NH: Heinemann.

Jackson, Philip. 1968. *Life in Classrooms.* New York: Holt, Rinehart, and Winston.

Kemmis, Stephen, and Robin McTaggart, eds. 1988. *The Action Research Planner.* Victoria: Deakin University Press.

Kincheloe, Joe. 1991. *Teachers as Researchers: Qualitative Inquiry as a Path to Empowerment.* London: Falmer Press.

Leglar, Mary, and Michelle Collay. 2002. "Research by Teachers on Teacher Education." In *The New Handbook of Research on Music Teaching and Learning*, edited by R. Colwell and C. Richardson, 855–73. Oxford: Oxford University Press.

Lieberman, Ann, and Désirée Mace. 2010. "Making Practice Public: Teacher Learning in the 21st Century." *Journal of Teacher Education* 61 (1): 77.

Lortie, Dan. 1975. *Schoolteacher: A Sociological Study.* Chicago: University of Chicago Press.

Loughran, John, and Tom Russell. 2007. "Beginning to Understand Teaching as a Discipline." *Studying Teacher Education* 3 (2): 217–27.

McDonald, Joseph. 1986. "Raising the Teacher's Voice and the Ironic Role of Theory." *Harvard Educational Review* 56 (4): 355–78.

Miller, Beth Ann. 1996. "Integrating Elementary General Music: A Collaborative Action Research Study." *Bulletin of the Council for Research in Music Education* 130: 100–15.

Miller, Beth Ann. 2003. "Integrating Elementary General Music Instruction with a First Grade Whole Language Classroom." *Bulletin of the Council for Research in Music Education* 156: 43–62.

Mills, Susan. 2001. "The World Music Ensemble: My Journey with Elementary Preservice Educators." *The Mountain Lake Reader* 2: 18–21.

Montgomery, Amanda, Robert deFrece, and Kathy Robinson. 2010. "Supporting Elementary Music Mentor Teachers: Learning Through a Collaborative Inquiry Group." In *Collaborative Action for Change: Selected Proceedings from the 2007 Symposium on Music Teacher Education*, edited by Margaret Schmidt, 231–50. Lanham, MD: Rowman and Littlefield.

Nelson, Tamara, Angie Deuel, David Slavit, and Anne Kennedy. 2010. "Leading Deep Conversations in Collaborative Inquiry Groups." *The Clearing House* 83 (5): 175–79.

Noffke, Susan. 1994: "Action Research: Towards the Next Generation." *Educational Action Research* 2 (1): 9–21.

Noffke, Susan. 2009. "Revisiting the Professional, Personal, and Political Dimensions of Action Research." In *The Sage Handbook of Educational Action Research*, edited by Susan Noffke and Bridget Somekh, 6–23. Los Angeles: Sage Publications.

Paley, Vivian. 1997. *The Girl with the Brown Crayon: How Children Use Stories to Shape Their Lives*. Cambridge, MA: Harvard University Press.

Parker, Elizabeth. 2010. "Exploring Student Experiences of Belonging within an Urban High School Choral Ensemble: An Action Research Study." *Music Education Research* 12 (4): 339–52.

Perl, Sondra, and Nancy Wilson. 1988. *Through Teachers' Eyes: Portraits of Writing Teachers at Work*. Portsmouth, NH: Heinemann.

Pernecky, Jack. 1963. "Action Research Methodology." *Bulletin of the Council for Research in Music Education* 1: 33–37.

Reimer, Bennett. 1992. "An Agenda for Music Teacher Education: Part II." *Journal of Music Teacher Education* 1: 5–11.

Reynolds, Alison, and Nancy Beitler. 2007. "Reflective Practice in a Middle-School Instrumental Setting." *Bulletin of the Council for Research in Music Education* 174: 55–69.

Robbins, Janet. 1994/1995. "Levels of Learning in Orff SPIEL." *Bulletin of the Council for Research in Music Education* 123: 47–53.

Robbins, Janet. 1999. "Getting Set and Letting Go: Pre-service Teachers' In-Flight Decision Making." *The Mountain Lake Reader* 1: 26–32.

Robbins, Janet, Mary Kathryn Burbank, and Heidi Dunkle. 2006. "Teacher Research: Tales from the Field." *The Mountain Lake Reader* 4: 60–68.

Rosiek, Jerry, and Becky Atkinson. 2005. "Bridging the Divides: The Need for a Pragmatic Semiotics of Teaching Knowledge Research." *Educational Theory* 55 (4): 421–42.

Roulston, Kathryn, Roy Legette, Monica DeLoach, Celeste Buckhalter-Pittman, Lynne Cory, and Robin Grenier. 2005. "Education: Mentoring and Community through Research." *Research Studies in Music Education* 25: 1–22.

Samaras, Anastasia, and Anne Freese. 2009. "Looking Back and Looking Forward." In *Self-Study Research Methodologies for Teacher Educators*, edited by Cynthia Lassonde, Sally Galman, and Claire Kosnik, 3–19. Rotterdam: Sense.

Schmidt, Patrick, and Janet Robbins. 2011. "Looking Backwards to Reach Forward: A Strategic Architecture for Professional Development in Music Education." *Arts Education Policy Review* 112: 95–103.

Shulman, Lee. 2011. "The Scholarship of Teaching and Learning: A Personal Account and Reflection." *International Journal for the Scholarship of Teaching and Learning* 5 (1): 1–7. http://academics.georgiasouthern.edu/ijsotl/v5n1.html.

Somekh, Bridgette, and Ken Zeichner. 2009: "Action Research for Educational Reform: Remodeling Action Research Theories and Practices in Local Contexts." *Educational Action Research* 17 (1): 5–21.

Stanley, Ann Marie. 2009. "The Experiences of Elementary Music Teachers in a Collaborative Teacher Study Group." Order No. 3354182, University of Michigan. http://search.proquest.com/docview/304929031?accountid=2837.

Strand, Katherine. 2003. "Nurturing Young Composers: Exploring the Relationship between Instruction and Transfer in 9-to 12-year Old Students." ProQuest Dissertations and Theses (PQDT).

Strand, Katherine. 2005. "Nurturing Young Composers: Exploring the Relationship between Instruction and Transfer in 9–12 Year-Old Students." *Bulletin of the Council for Research in Music Education* 165: 17–36.

Strand, Katherine. 2006. Learning to Inquire: Teacher Research in Undergraduate Teacher Training. *Journal of Music Teacher Education* 15 (2), 29–42.

Strand, Katherine. 2009. A narrative analysis of action research on teaching composition. *Music Education Research* 11(3): 349–63.

Thompson, Anne. 1990. "Letters to a Math Teacher." In *Coming to Know: Writing to Learn in the Intermediate Grades*, edited by Nancie Atwell, 87–93. Portsmouth, NH: Heinemann.

Walls, Kimberly, and Sue Samuels. 2011. "Collaborative Design in Processes for Authentic Preservice Music Teacher Observations." *Journal of Music Teacher Education* 20 (2): 24–39.

Warner, Sylvia Ashton. 1963. *Teacher*. New York: Simon and Schuster.

Wenger, Etienne, Richard McDermott, and Williams Snyder. 2002. *Cultivating Communities of Practice: A Guide to Managing Knowledge*. Boston: Harvard Business School Press.

Wiggins, Jacqueline. 1993. "The Nature of Children's Musical Learning in the Context of a Music Classroom." *Dissertation Abstracts International* 53 (11): 3838.

Wiggins, Jacqueline H. 1994. "Children's Strategies for Solving Compositional Problems with Peers." *Journal of Research in Music Education* 42 (3): 232–52.

Wiggins, Jacqueline. Winter, 1994/1995. "Teacher-Research in a General Music Classroom: Effects on the Teacher." *Bulletin of the Council for Research in Music Education* 123: 31–35.

Wiggins, Jacqueline. 1995. "Building Structural Understanding: Sam's Story." *Quarterly Journal of Music Teaching and Learning* 6 (3): 57–75.

Wiggins, Jacqueline. 1999/2000. "The Nature of Shared Musical Understanding and Its Role in Empowering Independent Musical Thinking." *Bulletin of the Council for Research in Music Education* 143: 65–90.

Zeichner, Kenneth. 1993. "Action Research: Personal Renewal and Social Reconstruction." *Educational Action Research* 1 (2): 199–219.

Zeichner, Kenneth, and Susan Noffke. 2001. "Practitioner Research." In *Handbook of Research on Teaching*, edited by V. Richardson, 298–330. Washington, DC: American Educational Research Association.

CHAPTER 10

....

MIXED METHODS RESEARCH IN MUSIC EDUCATION

....

KATE R. FITZPATRICK

ALTHOUGH many studies in music education research utilize singular qualitative or quantitative methods, researchers have been increasingly using a combination of methodological approaches to answer complex research questions. As music teaching and learning is a complex human endeavor, mixed methods researchers in our field attempt to illustrate these complexities with research that is both meaningfully contextual and also sufficiently illustrative of broader trends. Mixed methods researchers value both the tension and the complementarity that often emerges with the mixing of methods as a means to learning more about the subject at hand. According to Creswell (2011), a mixed methods researcher does the following:

- Collects and analyzes persuasively and rigorously both qualitative and quantitative data (based on research questions);
- Mixes (or integrates or links) the two forms of data concurrently by combining them (or merging them), or sequentially by having one build on the other, and in a way that gives priority to one or two both;
- Uses these procedures in a single study or in multiples phases of a program of study;
- Frames these procedures within philosophical worldviews and a theoretical lens; and
- Combines the procedures into specific research designs that direct the plan for conducting the study.

The central premise of such research is that "the use of quantitative and qualitative approaches in combination provides a better understanding of research problems than either approach alone" (Creswell and Plano Clark 2007). A full discussion of mixed methods research is beyond the scope of this chapter. Instead, this chapter will begin with a discussion of the emergence of mixed methods research in music education, followed by an overview of the basic foundations of mixed methods research. Then, in alignment with the purpose of this book, the final part of the chapter will raise issues for consideration within the qualitative research community regarding the emergence of mixed methods research in music education.

10.1. MIXED METHODS RESEARCH IN MUSIC EDUCATION

Although the emergence of mixed methods research as a viable alternative to monoistic designs has been relatively recent in music education, it has certainly been more widely utilized within other fields of educational research. For examples, Hart et al. (2009) and Onwuegbuzie and Ross (2010) have found rates of mixed methods publication in educational journals from other fields to range from 24 percent to 33 percent of all published journal articles. Despite its growing presence in other educational fields, published mixed methods research remains rare in the field of music education, perhaps due to the historic dominance of quantitative research within the field of music education and relatively recent emergence of qualitative research (Roulston 2006; Yarbrough 1984, 1996). Also, as stated by Panaiotidi (2005):

> The enduring dominance of one paradigm is more properly to be seen as a result of social-political influences and/or the immaturity—or more precisely, insufficient maturity—of the discipline. In regard to the current situation, holding to the monistic scheme seems to be extremely counter-productive from epistemological, methodological, and pragmatic points of view. (51)

In 2002, Campbell called for the integration of a variety of research perspectives and methods within the field:

> Not an aside nor afterthought, our sensitivity to diversity and to individual human perspective will require diligence in the application of suitable statistical analyses of considerable power and also careful attention to a verstehen approach that comprises thick descriptions. The beauty of embracing the study of groups and isolates, of those at the center and the sides of the population graph, and by way of positivist and postmodern approaches, is an enriched understanding of the spectrum of our profession. (199)

However, it is only recently that mixed methods articles have been published in our field (Austin and Berg 2006; Fitzpatrick 2011; Bazan 2011). Historically, of course, music education authors who have primarily utilized one broader methodological framework have also included elements of another method within their studies. For example, many qualitative studies in music education have included questionnaires as a component of their study's design (Conway, Eros, and Stanley 2008; Conway et al. 2010;

Carlisle 2008), used frequently to collect demographic data or ask initial questions. However, such research is generally not considered to be mixed methods research because the quantitative results are often not included in the presentation of data, nor are they integrated in any form with the qualitative data to form a larger understanding of the phenomenon.

Some of the earliest mixed methods publications within the field of music education include those by Austin and Berg (2006), Bazan (2011), and Fitzpatrick (2011). Austin and Berg (2006) investigated music practice among sixth-grade band and orchestra students. Although they utilized the quantitative "Music Practice Inventory" as their primary data collection instrument, they also collected narrative data about students' practice experiences, which were coded and subsequently compared to the quantitative data in order to enrich the findings.

Bazan's (2011) study, published in the *Bulletin of the Council for Research in Music Education*, presents the results of his 2007 mixed methods dissertation on the teaching and learning strategies of middle school band teachers. His mixed methods design was a two-stage, sequential study that placed emphasis on quantitative data but also collected qualitative data to "provide a deeper perspective."

Fitzpatrick's (2011) study of secondary urban instrumental teachers utilized a Triangulation Convergence mixed methods design with focus group, survey, and interview/observation phases and appeared in the *Journal of Research in Music Education* (*JRME*). Introducing the issue of the journal was a piece written by the editor of the *JRME*, Wendy Sims (2011), that specifically addressed the publication of mixed methods studies:

> The guiding principle for this type of research is that when authors synthesize the findings generated from analyses of both type of data, they gain insights that are greater than those that might be obtained from either analysis alone—in other words, the whole is greater than the sum of parts. (227)

In addition to these published studies, there are increasingly more dissertations in the field of music education that utilize a mixed methods approach. Table 10.1 presents a list of the earliest dissertations to emerge in the field of music education, from 2004 to 2010. The growing popularity of such research approaches suggests that mixed methods research is having its "dawn" in the music education field, and this prompts questions that need to be addressed by our research community. To assure that the integrity of qualitative research will be maintained within this newest research paradigm, it is important to consider the background, assumptions, purpose, and design of mixed methods research, and thus how these elements can be more successfully utilized within music education research settings. Before proceeding, it is important to note that the field of mixed methods research is still in its "adolescence" (Tashakkori and Teddlie 2003). Thus, many of the terms and concepts presented here will change in the coming years; this is an exciting yet bewildering time for mixed methods researchers.

Table 10.1 Early U.S.–Based Mixed Methods Dissertations in the Field of Music Education (to 2010)

2010	Baer, J.	Walden University	The relationship of multiple intelligence instruction to sight singing achievement of middle school choral students
2010	Gavin, R. B.	Florida State University	An exploration of potential factors affecting persistence to degree completion in undergraduate music teacher education students
2010	Neokleous, R.	Boston University	Tracking preservice kindergarten teachers' development of singing skills and confidence: An applied study
2010	Rummel, J. R.	Boston University	Perceptions of jazz improvisation among Pennsylvania music educators
2010	Stringham, D.	Eastman	Improvisation and composition in a high school instrumental music curriculum
2009	Hendricks, K.	University of Illinois, Urbana-Champaign	Relationships between the sources of self-efficacy and changes in competence perceptions of music students during an all-state orchestra event
2009	Scruggs, B.	Georgia State University	Learning outcomes in two divergent middle school string orchestra classroom environments: A comparison of a learner-centered and a teacher-centered approach
2008	Fitzpatrick, K.	Northwestern University	A mixed methods portrait of urban instrumental music teaching
2007	Bazan, D.	Case Western Reserve	Teaching and learning strategies used by student-directed teachers of middle school band
2007	Thomas, M. P.	Walden University	Effects of team teaching in the massed secondary choral setting
2005	Saunders, A.	The University of Utah	The role of motivation in the choral setting: Teacher beliefs and their impact on choral conductor behavior and choral student motivation
2005	Dansereau, D.	Georgia State University	The musicality of 3-year-old children within the context of research-based musical engagement
2004	Huang, H.	University of Idaho	A study of the relationship between music learning and school achievement of sixth-grade students

Note: Dissertations retrieved from the Proquest: Digital Dissertations and Theses database, using the search terms "mixed methods" and "music" or "music education" and the date range 2000–2010.

10.2. FOUNDATIONS OF MIXED METHODS RESEARCH

10.2.1. Foundational Paradigms

It is often difficult for researchers steeped in either positivist/postpositivist or constructivist paradigms to imagine how mixed methods researchers might orient themselves with regard to epistemology. For qualitative researchers in the field of music education who have rejected the postpositivist paradigm as being insufficient to illustrate the entirety of the music education experience, such questions may be especially relevant. Criticisms of mixed methods research have included the concern that mixed methods research involves the interplay of two paradigms that are incompatible. However, looking at the extant literature in music education journals, one sees quantitative and qualitative data appearing side by side, and frequently the two methods address the same topic, albeit in separate articles. According to Brewer and Hunter (2006):

> There is now virtually no major problem area that is studied exclusively with one method. While the social sciences have remained largely single method in approach at the level of the individual investigator and the individual research project, the sum of individual efforts has resulted in a multimethod approach to problems.... A major benefit of adapting the multimethod approach is that the approach begins the task of integration from the ground up by calling upon individual social scientists to integrate methods throughout the course of their individual investigations. (10–11)

Mixed methods researchers generally utilize methodological eclecticism (Teddlie and Tashakkori 2011), which contends that "we are free to combine the best methodological tools in answering our research questions" (295). Such an approach is often based on the philosophy of pragmatism. The pragmatist philosophy, based on the work of such authors as Pierce, Mead, James, Dewey, Rorty, Murphy, Patton, and Cherryholmes (Creswell 2003), posits that finding solutions to problems is of greater importance than the method used to solve those problems. Pragmatists adhere to a philosophy of paradigm relativism (Tashakkori and Teddlie 1998), which encourages the use of whatever methodological approach works for the particular problem under study. Pragmatism does not claim that any one philosophy of the nature of knowledge and reality is correct, but rather allows for utilization of many techniques and methodologies in the service of solving a problem. The problem, therefore, is of primary importance, and truth is "what works at the time" (Creswell 2003). Thus, pragmatism allows for the utilization of mixed methods to serve the needs of the problem at hand. Besides pragmatism, Teddlie and Tashakkori (2011) suggest that the other most commonly accepted paradigmatic frameworks used in mixed methods research are frameworks associated with the axiological assumption (Mertens 2007) and the dialectical stance, which involves using multiple assumptive frameworks within the same study (Greene 2007; Greene and Caracelli 2003).

10.2.2. Purposes of Mixed Methods Research

The decision to utilize a mixed methods research design should be made when the research questions would be "best and most efficiently answered" (Teddlie and Tashakkori 2011) through such a design. Thus, when deciding whether to use a mixed methods design, the research questions are of primary importance, and the method utilized to answer them secondary. There are certainly many cases where a question is best and most efficiently answered through a qualitative-only or quantitative-only design rather than through a mixed methods design.

When the research question does substantiate the use of mixed methods designs, it is important to consider the purpose of such designs. The main purpose for the utilization of multiple methods is to recognize that all methods have limitations. Through the use of at least two different methods within a single study, it is hoped that the weaknesses of each might be reduced by the strengths of the other. This strategy is titled "between-methods triangulation" (Denzin 1978). Such triangulation attempts to prevent any problems stemming from the use of a single method, wherein "any inherent weakness stemming from the paradigm used will prevail regardless of the specific research design used within that paradigm" (Onwuegbuzie 2000, 13). It is important to clarify the meaning of the word "triangulation" with regard to mixed methods studies. As Woolley (2009) points out:

> Triangulation is a term that has been used in a variety of ways, including in the sense of using mixed methods to produce a fuller account. Unfortunately, however, its use also appears to have resulted in a common misconception, presumably stemming from its original referent, that mutual validation is the goal in mixed methods studies (Gorard and Taylor, 2004; Kelle, 2001). On the contrary, quantitative and qualitative methods provide differing perspectives on a subject and this is why the use of both may be viewed as complementary rather than validatory. The quantitative approach is characteristically indirect and reductive; the qualitative approach is characteristically direct and holistic. These are the strengths of each; these are the different levels of inquiry at which they are directed. (8)

In addition to triangulation, Rossman and Wilson (1991) offer four purposes for mixed methods research. In the first, corroboration, multiple methods are utilized simultaneously but independently to test consistency of findings. The second, elaboration, utilizes two approaches to enhance and enrich the findings of one method with another. Development is a third purpose for mixed methods research, and utilizes the results from one method to shape the design of the next method. The fourth purpose is initiation, wherein a second methodology is utilized to challenge the original conception

Table 10.2 Justifications for Undertaking Mixed Methods Studies (O'Cathain, Nicholl, and Murphy 2007, 148)

1. Comprehensiveness, where using both qualitative and quantitative methods allows an issue to be addressed more widely and more completely (Morse 2003).

2. Increased validity, when the findings from two different methods agree (Glik et al. 1986).

3. Development or facilitation in that one method is improved due to the existence of the other, for example, one method guides the sampling, data collection, or analysis of the other (Sandelowski 2000).

4. Emancipation, where the use of a variety of methods ensures that marginalized voices are given space, offering a more equitable or ethical approach to research (Mertens 2003).

5. "Satisficing," or second best because it may be impractical to undertake the single-method study ideally required (Datta 1997).

6. "Salvaging," where one method saves another that has floundered (Sandelowski 2000; Weinholtz, Kacer, and Rocklin 1995).

of the research problem and to suggest ways in which it may be reframed. In addition, Table 10.2 presents O'Cathain, Nicholl, and Murphy's (2007) summary of literature that discusses other purposes for the use of mixed methods research.

10.2.3. Mixed Methods Designs

With regard to selecting a mixed methods research design, the question is key. Mixed methods approaches are most appropriate for studies where the purpose and research questions require answers that are both meaningfully contextual and also sufficiently illustrative of broader trends. The selection of a mixed methods design, however, may not be a simple task. As the mixed methods field continues to evolve and develop, so do mixed methods designs continue to change. In fact, "many believe that a complete typology of MMR [mixed methods research] designs is not possible due to the emergent nature of the QUAL component of the research and the ability of MMR designs to mutate, while others seek agreement on a set number of basic designs for the sake of simplicity and pedagogy" (Teddlie and Tashakkori 2011, 289).

According to Creswell (2003), four main choices need to be made with regard to implementation, priority, integration, and theoretical perspective. First, the researcher needs to decide the sequence in which the methods will be utilized. For example, both methods may be used concurrently, or one method may be used first, followed by the other. The researcher next needs to decide what priority will be given to the different methods: Will one method predominate in importance, with the other playing a supporting role? Or, will both methods be used equally? Third, the researcher must decide at what stage in the research project (data collection, data analysis, data interpretation, or some combination of these) the methods will be integrated. Finally, the researcher must decide if an explicit theoretical framework (such as an advocacy lens or a theoretical perspective from the social sciences) will be utilized to guide the use of both methods.

The choices that the researcher makes leads to the study being classified according to five different categories of mixed method designs (Tashakkori and Teddlie 1998; Creswell 1995; Morse 1991). The following design categories are provided for the purpose of providing a baseline understanding of mixed methods designs; mixed methods researchers should be encouraged to thoughtfully develop other designs that best serve the purposes of their individual studies:

1. Sequential studies, which consist of two consecutive phases of research—one quantitative and one qualitative;
2. Parallel/simultaneous studies, in which both quantitative and qualitative phases are conducted at the same time;
3. Equivalent status designs, which utilize the qualitative and quantitative approaches equally to investigate the same phenomenon;
4. Dominant/less-dominant studies, in which most of the study is undertaken within either a quantitative or qualitative approach, but the other method is used supportively;
5. Designs with multilevel use of approaches, which utilize both methods at different levels of data aggregation.

These different aspects of design can be combined, as an equivalent design may be conducted sequentially, and a dominant/less-dominant design may be conducted in parallel/simultaneously.

10.2.4. Data Mixing or Integration

When mixed methods research was first emerging as an accepted mode of inquiry, Greene, Caracelli, and Graham (1989) defined mixed methods designs as "those that include at least one quantitative method (designed to collect numbers) and one qualitative method (designed to collect words)" (256). In recent years, however, this definition has been questioned, and those types of research designs that simply present quantitative and qualitative research as two distinct strands without explicit integration have been labeled as "quasimixed" (Teddlie and Tashakkori 2006). According to Bazeley (2009), "Integration requires interdependence in reaching a common theoretical or research goal, so that complementary or sequenced components in a study, not necessarily involving integration, may consequently not be considered to be mixed methods" (204). Integration, or mixing, of qualitative and quantitative data sets is now considered to be an essential component of mixed methods designs:

Mixed methods research is simply more than reporting two distinct "strands" of quantitative and qualitative research; these studies must also integrate, link, or connect these "strands" in some way. The expectation is that by the end of the manuscript, conclusions gleaned from the two strands are integrated to provide a fuller understanding of the phenomenon under study. (Creswell and Tashakkori 2007)

The successful integration of qualitative and quantitative data is directly related to the concept of mixed methods validity (also called inference quality or legitimation), a concept that "addresses the ability of the researcher to draw meaningful and accurate conclusions from all of the data in the study" (Creswell and Plano Clark 2007, 146). Mixed methods researchers use many strategies to mix or integrate data from quantitative and qualitative sources. The most common method utilized for direct integration is the use of a discussion or matrix. Within a mixed methods discussion section of an article, thesis, or dissertation, a researcher may choose to present qualitative quotes, codes, or themes alongside specific statistical results that align topically. A matrix may be used to present both qualitative and quantitative results directly alongside one another for easy comparison and contrast (see Fitzpatrick 2008).

Another technique that is more rarely used is data transformation. Researchers use data transformation to convert one form of data into another. For example, a researcher may count the instances or prevalence of qualitative themes or codes, analyze them statistically, and then compare them with quantitative data (Creswell and Plano Clark 2007). Or, a researcher may conduct a quantitative factor analysis to develop factors that could then be compared with qualitative themes (Punch 1998). Some sequential or embedded mixed methods designs are integrated directly through the use of one form of data to shape another. For example, in an instrument development design, an initial qualitative phase may lead to the development of a quantitative instrument, with the mixing of the two phases happening at the point of the construction of the new instrument.

The development of new techniques for the integration of quantitative and qualitative data sets will be a priority for mixed methods researchers in the coming years, According to O'Cathain, Nicholl, and Murphy (2007), it is this vital aspect of integration that distinguishes mixed methods studies from a set of monomethod studies undertaken independently.

10.3. Considering Qualitative Research in Mixed Methods Studies

Creswell (2011) points out that qualitative researchers have long embraced the complementary use of quantitative data, even before the emergence of a full mixed methods scholarly dialogue in the 1980s. For example, in Denzin's seminal 1978 book, *The Research Act: A Theoretical Introduction to Sociological Methods*, he suggests the use of various data sources in a study under the umbrella term "data triangulation," saying: "I now offer as a final methodological rule the principle that multiple methods should be used in every investigation" (28). Sieber (1973) discussed and developed procedures for the "interplay" of fieldwork and survey methods. Patton (1980) advanced the use of "methodological mixes" and described four design models, some of which included the transformation of qualitative data into "counts." More recently, Morse and Niehaus (2009) described the work of ethnographers as being "mixed" in nature, due to the frequent collection of both quantitative and qualitative data in ethnographic work.

Still, many qualitative researchers question the use of mixed methods research. Such critics are concerned not only about the "incompatibility thesis" (Howe 2004), or the problems associated with mixing worldviews in a single study, but also the perceived prominence of postpositivist thinking in mixed methods research (Creswell 2011). This perception is logically grounded, given that most initial mixed methods studies involved the addition of a qualitative component to a study that was initially a quantitative project (Teddlie and Tashakkori 2011). According to Howe (2004), "It is not that qualitative methods can never be fruitfully and appropriately used in this way, but their natural home is within an interpretivist framework with the democratic aim of seeking to understand and give voice to the insider's perspective" (54). Denzin and Lincoln similarly discussed the need for qualitative methods to exist within their own domain of a "critical, interpretive framework" rather than within the framework of a mixed methods design. Giddings (2006) refers to mixed methods research as "positivism dressed in drag," with such positivistic thinking reflected in the design and analysis techniques described by mixed methods scholars.

Teddlie and Tashakkori (2011) address these concerns directly:

> We want to unambiguously express our regard for the powerful contributions of QUAL methods due to the concern that some scholars have expressed about MMR [mixed methods research] subordinating QUAL methods to a secondary role behind QUAN methods. This is not how we interpret the MMR literature from the past 30-plus years. In fact, QUAL + quan studies [those emphasizing the qualitative component over the quantitative] emphasizing the detailed, impressionistic perceptions of human "data-gathering instruments" and their interpretations of their outcomes are among the most valuable of all the extant MMR [mixed methods research] literature. (286)

Although mixed methods research has been emerging as a viable paradigm for some time, strategies to ensure the rigor of new mixed methods designs are still being developed. With regard to the use of qualitative research in mixed methods designs, there are important decisions that have yet to be made on important methodological issues. According to Morse (2005), it is qualitative researchers who must make these decisions:

> Qualitative researchers, therefore, have a choice: We can take control, or we can ignore this trend; we can step aside and let other researchers establish rules for the

use of qualitative data, or we ourselves can develop sound principles of appropriate use. (583)

Surely there are many questions that deserve consideration with regard to the development of mixed methods research in music education, and space here precludes the discussion of them all. To further the conversation within our field about the use of mixed methods research, I here present some emerging issues that deserve contemplation by the qualitative music education research community.

10.3.1. Lack of Qualitative Rigor

According to Creswell and Plano Clark (2007), studies that utilize minimal qualitative research, such as those survey studies that ask a few open-ended questions as a part of the survey, can still be considered mixed methods research, even though "the qualitative data may consist of short sentences and brief comments, hardly the type of qualitative data that involves rich context and detailed information from participants" (11). To me, this is a problematic assertion that needs to be addressed by the qualitative research community.

There is concern among mixed methods scholars (Teddlie and Tashakkori 2011) that such issues of lack of rigor may be due in part to researchers who undertake such research with primary training in one tradition and minimal competence or education with regard to the other. Similarly, there is a concern that the ability to be a "methodological connoisseur" requires a depth of experience in both methodological traditions that novice researchers may not have. Teddlie and Tashakkori (2011) suggest that one remedy will need to be the provision of better and deeper experiences at the doctoral level, where students work in the field alongside their quantitative, qualitative, and mixed methods mentors. As mixed methods research continues to evolve as an accepted domain and doctoral students increasingly require better experiences with both qualitative and qualitative techniques, the necessity of methodological diversity within faculties may increase.

I would assert instead that all mixed methods data, whether qualitative or quantitative, should be collected and analyzed according to the traditions of that particular methodology. Within mixed methods designs, it is possible, for practical purposes, that some phases of study will be more abbreviated than would normally occur with a larger singular study. However, each phase of the research design, even if abbreviated, should align with the expectations of rigor that each method requires. The primary question to be asked is "Would the design of this portion of the study be able to stand alone were it not part of a mixed methods study?" With regard to the use of an open-ended question at the end of a survey, I would argue that this would not be sufficient to constitute the qualitative phase of a mixed methods study, as the foundations of qualitative research, including standards of trustworthiness, do not typically justify stand-alone "open-ended questionnaire" studies.

10.3.2. Use of Data Transformation Techniques

The use of data transformation techniques has its origins in the quantitizing of qualitative data, or the process of converting qualitative data to numerical codes that can be statistically analyzed (Miles and Huberman 1994). The process of qualitizing (Tashakkori and Teddlie 1998), or the process by which quantitative data are transformed into data that can be analyzed qualitatively, is also used, albeit more rarely, in mixed methods research.

Many qualitative researchers will argue with the basis for conducting such transformations of data, and the discussion and debate of the proper use of this technique should continue. Does the quantifying of qualitative data undermine the purpose and trustworthiness of qualitative research? Are there ways to better adapt such techniques to allow for the better representation of data in its original form? For example, perhaps researchers who utilize such techniques might first be asked to present both qualitative and quantitative data in the manner associated with each paradigm's traditional modes of representation (i.e., presentation of within-case and cross-case themes) prior to the transformation of any one form of data into another (i.e., counting of instances of a case). Hindering such full presentations of data, of course, are the page-length restrictions of most peer-reviewed journals in music education. Such issues deserve further discussion among qualitative researchers in our field.

10.3.3. Publication of Mixed Methods Studies in Music Education Journals

There are far fewer instances of mixed methods research published in our field than there are mixed methods dissertations. One apparent reason for this discrepancy is the issue of how to successfully report the findings of such studies, which can be significantly longer and more complex than mono-method studies, within the typical page constraints of music education journals. This issue may be especially problematic for the full representation of qualitative data within a published article, as authors struggle to provide rich and thick description of their participants' experiences while also accommodating both quantitative data and the merged "mixed" data analysis. Understandably, authors are often tempted to publish the qualitative and quantitative components of their studies separately.

However, according to O'Cathain, Nicholl, and Murphy (2007), such separate publication may produce decreased "yield" from the mixed methods study: "A study with separate articles from both components might be considered to have produced 'the sum of its parts' and might arguably be no better than if independent qualitative and quantitative studies had been undertaken" (151). Sims (2011) echoes these thoughts in her previously mentioned "Forum" piece addressing the publication of mixed methods research in the *JRME*: "True mixed methods research cannot be divided into two articles for publication without losing an important, arguably the *most* important, aspect of the analysis" (227).

Given that research using a mixed methods approach consists of both the qualitative and quantitative components as well as the integrated analysis, it may indeed require more space to report than other types of research. What types of solutions can our professional community develop to make the publication of mixed methods research easier? For example, Sims (2011) suggests the use of, and Fitzpatrick (2011) utilizes, supplemental online Web space to present data that could not be fitted within the page constraints of the journal. What other strategies can be developed by our research community?

10.3.4. Future Directions: Maintaining Creativity and Openness

Besides addressing some of the previously discussed issues, there are many exciting contributions that the qualitative research community can make to the future of mixed methods research in music education. For example, how can mixed methods research designs be adapted to address the richness of the arts? How can mixed methods researchers utilize arts-based approaches (Barone 2001) within mixed methods designs to enrich our understanding of phenomena? The music education community could provide tremendous leadership with regard to this issue.

In addition, how can we better foster collaborations between qualitatively trained music education researchers and their like-minded quantitatively trained colleagues? Can such collaborations allow for fruitful mixed methods collaborations to emerge? As Reimer stated, such collaborations "would allow us to tackle the larger issues, rescuing us from our tendency to deal only with those small enough to be handled in single, one-shot studies" (2008, 200–01). The resulting interactions and publications may also help to develop mutual understanding within our research community: "Interaction between colleagues—even colleagues of quite different methodological persuasions—can be a powerful integrative force" (Brewer and Hunter 2006, 12).

Many exciting possibilities are emerging with regard to the use of mixed methods research in music education. However, there are also many questions that remain. The successful development of mixed methods research within our field will rely upon the emergence of a dialogue that attempts to honor the integrity of both qualitative and quantitative research traditions. Such a dialogue requires a level of creativity and openness, and the thoughtful contributions of the qualitative research community in music education.

10.4. Moving Forward

Within the music education community, there is no doubt that mono-method designs predominate, and there are, of course, many research questions that are best addressed using either a singular quantitative or qualitative approach. However, increasingly, music education researchers are exploring ways to use mixed methods designs within their studies. The use of multiple methods requires a thoughtful, well-crafted, and well-considered approach. As the use of mixed methods research increases within our field, there will be growing pains as the methodology evolves and adapts to the needs of the music education community. The development of better mixed methods research in music education and criteria for evaluating such designs will be aided by the thoughtful and creative contributions of the qualitative research community.

REFERENCES

Austin, J., and M. Berg. 2006. "Exploring Music Practice among Sixth-Grade Band and Orchestra Students." *Psychology of Music* 34: 535–58.

Baer, J. S. 2010. "The Relationship of Multiple Intelligence Instruction to Sight Singing Achievement of Middle School Choral Students." PhD diss., Walden University.

Barone, T. 2001. "Science, Art, and the Predispositions of Educational Researchers." *Educational Researcher* 30 (7): 24–28.

Bazan, D. 2007. "Teaching and Learning Strategies Used by Student-Directed Teachers of Middle School Band." PhD diss., Case Western Reserve University.

Bazan, D. 2011. "The Use of Student-Directed Instruction by Middle School Band Teachers." *Bulletin of the Council for Research in Music Education* 189: 23–56.

Bazeley, P. 2009. "Editorial: Integrating Data Analyses in Mixed Methods Research." *Journal of Mixed Methods Research* 3 (3): 203.

Brewer, J., and A. Hunter. 2006. *Foundations of Multimethod Research: Synthesizing Styles.* Thousand Oaks, CA: Sage Publications.

Campbell, P. S. 2002. "Senior Researcher Award Acceptance Speech: A Matter of Perspective: Thoughts on the Multiple Realities of Research." *Journal of Research in Music Education* 50: 191–201.

Carlisle, K. J. 2008. "A Study of Social-Emotional Climate within Secondary School Music Classrooms Settings." PhD diss., University of Toronto.

Conway, C., J. Eros, K. Pellegrino, and C. West. 2010. "The Role of Graduate and Undergraduate Interactions in the Development of Preservice Music Teachers and Music Teacher Educators: A Self-Study in Music Teacher Education." *Bulletin of the Council for Research in Music Education* 183: 49–64.

Conway, C., J. Eros, and A. M. Stanley. 2008. "Summers-Only versus the Academic Year Master of Music in Music Education Degree: Perceptions of Program Graduates." *Bulletin of the Council for Research in Music Education* 178: 21–34.

Creswell, J. 1995. *Research Design: Qualitative and Quantitative Approaches.* Thousand Oaks, CA: Sage Publications.

Creswell, J. 2003. *Research Design: Qualitative, Quantitative, and Mixed Methods Approaches.* Thousand Oaks, CA: Sage Publications.

Creswell, J. 2011. "Controversies in Mixed Methods Research." In *The Sage Handbook of Qualitative Research*, edited by N. K. Denzin and Y. S. Lincoln, 269–84. Thousand Oaks, CA: Sage Publications.

Creswell, J., and V. Plano Clark. 2007. *Designing and Conducting Mixed Methods Research.* Thousand Oaks, CA: Sage Publications.

Creswell, J., and A. Tashakkori. 2007. "Developing Publishable Mixed Methods Manuscripts." *Journal of Mixed Methods Research* 1 (2): 107–11.

Dansereau, D. R. 2005. "*The Musicality of 3-Year-Old Children within the Context of Research-Based Musical Engagement.*" PhD diss., Georgia State University.

Datta, L. 1997. "A Pragmatic Basis for Mixed-Methods Designs." In *Advances in Mixed-Method Evaluation: The Challenges and Benefits of Integrating Diverse Paradigms*, edited by J. C. Greene and V. Caracelli, 33–46. San Francisco: Jossey-Bass.

Denzin, N. K. 1978. *The Research Act: A Theoretical Introduction to Sociological Methods.* New York: Praeger.

Fitzpatrick, K. A. 2008. "Mixed Methods Portrait of Urban Instrumental Music Teaching." PhD diss., Northwestern University.

Fitzpatrick, K. A. 2011. "A Mixed Methods Portrait of Urban Instrumental Music Teaching." *Journal of Research in Music Education* 59: 229–56.

Gavin, Russell B. 2010. "An Exploration of Potential Factors Affecting Persistence to Degree Completion in Undergraduate Music Teacher Education Students." PhD diss., The Florida State University.

Giddings, L. S. 2006. "Mixed-Methods Research: Positivism Dressed in Drag?" *Journal of Research in Nursing* 11 (3): 195–203.

Glik, D. C., K. Parker, G. Muligande, and B. Hategikamana. 1986. "Integrating Quantitative and Qualitative Survey Techniques." *International Quarterly of Community Health Education* 7 (3): 181–200.

Greene, J. C. 2007. *Mixed Methods in Social Inquiry.* San Francisco: Jossey-Bass.

Greene, J. C., and V. Caracelli. 2003. "Making Paradigmatic Sense of Mixed Methods Practice." In *Handbook of Mixed Methods on Social and Behavioral Research*, edited by A. Tashakkori and C. Teddlie, 91–110. Thousand Oaks, CA: Sage Publications.

Greene, J. C., V. Caracelli, and W. Graham. 1989. "Toward a Conceptual Framework for Mixed-Method Evaluation Designs." *Educational Evaluation and Policy Analysis* 11 (3): 255–74.

Hart, L. C., S. Z. Smith, S. L. Swats, and M. E. Smith. 2009. "An Examination of Research Methods in Mathematics Education." *Journal of Mixed Methods Research* 3: 26–41.

Howe, K. R. 2004. "A Critique of Experimentalism." *Qualitative Inquiry* 10: 42–61.

Huang, H. J. 2004. "A Study of the Relationship between Music Learning and School Achievement of Sixth-Grade Students." PhD diss., University of Idaho.

Mertens, D. M. 2003. "Mixed Methods and the Politics of Human Research: The Transformative-Emancipatory Perspective." In *Handbook of Mixed Methods in Social and Behavioral Research*, edited by A. Tashakkori and C. Teddlie, 135–66. London: Sage Publications.

Mertens, D. M. 2007. "Transformative Paradigm: Mixed Methods and Social Justice." *Journal of Mixed Methods Research* 1 (3): 212–25.

Miles, M. B., and A. M. Huberman. 1994. *Qualitative Data Analysis: A Sourcebook of New Methods.* 2nd ed. Thousand Oaks, CA: Sage Publications.

Morse, J. 1991. "Approaches to Qualitative-Quantitative Methodological Triangulation." *Nursing Research* 40: 120–23.

Morse, J. 2002. "Principles of Mixed Methods and Multimethod Research Design." In *Handbook of Mixed Methods in Social and Behavioral Research*, edited by A. Tashakkori and C. Teddlie, 189–208. London: Sage Publications.

Morse, J. 2005. "Evolving Trends in Qualitative Research: Advances in Mixed-Methods Design." *Qualitative Health Research* 15 (5): 583–85.

Morse, J., and L. Niehaus. 2009. *Mixed Method Design: Principles and Procedures.* Walnut Creek, CA: Left Coast Press.

Neokleous, R. 2010. "Tracking Preservice Kindergarten Teachers' Development of Singing Skills and Confidence: An Applied Study." PhD diss., Boston University.

O'Cathain, A., J. Nicholl, and E. Murphy. 2007. "Integration and Publications as Indicators of 'Yield' from Mixed Methods Studies." *Journal of Mixed Methods Research* 1 (2): 147.

Onwuegbuzie, A. 2000. "Positivists, Post-Positivists, Post-Structuralists, and Post-Modernists: Why Can't We All Get Along? Towards a Framework for Unifying Research Paradigms." Paper presented at the annual meeting of the Association for the Advancement of Educational Research (AAER), November, 18, Ponte Vedra, Florida. Access ERIC: FullText. Georgia.

Onwuegbuzie, A., and A. Ross. 2010. "Mixed Methods Research Design: A Comparison of Prevalence in JRME and AERJ." *International Journal of Multiple Research Approaches* 4 (3): 233–45.

Panaiotidi, E. 2005. "The Nature of Paradigms and Paradigm Shifts in Music Education." *Philosophy of Music Education Review* 13 (1): 37–75.

Patton, M. 1980. *Qualitative Evaluation Methods.* Beverly Hills, CA: Sage Publications.

Punch, K. F. 1998. *Introduction to Social Research: Quantitative and Qualitative Approaches.* London: Sage Publications.

Reimer, B. 2008. "Research in Music Education: Personal and Professional Reflections in a Time of Perplexity." *Journal of Research in Music Education* 56 (3): 190–203.

Rossman, G. B., and B. L. Wilson. 1991. "Numbers and Words Revisited: Being 'Shamelessly Eclectic.'" *Quality and Quantity* 28 (3): 315–27.

Roulston, K. 2006. "Mapping the Possibilities of Qualitative Research in Music Education: A Primer." *Music Education Research* 8 (2): 153–73.

Rummel, J. R. 2010. "Perceptions of Jazz Improvisation among Pennsylvania Music Educators." PhD diss., Boston University.

Sandelowski, M. 2000. "Combining Qualitative and Quantitative Sampling, Data Collection, and Analysis Techniques in Mixed-Method Studies." *Research in Nursing and Health* 23: 246–55.

Saunders, A. T. 2005. "The Role of Motivation in the Choral Setting: Teacher Beliefs and their Impact on Choral Conductor Behavior and Choral Student Motivation." PhD diss., The University of Utah.

Scruggs, B. B. 2009. "Learning Outcomes in Two Divergent Middle School String Orchestra Classroom Environments: A Comparison of a Learner-Centered and a Teacher-Centered Approach." PhD diss., Georgia State University.

Sieber, S. D. 1973. "The Integration of Fieldwork and Survey Methods." *American Journal of Sociology* 78: 1335–59.

Sims, W. 2011. "Forum." *Journal of Research in Music Education* 59: 227–28.

Stringham, D. A. 2010. "Improvisation and Composition in a High School Instrumental Music Curriculum." PhD diss., University of Rochester, Eastman School of Music.

Tashakkori, A., and C. Teddlie. 1998. *Mixed Methodology: Combining Qualitative and Quantitative Approaches.* Thousand Oaks, CA: Sage Publications.

Tashakkori, A., and C. Teddlie, eds. 2003. *Handbook of Mixed Methods in Social and Behavioral Research.* Thousand Oaks, CA: Sage Publications.

Teddlie, C., and A. Tashakkori. 2006. "A Genera: Typology of Research Designs Featuring Mixed Methods." *Research in Schools* 13 (1): 12–28.

Teddlie, C., and A. Tashakkori. 2011. "Mixed Methods Research: Contemporary Issues in an Emerging Field." In *The Sage Handbook of Qualitative Research*, edited by N. K. Denzin and Y. S. Lincoln, 285–300. Thousand Oaks, CA: Sage Publications.

Thomas, M. P. 2007. "Effects of Team Teaching in the Massed Secondary Choral Setting." PhD diss., Walden University.

Weinholtz, D., B. Kacer, and T. Rocklin. 1995. "Salvaging Quantitative Research with Qualitative Data." *Qualitative Health Research* 5 (3): 388–97.

Woolley, C. M. 2009. "Meeting the Mixed Methods Challenge of Integration in a Sociological Study of Structure and Agency." *Journal of Mixed Methods Research* 3 (1): 7.

Yarbrough, C. 1984. "A Content Analysis of the 'Journal of Research in Music Education,' 1953– 1983." *Journal of Research in Music Education* 32 (4): 213–22.

Yarbrough, C. 1996. "The Future of Scholarly Inquiry in Music Education: 1996 Senior Researcher Award Acceptance Address." *Journal of Research in Music Education* 44: 190–203.

CHAPTER 11

FUTURE POSSIBILITIES FOR QUALITATIVE RESEARCH IN MUSIC EDUCATION

JANET R. BARRETT

TITLING a chapter "future possibilities" calls for prescient acts of prognostication. At the very least, such a title suggests that qualitative research in music education has developed to the point that one can sense larger patterns at play within the field and that these larger patterns have gained enough momentum and heft to warrant their development, refinement, and expansion. Before pointing to future directions, it seems wise to first look back, if only briefly and perhaps indulgently (metanarratives of "progress" notwithstanding). During the 1980s and 1990s, qualitative research in education was finding its voice. The American Educational Research Association's *Educational Researcher* served as a bellwether to presage what was to come. Derived from Middle English, a bellwether is the lead sheep in a flock, around whose neck a bell is hung so that you hear the flock coming before you can actually see the herd. Through that period, qualitative researchers in education at large made their way through rough terrain in an attempt to distinguish the epistemological groundings of qualitative work from the easier to locate and safer footings of quantitative research. In music education, there were stirrings and wanderings, although there was clearly no organized herd, or prominent group of researchers at the forefront. I read through the draft chapters for this *Handbook* in light of this historical trajectory, recalling how, in the late 1980s when I was a doctoral student, qualitative inquiry seemed to be forming in front of our eyes. In music education, there were few studies to be used as examples and few proponents who could serve as mentors. We could hear the bell, faintly at times, but we certainly couldn't see the herd. We weren't even sure if there were enough researchers doing qualitative research in music education to justify calling ourselves a herd. Stepping out to propose a qualitative dissertation or study felt treacherous, probably just as much for those of us writing dissertations as those who were advising them, and together we expected to encounter boulders and ravines and unimaginable obstacles in our path. Put in this context, this volume represents considerable accomplishments for music education, as relatively small as we are as a field. Our growth has been organic rather than organized, moving in fits and starts, but notable nonetheless. To echo Conway and West's observation in this volume, we have come a long way in 20 years from one chapter in the 1992 *Handbook* and qualitative "sightings" along the way to the body of research represented by this entire project.

Recall the common justificatory language that served as a prologue for earlier dissertations and journal articles in which the researcher felt compelled to explain basic concepts of qualitative inquiry and argue for its validity and rigor before finally reaching the rationale for the actual study. It was as if each study required an overture of legitimizing explanation before establishing central phenomena and purpose statements. This era has passed. Although the paradigm wars still rage outside (fueled by the politicization of so-called scientific research), within music education, qualitative research has earned respectability. I recall as well my own process of proposing a qualitative dissertation on the cognitive processes children use to play by ear, completed in 1990, when qualitative work was just cresting on the horizon. I felt as if I were inventing a procedure for analysis (with some key structural support from Miles and Huberman), investigating a relatively underexamined area of study, while simultaneously convincing my committee of the project's viability. My committee was split down the middle on the use of the word "hypothesis," and as hard as I persisted that the term was not appropriate for the study, I lost the argument. I relied heavily on the volume on disciplined inquiry, *Complementary Methods for Research in Education*, published by AERA and edited by Lee Shulman, when I needed reassurance. Many years later, I found myself in the fortuitous position of teaching a qualitative research methods course, feeling again like a pioneer. Gracious gifts of syllabi from other colleagues helped to establish some principles for structuring a course. The pedagogy of qualitative research has become far more established and variegated in recent years. The challenge of teaching methods has been intensified by the proliferation of methods texts and multiple decisions regarding the alignment of the epistemological fit with the method and the type of study proposed. We now have a wealth of methodological literature at hand, and the challenge is to choose wisely and to remain aligned with the underlying principles suggested by these perspectives.

To prepare for writing this chapter, I read the chapters in the 2014 *Handbook* sequentially (which few readers are likely to do, I suspect). This overview revealed some patterns, particularly in noting which studies and researchers are cited regularly by others. Another theme was seeing whose work outside the field has served as a beacon within. As a hybrid field ourselves (music and education), we thrive by borrowing from other traditions, scholars, and communities. I was most surprised that enough work can be cited to justify the syntheses of work in the content areas cited as models (early childhood, general music, strings, band, etc.), and although nearly each chapter author called for more development, each subject area can legitimately claim a base of studies as starting points. Chapters on overarching issues and designs point toward a greater maturity of thought and oversight, and I suspect they will be consulted frequently in courses and seminars.

The past, present, and future of qualitative research in general can be grasped, at least partially, by reading the prologues and epilogues that frame the four *Sage Handbooks of Qualitative Research*. For each synoptic volume, Norman Denzin and Yvonna Lincoln situate the current status of qualitative inquiry and dialogue among qualitative researchers as a series of moments or turns in which new vistas come into view, or segments of the journey are seen more clearly in retrospect. These include:

- The traditional (1900–1950)
- The modernist or golden age (1950–1970)
- Blurred genres (1970–1986)
- The crisis of representation (1986–1990)
- The postmodern (1990–1995)
- Post-experimental inquiry (1995–2000)
- The methodologically contested present (2000–2010)
- The future (2010–) (2011, 3)

I wondered if qualitative work in music education could be similarly partitioned, or whether it paralleled some of the distinctive yet overlapping phases that Denzin and Lincoln describe. I cannot find clear parallels or provide tidy synopses of where we have been, but as a result of reading the chapters in the entire project, it is safe to say that we have passed through infancy and childhood and we may have arrived somewhere in adolescence, headed toward greater maturity. I also looked to Denzin and Lincoln's notions of the "eighth moment," the future that is enmeshed in arguments related to the evidence-based neoliberal ideologies of national educational policy, a leaning toward "moral discourse, with the development of sacred textualities," and a dynamic surge of questions related to "democracy, race, gender, class, nation-states, globalization, freedom, and community" (2011, 3). Music education, in my reading, has not yet caught up with or fully confronted the future that Denzin and Lincoln envision, although the call for social justice is becoming louder. The challenge of this epilogue, then, is to sketch out some of the challenges and opportunities facing qualitative research in music education that make sense for this particular moment in our field, amplified by the work in this first discipline-specific handbook. To use a favored word, the section headings for the remainder of this chapter were derived from the emergent themes seen across the *Handbook*.[1] Seven future directions are proposed, in which qualitative research in music education will:

- Attain greater clarity in aligning our research activities with wisely chosen and pressing aims, *strong purposes*;
- Attend more closely to the epistemological coherence of our theoretical and analytical frameworks, *strong footings*;
- Situate inquiry in new contexts, engaging new voices, and pursuing compelling *new realms* of study;

- Utilize *new affordances* of technology and social media as strategic tools and environments for qualitative work;
- Seek greater *resonance and rigor* through attending to writing and scholarly critique;
- Integrate *the community of qualitative researchers* in order to build our professional capacity and collaborative power; and
- Expand the *reach of qualitative inquiry* by attending to its overall impact on practitioners, scholars, and communities.

11.1. STRONG PURPOSES

No longer is it sufficient to propose a research study simply because no one else has investigated a particular topic, event, or context. There may be legitimate reasons that no one has invested the care and effort to do so. As a field, we must challenge ourselves to ask questions that will lead to substantive understanding, deep insight, and greater professional capacity. Each published study represents a precious investment of intellect, resources, time, and commitment both for those who collaborated in its genesis and for those enter into the text as readers. The care we take in framing and forming our questions, no matter how emergent and dynamic, is essential.

An essay on the future of qualitative research in psychology borrows from popular culture, quoting an especially famous split infinitive—"to boldly go" . . . "Like the Starship Enterprise using warp drive to cover the immense distances involved in intergalactic exploration, qualitative researchers want to do things and go places that psychology has not been able to reach before" (Willig and Stainton-Rogers 2008, 591). So it is with music education. Through our research efforts, we have entered into lived worlds that have been unseen, unheard, and ungraspable before now. Inquiry has been directed toward the multiple ways that individuals experience and value music in their lives, the social surrounds that enable or constrict musical growth, the ways that music both shapes and shifts identities, the processes and pathways of teaching music. Through an array of studies, greater understanding of the complexities, particularities, nuances, and paths of musical engagement has developed.

Qualitative research is also beginning to address the conundrums facing our field that resist facile solutions, such as the disjunctures between school music and music in society, attempts to reconceptualize the music curriculum to broaden its reach and impact, and perennial crises of access and legitimization. Yvonna Lincoln speaks of "the clandestine disfigurements and outrages of racism, sexism, homophobia, and class injuries" (2010, 4) that have been exposed through interpretive work in the larger qualitative community. Together with Norman Denzin, she adopts a nearly evangelical tone in the prologue and epilogue to the fourth qualitative handbook, calling researchers to commit to critical projects directed toward social justice. Their call is plain, clear, and straightforward:

There is a pressing need to show how the practices of qualitative research can help change the world in positive ways. It is necessary to continue to engage the pedagogical, theoretical, and practical promise of qualitative research as a form of radical democratic practice. (2011, x)

A socially situated, critical perspective within music education has arisen to engage themes of race, class, gender, ability/disability; researchers will continue to pursue this critical work toward larger moral purposes.

I am reminded of an essay written by Alan "Buddy" Peshkin that I frequently consult in teaching qualitative research methods. Moved to defend the goodness of qualitative research on behalf of his students, whose proposals had been criticized by departmental colleagues for failing to be sufficiently "theory driven, hypothesis testing, or generalization producing," he was inspired instead to address a different question, "What is its generative promise?" (1993, 23), allowing him to turn from a more defensive posture. In other words, what is qualitative research good for? He develops the essay by explaining various outcomes or functions of qualitative research for description, interpretation, verification, and evaluation, taking care to address how these categorical distinctions are often blended and interrelated. The goodness of qualitative research in music education can be judged by considering the wisdom and care involved in naming and framing projects, forming questions, and aligning these research questions with the pressing needs and issues of our contemporary experience.

11.2. STRONG FOOTINGS

Qualitative researchers would be well-advised to read and re-read the initial chapters in this volume, Matsunobu and Bresler, Conway and West, Allsup, and Scheib, to develop greater discernment and judgment about the frameworks of ideas that undergird inquiry. Well-articulated foundations, the principled systems of ideas that convey distinct epistemological, ontological, and methodological beliefs about the nature of knowledge, reality, and modes of inquiry, distinguish various families of qualitative work from other paradigms of research. Lincoln, Lynham, and Guba review earlier work related to research paradigms: positivism, postpositivism, critical theory, and constructivism, while adding a fifth, the participatory paradigm (2011, 98). Situating work within various "ontologies and epistemologies that differ sharply from those undergirding conventional social science" (97), they list a corresponding variety of perspectives including feminist theories, critical race and ethnic studies, queer theory, border theories, postcolonial ontologies and epistemologies, and post-structural and postmodern work.

In chapter 1, Matsunobu and Bresler describe how music education has borrowed from research traditions rooted in anthropology, philosophy, action research, ethnography, ethnomusicology, and hermeneutics. Generous appropriation from other traditions has informed and enabled many music education researchers to develop discipline-specific studies. Drawing liberally from other research methods, strategies, and techniques, however, can be counterproductive as well if the underlying assumptions and premises are at odds. Imagine a foundation consisting of a little poured concrete, some glass and chrome, a few weathered pine boards, mixed with recycled cardboard boxes. Such a foundation cannot hold. Instead, we strive for coherence and good fit without restriction, articulating clear organizing premises. Although it is challenging to sort through large systems or paradigms, epistemologies, frameworks, and perspectives, we notice the difference in tightly reasoned, analyzed, and reported studies. As Allsup reminds us in chapter 3, epistemology is the bedrock upon which our claims rest. He argues for thoughtful coherence when he says: "the relationship between one's epistemological view of education must be consistent with the design of one's research." Educational thinking is intertwined with systems of thought that, whether articulated or tacit, influence how we approach music teaching and learning. Using Bruner as a case, Allsup traces the shifts in epistemological thought that have characterized Bruner's leading voice in education. Moving toward this coherence while avoiding rigidity is a sign of growing maturity within the field.

Scheib, in chapter 4, sorts through the panoramic array of superordinate and subordinate categorizations related to worldviews, orientations, perspectives, paradigms, theoretical frameworks, conceptual frameworks, models. At heart is the notion that qualitative research is informed by the researcher's stance and beliefs as well as the sets of ideas derived from empirical inquiry and analytical theorizing. In every phase of the qualitative research process, a dynamic synergy between the abstract and the particular is at play. A counterpoint of ideas arises as the researcher sorts and sifts, names and labels, groups and clusters, annotates and comments on the data in correspondence with key ideas drawn into the mix from "outside" the study. New findings are situated into preexisting theories; new theoretical propositions emerge from key findings. As one instance, consider the constructivist orientation of many studies in music education and the way these studies have dovetailed closely through an emergent relationship of theory and data.

Careful consideration of theoretical foundations and frameworks comes sharply to attention when contemplating the "new kid on the block," mixed methods. Fitzpatrick, in chapter 10 cites Woolley's distinctions of quantitative as "indirect and reductive"; qualitative as "direct and holistic," a vivid conflict of worldviews. This is the crux of the incommensurability argument that suggests deep rifts in knowledge claims that cannot be held in view simultaneously because of their fundamentally irreconcilable positions. In the pragmatist's view, these central tensions not only coexist, they inform one another. Methodological eclecticism is valued. Debates and dialogues about frameworks—their compatibilities and concordances—are of vital importance as a future direction for qualitative inquiry in our field. I can foresee lively debate as more solid mixed methods studies are proposed, conducted, and disseminated and these concordances interrogated.

11.3. NEW REALMS

Qualitative researchers in music education are called to situate inquiry in new contexts, engaging new voices and pursuing compelling realms of study. Many prompts for expansiveness appear throughout the perspectives of the entire *Handbook*, most often based on the author's realization that reviews of extant studies revealed gaps and lacunae. Among these compelling calls is the recurrent invitation for researchers to reach out to underrepresented groups. Carter, in the third volume, wisely acknowledges the "inherent problems associated with established social categories" as he draws attention to the ways that any social category, however well-intentioned and clearly defined, is itself an abstraction when situated in complex human experience, especially at the overlapping and fluid intersections of socially constructed and maintained categorical distinctions. Nonetheless, qualitative researchers are charged with giving voice to those who are silenced, marginalized, or misunderstood, especially related to issues of race, class, gender, dis/ability. Research in music education has interrogated questions related to power, access, poverty, privilege, oppression, injustice, and invisibility. Equity is an aim for us all. To pursue systematic inquiry involves entering into the realm of the political, where inequity is unveiled and confronted. It requires attending to "what is not yet seen or heard."

Elementary and secondary classrooms have traditionally been and will remain inviting contexts of inquiry in probing musical understanding, the reciprocality of teaching and learning, processes of social interaction, and especially the influences of educational policy on music education. Within schools, opportunities for collaboration are plentiful. Robbins, in chapter 9, speaks to the "democratic validity" of practitioner research, fostering shared inquiry with teachers in the field. In this regard, the intimate relationship of teaching as a form of inquiry and inquiry on forms of teaching can be explored. Given the inhospitable conditions that face music teachers in many school settings, employing teacher research as a form of professional agency seems an especially urgent need.

A socially just orientation also takes qualitative researchers into new contexts of preschools, prisons, community schools, eldercare, and juvenile detention facilities, as well as churches, concert halls, street corners, ethnic fairs and festivals, and sites beyond. Several authors represented in this project have beckoned researchers to consider virtual worlds of social media as multiple, simultaneous, and complex worlds of musical engagement. Music's ubiquitous presence in the lives of children, adolescents, and adults is not contained within classrooms walls. The fullness of culture and community complements and often overlaps with the study of music in school settings.

A frequently cited notion that corresponds to the emancipatory potential of qualitative research is that it "gives voice" to those whose voices go unheard. As the realms and contexts of inquiry are broadened, ethical considerations multiply in giving voice to children and adults in ways that protect their identities and acknowledge the ownership of their ideas.

11.4. New Affordances

The processes of qualitative research are enabled through the use of strategies, tools, designs, and methodological guidebooks that enable inquiry; many such affordances will influence future work. I have written elsewhere about how conducting qualitative research requires a series of transformations (Barrett 2007). Each transformative move—from the lived world of participants to data generation, from data generation to permanent data records, from data records to a complex theorized report—depends upon the researcher's wise and skillful use of a vast array of personal and professional resources. The chapters in this volume on approaches and designs, as well as the chapters in volume 2 on data collection and analysis, will be invaluable in supporting the complex inner workings of a study that so often are mentioned in terse, telegraphic ways in articles, rarely laying open the rigorous systematic thinking governing the process of qualitative inquiry.

Certainly a future direction for qualitative researchers points to greater use of music as data, as Pellegrino (volume 2) and others mention. Sounds shape our experiences and identities, but when the lived world of participants is represented in research reports, the very sounds at the center of these worlds are often difficult to capture or convey. Few journal articles supplement textual data through the use of photographs, video, audio, digital media, movement, and gestures, but this is likely to change. The affordances of technology in particular will allow a greater profusion of representational forms, requiring skillful analysis and interpretation, but leading to a deeper, richer engagement with the "primary sources" of sound, image, gesture, and text. Tobias, in volume 2, reminds us that these data types are both researcher-generated and participant-generated, allowing the reader to move fluidly back and forth.

At the same time as we contemplate new data sources and means of analysis, we look to underutilized approaches for their potential to inform. A perusal of the chapters across this *Handbook* shows that music education researchers have been drawn to case study and ethnography, with narrative and phenomenology less prevalent. Grounded theory, discourse analysis, and autoethnography are even less common. Methodological eclecticism is probably a sign of health, but not simply for the sake of eclecticism.

Webster, in volume 2, asks whether we are using all of the tools at our command to assist inquiry. Certainly, qualitative data analysis software enables researchers to organize, examine, annotate, manipulate, and search for patterns in complex data sets, but as I am always reminded when my students review these programs, each software program both enables and constrains what one is able to do with the data. The researcher's sensibilities surpass all. The profusion of methodological literature in qualitative research also challenges us to choose wisely the kind of handbooks, guides, and manuals that provide guidance in learning useful techniques.

11.5. RESONANCE AND RIGOR

Verisimilitude, when a research report "rings true" to the lived experience of participants and readers, is also a sign of its resonance with music teaching and learning. The quality of writing is of paramount importance to individual researchers, faculty members who teach qualitative methods, reviewers, and the broad scholarly community, and perhaps most keenly to any reader, far and wide, who may engage with a text. Eisner writes, "words, except when they are used artistically, are proxies for direct experience. They point us in the direction in which we can undergo what the words purport to reveal. Words, in this sense, are like cues to guide us on a journey" (2008, 5). Eisner makes this compelling point before enlarging his scope to argue for additional forms of representation through arts-based research, but his observation about the power of words still obtains whatever the form or type. The central body of work in music education is inextricably bound to words as prompts for the journey. The researcher must carry meaning through sufficiently evocative, challenging, well-reasoned, and articulate prose. A well-crafted piece of writing enables the reader to enter into conversation with the ideas with clarity of focus and without distraction. Laurel Richardson, cited by Robinson elsewhere, points to common problems, however, as she reveals: "I have a confession to make. For thirty years, I have yawned my way through numerous supposedly exemplary qualitative studies. Countless numbers of texts have I abandoned half-read, half-scanned" (1997, 87). She hones in on a key dilemma: "Qualitative work depends upon people's reading it . . . [it] has to be read, not scanned; its meaning is in the reading" (87). She speaks to professional socialization that "homogenizes" the text through use of common patterns derived from the social sciences. Richardson calls for attention to writing as a mode of inquiry, arguing for more imaginative, yet prismatically coherent, forms through the processes of crystallization. Her ideas, like those of other scholars in narrative and arts-based inquiry, challenge researchers, reviewers, and readers to pursue writing that is deep, complex, grounded, multifaceted, provocative. As qualitative research continues to develop in music education, so will the forms, structures, and means of representation employed.

As a field, we continue to expand our capacities to foster more imaginative, socially meaningful, and rigorous projects. We have reached a point at which there is a critical mass of researchers in music education who are knowledgeable, widely read, and sufficiently established to provide the kind of scholarly critique to support and elevate professional discourse. Criticism, says Colwell, "implies an awareness of antecedents and consequence, means and ends; and comments need to be based on an understanding of the history and the purpose of the effort criticized" (2005, 76). With the scholarship cited in the overall *Handbook*, we now have a far keener awareness of the foundational grounding to enable informed criticism. Colwell cites a definition of "critical friend" by David Myers: "a critical friend can be defined as a trusted person who asks provocative questions, provides data to be examined through another lens, and offers critiques of a person's work as a friend. A critical friend takes the time to fully understand the context of the work presented and the outcomes that the person or group is working toward. The friend is an advocate for the success of that work" (76). In many ways, doctoral advisors serve as critical friends, as can reviewers and editors when the purpose of the exchange is to help focus and shape more rigorous and resonant reports. At this point in time, much of the careful analytical and interpretive work of the researcher is frequently compressed into a short paragraph or two in the published document; the affordances of technology may help us to make these processes more transparent and available for the consideration of those who want to learn more. Editorial work often goes unsung. The overall maturity of qualitative work is enhanced through the diverse lenses, perspectives, and sophisticated commentary provided by critical friends, reviewers, editors, and doctoral advisors.

11.6. COMMUNITY

Many of us who count ourselves part of the community of qualitative researchers in music education have grown up as "school music people," acclimated to the routines and grammars of music teaching and learning in powerful but often tacit ways. We can hold one another accountable as we probe normative assumptions, just as we benefit greatly from the cross-fertilization of collaboration with others outside the field. Music educators in higher education tend to be well-connected through regular participation in conferences, professional societies, and editorial activities. Eavesdropping on professional conversations at conferences, however, one often hears labels that sort individuals into neat and tidy categories as "quantitative" or "qualitative" researchers, as if these powerful identities, alliances, and affiliations are distinct and invariant. A key question for research education is whether this categorization is healthy. For example, the overall field of research may be strengthened if doctoral programs emphasize the development of research capabilities in multiple designs and across paradigms. Such methodological eclecticism must be balanced with the realization that a steep learning curve is often necessary to produce high-quality work using particular approaches.

Campbell and Thompson (volume 3) note how qualitative work in music teacher education is quite prevalent, yet remains largely uncoordinated. Clearly, the field would benefit from addressing collaboration and coordinated efforts in nearly every sub-area of scholarship. As universities establish centers for collaborative research, so might cross-university consortia be established to pursue agendas for inquiry across types and designs. Centered in powerful organizing questions, such consortia could contribute depth and breadth of understanding built from diverse forms of inquiry. In his senior researcher address, Bennett Reimer challenged the research community at large along these lines:

We need to develop ways for individual researchers, steeped in a particular research methodology by their training and experience, to work in close cooperation with others who are expert in their particular mode of research, all of them focusing on the very same issue, aiming for the very same goal—each in his or her own way but in close contact and coordinative interactions with each of the others—with at least some of such projects (perhaps many) being longitudinal. (2008, 200)

In this manner, vital symbiotic understandings can be achieved. Patricia Shehan Campbell, in her senior researcher address to the Society for Research in Music Education, spoke to professional socialization, inviting music educators to seek broader realms of scholarly inquiry:

As in the case of all institutions, societies, and culture, we have created in our research what Michael Foucault called "the norms of our discourse" (1988). It is a solid training that we have known, a dynamic community into which we have been socialized, and a clear and concise style of discourse that we articulate and uphold. Yet, as Marcel Proust declared, "the voyage of discovery is not just in seeing new landscapes but in having new eyes" (1948). Having new eyes (and new ears) equates with the acceptance and application of a wider palette of possibilities relative to the subcultures within our midst, to the designs we use, to the techniques of information-gathering and analysis, and to the interpretive styles and forms of our published work. (2002, 94)

The infrastructures that support research in music education, including professional societies, editors and editorial boards, publishers, colleges and universities, conference organizers, and grant agencies can foster greater coordination and alignment toward broad and meaningful research initiatives. Such initiatives augur well for the development and dissemination of qualitative research, and for building greater awareness across the profession of the contributions to knowledge made by qualitative inquiry.

11.7. BROADER REACH

In this last section, I will address expanding the reach of qualitative inquiry by attending to its overall impact on practitioners, scholars, and communities. We have long yearned for a closer integration of the worlds of research and practice. We aspire to impact. Impact has multiple dimensions—on the researcher, the academic community, the field of study, the practitioners we aim to serve. Richardson captures this succinctly when she asks of the studies she reads: "Does this affect me? Emotionally? Intellectually? Generate new questions? Move me to write? Move me to try new research practices? Move me to action?" (2000, 254).

A larger picture of impact speaks to a recurrent dilemma of qualitative work. In its particularity and complexity, qualitative studies are difficult to "sum up," what Lincoln identifies as the "cumulation" problem. "The question of cumulation," she writes, "revolves about how we know what we know with the knowledge we generate, what that knowledge means when we add it up, and for what purposes it will be used" (2010, 5). Unlike much quantitative research that can be synthesized and analyzed across data sets for meta-analyses of findings, qualitative research resists such summing up. How do we draw upon multiple studies that together constitute a larger gestalt without somehow compromising their particular insights? Lincoln challenges us to consider how knowledge gleaned through qualitative means "accumulates, philosophically, theoretically, metaphorically, pragmatically, because surely those who bury themselves in qualitative research know much about the world" (6). Keen imagination is needed to develop ways to represent the fund of knowledge without decontextualizing, reducing, or trivializing the work.

Cumulation speaks to the use of qualitative research as a powerful means for transforming understanding, through conventional means of dissemination, including teaching broadly construed. I am reminded of the Carnegie Initiative on the Doctorate project, which calls for newly minted PhD recipients committed to:

> *Generating* new knowledge and defending knowledge claims against challenges and criticism, *conserving* the most important ideas and findings that are a legacy of past and current work, and *transforming* knowledge that has been generated and conserved by explaining and connecting it to ideas from other fields. All of this implies to the ability to teach well to a variety of audiences, including those outside formal classrooms. (Golde 2006, 10)

Future possibilities in qualitative research build on researchers' attention to strong purposes, strong foundations, new realms, new affordances, greater resonance and rigor, integration of the research community, and concern for impact. As qualitative researchers consider the moral obligations, ethical considerations, methodological commitments, communicative potentials, and aesthetic dimensions of their work, we will contribute to the vitality of qualitative inquiry in the field of music education.

NOTE

1. This chapter, which was conceived as an overview of the 2014 edition, will refer to chapters that can be found in all three paperback editions of the *Oxford Handbook of Qualitative Research in American Music Education*.

REFERENCES

Barrett, Janet R. 2007. "The Researcher as Instrument: Learning to Conduct Qualitative Research through Analyzing and Interpreting a Choral Rehearsal." *Music Education Research* 9 (3): 417–33.

Campbell, Patricia Shehan. 2002. "A Matter of Perspective: Thoughts on the Multiple Realities of Research." *Journal of Research in Music Education* 50 (3): 191–201.

Colwell, Richard. 2005. "Can We Be Friends?" *Bulletin of the Council for Research in Music Education* 166: 75–91.

Denzin, Norman K., and Yvonna S. Lincoln. 2011. "Introduction: The Discipline and Practice of Qualitative Research." In *The Sage Handbook of Qualitative Research*, edited by Norman K. Denzin and Yvonna S. Lincoln, 1–19. Los Angeles: Sage Publications.

Denzin, Norman K., and Yvonna S. Lincoln. "Preface." 2011. In *The Sage Handbook of Qualitative Research*, edited by Norman K. Denzin and Yvonna S. Lincoln, ix–xvi. Los Angeles: Sage Publications.

Denzin, Norman K., and Yvonna S. Lincoln, eds. 2011. *The Sage Handbook of Qualitative Research*. 4th ed. Thousand Oaks, CA: Sage Publications.

Eisner, Elliot. "Art and Knowledge." 2008. In *Handbook of the Arts in Qualitative Research*, edited by J. Gary Knowles and Ardra L. Cole, 1–12. Thousand Oaks, CA: Sage Publications.

Golde, Chris M. 2006. "Preparing Stewards of the Discipline." In *Envisioning the Future of Doctoral Education: Preparing Stewards of the Discipine, Carnegie Essays on the Doctorate*, edited by Chris M. Golde, George E. Walker, and Associates, 3–22. San Francisco, CA: Jossey-Bass.

Lincoln, Yvonna S. 2010. " 'What a Long Strange Trip It's Been . . .': Twenty-Five Years of Qualitative and New Paradigm Research." *Qualitative Inquiry* 16 (1): 3–9.

Lincoln, Yvonna S., Susan A. Lynham, and Egon G. Guba. 2011. "Paradigmatic Controversies, Contradictions, and Emerging Confluences Revisited." In *The Sage Handbook of Qualitative Research*, edited by Norman K. Denzin and Yvonna S. Lincoln, 97–128. Los Angeles: Sage Publications.

Peshkin, Alan. 1993. "The Goodness of Qualitative Research." *Educational Researcher* 22 (2): 23–29.

Reimer, Bennett. 2008. "Research in Music Education: Personal and Professional Reflections in a Time of Perplexity." *Journal of Research in Music Education* 56 (3): 190–203.

Richardson, Laurel. 2000. "Evaluating Ethnography." *Qualitative Inquiry* 6 (2): 253–55.

Richardson, Laurel. 1997. *Fields of Play: Constructing an Academic Life*. New Brunswick, NJ: Rutgers University Press.

Willig, Carla, and Wendy Stainton-Rogers. 2008. "Review and Prospect." In *The Sage Handbook of Qualitative Research in Psychology*, edited by Carla Willig and Wendy Stainton-Rogers, 590–604. London: Sage Publications.

Index

Page numbers followed by *b*, *t*, and *f* indicate boxes, tables, and figures. Numbers followed by "n" indicate notes.